DERBYSHIRE

THE KING'S ENGLAND

Edited by Arthur Mee

In 41 Volumes

ENCHANTED LAND (INTRODUCTORY VOLUME)

Bedfordshire and
  Huntingdonshire
Berkshire
Buckinghamshire
Cambridgeshire
Cheshire
Cornwall
Derbyshire
Devon
Dorset
Durham
Essex
Gloucestershire
Hampshire with the Isle of
  Wight
Herefordshire
Hertfordshire
Kent
Lake Counties
Lancashire
Leicestershire and
  Rutland

Lincolnshire
London
Middlesex
Monmouthshire
Norfolk
Northamptonshire
Northumberland
Nottinghamshire
Oxfordshire
Shropshire
Somerset
Staffordshire
Suffolk
Surrey
Sussex
Warwickshire
Wiltshire
Worcestershire
Yorkshire—East Riding
Yorkshire—North Riding
Yorkshire—West Riding

THE KING'S ENGLAND

DERBYSHIRE

By
ARTHUR MEE

fully revised and edited by
F. R. BANKS

Illustrated with new photographs by
A. F. KERSTING

HODDER AND STOUGHTON
LONDON   SYDNEY   AUCKLAND   TORONTO

COPYRIGHT © 1969 BY HODDER AND STOUGHTON LTD
AND THE EXECUTORS OF THE LATE ARTHUR MEE

ILLUSTRATIONS © 1969 BY A. F. KERSTING

FIRST PUBLISHED JUNE 1937
NEW EDITION REVISED AND RESET 1969
SECOND IMPRESSION 1974

ISBN 0 340 00077 5

Printed in Great Britain
for Hodder and Stoughton Limited,
St. Paul's House, Warwick Lane, London EC4P 4AH
by Fletcher & Son Ltd, Norwich

INTRODUCTION TO REVISED EDITION

IN preparing the new edition of THE KING'S ENGLAND care has been taken to bring the books up to date as far as possible within the changes which have taken place since the series was originally planned. In addition the editor has made his revisions both in text and illustrations with a view to keeping the price of the books within reasonable limits, in spite of greatly increased production costs. But throughout the book, it has been the editor's special care to preserve Mr Arthur Mee's original intention of providing something more than just another guide book giving archaeological, ecclesiastical, and topographical information.

In the case of every town and village mentioned in the King's England Series, it has been the intention not only to indicate its position on the map, but to convey something of its atmosphere. And the biographical selections about people who are ever associated with that part of the country in which they lived, or who are commemorated in the parish church—which was such a popular feature of the former edition—have been retained and in some cases supplemented.

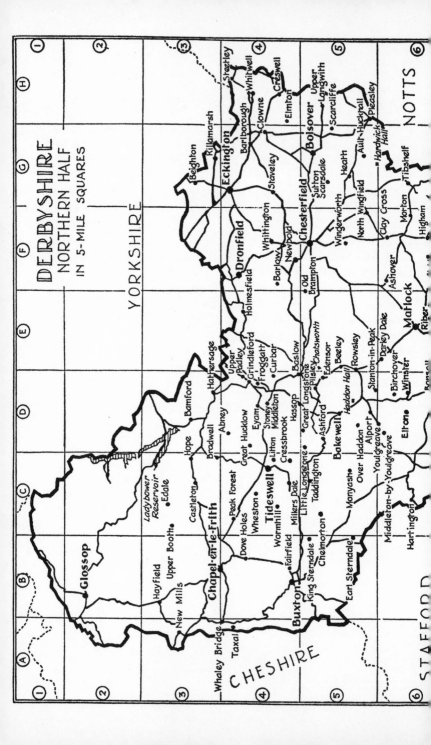

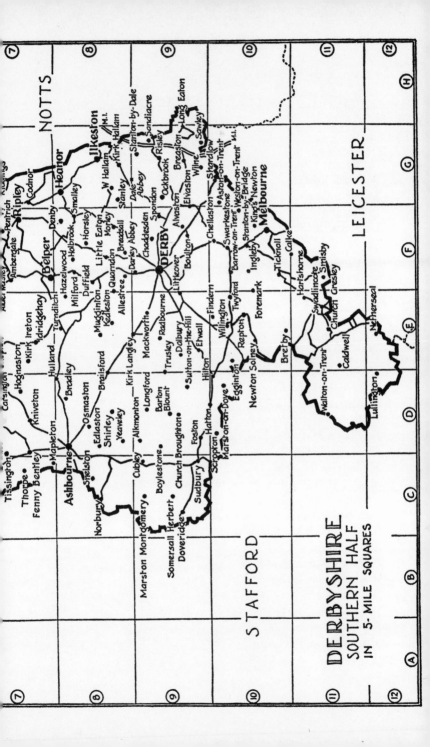

DERBYSHIRE
SOUTHERN HALF
IN 5-MILE SQUARES

ILLUSTRATIONS

INTRODUCTION

DERBYSHIRE is one of the delightful counties, not overpowering with history, but filled with nature's lovely places, packed with natural beauty in infinite variety, from magnificent Peakland heights to caverns deep in the heart of the rock.

It teems with interest for those who seek the story of the past in mineral and stone, in stone circles and burial mounds. It is watered by charming rivers spanned by lovely bridges, and has fine parks where historic families have lived for centuries. A place for everybody is Derbyshire, with more than a thousand square miles of wonderland almost in the heart of England, with about 900,000 people on 640,000 acres, and as fine a group of villages as any of our inland counties.

The oldest tale of Stone Age Derbyshire is told by Creswell Crags, where was found the first example of pictorial art in England. The great stones take up the tale of the prehistoric past, with Arbor Low stone circle, fortresses like Carl Wark, ruined chambers, and barrows where pottery and bronze have been found with the people who used them. There are traces of stations and roads made by the Romans who mined the lead they found in Derbyshire, and Saxon crosses among the finest in the land. Of feudal castles and keeps the most outstanding is Peveril Castle, crowning a high precipice at Castleton, the centre of government in Norman times for the High Peak Forest, and the setting for the submission of Malcolm IV, King of Scotland, to Henry II. The foundations of Duffield's massive keep are laid bare.

There are monastic ruins at Repton and Dale Abbey, and Haddon Hall is the finest mediaeval house for a hundred miles, if not in all England. Wingfield Manor, which held captive Mary, Queen of Scots, is the splendid ruin of the finest fortified house of the 15th century. Hardwick Hall is one of the most splendid Elizabethan mansions in England; Chatsworth, the Palace of the Peak, is one of the stateliest homes set in a glorious park and filled with treasures. Halls like stately Kedleston, Bolsover Castle, Sudbury, and Melbourne, the charming smaller halls of Tissington and Eyam, and

I

many a fine old manor house and farmhouse carry on the tale of the domestic architecture of this homely countryside. Lea Hurst at Holloway, of the 19th century, was the home of Florence Nightingale.

Here and there the old market-houses stand, as at Bakewell and Winster, and there are old village crosses—charming ones at Repton, Bonsall, and Higham. Some of the old villages keep green the spirit of the past with picturesque customs and famous events—the ringing of the curfew and the pancake bell at Ashford-in-the-Water, the great Well-Dressing festivals at Tissington and other places, the Garland Day festival at Castleton, the sheep-dog trials at Longshaw and elsewhere, and the remarkable Shrovetide football match at Ashbourne. There is a Roman Catholic pilgrimage in June to Padley Chapel in memory of two martyrs, and a service every August at Cucklet Delf in memory of the plague victims of Eyam. We come upon the memory of Little John, the friend of Robin Hood who is said to be buried at Hathersage. Fishermen follow the wake of Izaak Walton and Charles Cotton, and walkers tread the haunts beloved by John Ruskin, Charlotte Brontë, George Eliot, and Dr Johnson.

A marvellous place it is to walk or drive in, with the glories of Derbyshire scenery working up to its climax in 56 miles from south to north. The golden meadows of the south, watered by the Trent and the Dove, and the richly pastured farms give way to a charming countryside of green hills and dales, and then comes a world of stone-walled fields and treeless limestone uplands and the sky, bringing us to the wild grandeur of Kinder Scout and Bleaklow, with their windswept heights and trackless moorland wastes.

There are broad and beautiful dales where we may drive, looking up to heights all round; and exquisite dales where only feet may walk and no wheels run, dales like gems of rock and wood and water adorning the feet of the hills. There are dry dales like stark ravines, gaunt mountain passes and delightful dells, rocks in fantastic formation, and cliff-like edges overhanging the valleys. There are highways and views as surprising as they are entrancing—the Via Gellia riding through a lovely ravine shut in by cliffs mantled in green, the cornice road above the dale of the Wye, and the grand stretch of a dozen miles between the Ladybower Reservoir and

Glossop, climbing to nearly 1700 feet and crossing one of the wildest tracts in the country, between Bleaklow and Kinder Scout. Steeply edged by bold rocks, this high land, extending for miles at about 2000 feet above sea-level, gives the name of the High Peak to the most distinctive mass of the Pennine Chain before it sinks gradually into the undulating Midland plain.

One unforgettable Derbyshire view is from Monsal Head, where the Wye is seen swinging sharply round in its dale, a paradise into which the railway came in Ruskin's day, stirring him to mighty wrath. Another is the magnificent panorama from the summit of Win Hill, into which come the fine Ladybower Reservoir, the valleys of the Derwent, the Ashop, and the Noe, and the peaceful Hope Valley. A third is from Mam Tor above the vales of Hope and Edale; and a fourth the famous Surprise View from Millstone Edge Nick above Hathersage, where we see the Hope and Derwent Valleys framed in a fine array of moors and hills. For those who wander through the valleys and climb the hills there are a thousand kinds of wild flowers.

Derbyshire's unique beauty lies in the track of its streams, and must often be sought on foot. As every lover of the county knows, there is no other way by which we can make its full acquaintance. Nearly the whole of it is in the basin of the Trent, for, though this river crosses only the rich southern meadows, it takes to itself the three chief rivers and their countless tributaries gathered on their way. The Dove falls into the Trent at Newton Solney, and the Derwent (swelled by the Wye at Rowsley) between Wilne and Sawley.

The Derwent, the dominant river of Derbyshire, rises on the lofty pathless moorlands culminating in Bleaklow at a height of over 2000 feet and for most of its upper course to the Howden and Derwent Reservoirs it forms the boundary with Yorkshire. Then it flows down the middle of the county through scenes of great beauty —its moorland tributaries, the Westend, the Abbey Brook, the Alport, and the Noe, coming from wilds as remote in feeling as any in the British Isles. Engineering feats have transformed the Upper Derwent Valley above Bamford into Derbyshire's Lake Country, by damming the river into a chain of reservoirs. Below its junction with the Noe, at the end of the green Hope Valley, the Derwent is

3

escorted by ridges between 1200 and 1500 feet high on each side; then it winds through the magnificent Chatsworth Park and receives the Wye at Rowsley. Beyond Darley Dale it reaches the rocky limestone gorge of the Matlocks, the valley continuing wooded and picturesque by Cromford to Ambergate, where the river is joined by the Amber. The Derwent flows through Belper and Derby to the wide vale of the Trent, saying goodbye to its last mill-wheel at Wilne after collecting the waters of nearly 300,000 acres.

Charming as is the Derwent Valley, the Wye Valley equals it in beauty, though it lacks the broader views and the finer grouping of the hills around the Derwent's course. Impetuous and hurrying, the river helps in the making of delightful pictures in its short journey, which we can follow in the length of a summer's day. It flows in a deeply cut channel through narrow, steep, wooded dales; only here and there can they be seen well from above. Rising near Buxton, one of its springs on the slopes of Axe Edge, one in the neighbourhood of Combs Moss, another coming to life in the depths of Poole's Cavern, the Wye leaves the town through Ashwood Dale, and threads Wye Dale and the limestone ravines of Chee Dale, Millers Dale, and Monsal Dale, where it winds round the foot of Fin Cop. Here it is joined again by the highway which left Wye Dale to climb to Taddington and has come down the beautiful wooded Taddington Dale, and the river and the road go on as companions for the rest of the way. After passing through Ashford-in-the-Water and the old market town of Bakewell, the valley opens out a little into meadowy sweetness; the river passes Haddon Hall with its grey towers, receives the waters from two exquisite dales, and falls into the Derwent.

We are not alone in thinking that there is no river in England to compare with the Dove, which rises on the slopes of Axe Edge and becomes the county boundary with Staffordshire until it reaches the Trent. In spite of its peerless beauty it is the most modest of rivers, hiding itself where at its best in a deeply cleft passage of which the whereabouts cannot readily be seen. Dovedale, its most exquisite part, is matchless in delicate loveliness, and no highway quite reaches it. The dale is more easily missed than found by those who casually pass, and when found, it can only be seen by walking.

For the first part of its course the river is shut in on each side by a limestone plateau which rises now and then to greater heights. Its

4

stretch of great beauty comes with Beresford Dale, where the clear stream runs between green margins and limestone rocks, plentifully wooded and decked with flowers in the summer. Here the charming little fishing house Charles Cotton built for Izaak Walton is now hidden among trees. Then the Dove runs through the fine ravine of Wolfscote Dale, and into this near its southern end comes the dry windswept gorge of Biggin Dale. The river winds on to the secluded hamlet of Milldale and the picturesque little Viator's Bridge, then quite suddenly rocky portals are reached and the Dovedale which enchants everybody begins. We are now at one of the loveliest spots in the loveliest countryside in the land, and it continues for well over two miles as the crow flies.

It is a succession of scenes of dainty beauty set in a frame of rocky wildness. The sides of the sheer narrow gorge are constantly varying in outline, and are thickly wooded and clad with green, with wild flowers in every crevice. The stream runs clear, with little windings giving the view a perpetual freshness. It foams in shallows over the stony bed, and its still deep trout pools make it an angler's paradise. The footpath rises and falls, and there is no monotony. The whole scene is a rarity, complete, with no discordant feature. Seen in quietude, it is the choicest piece of England, and has laid its charm on every sensitive traveller who trod its slender path. At the end of the gorge come the stepping-stones, with the grassy Thorpe Cloud, rising like a cone to block the expanding view, and Bunster, guardian of the dale on the Staffordshire side. The Dove slips past to meet its first tributary, the River Manifold, beyond an open glade.

It is a heartening thing to remember that most of this enchanted vale belongs to the National Trust. Perhaps the most exquisitely English piece of England, it is fortunate, too, in being included in the first of our National Parks, for though so hidden away in the very heart of the land, it is within reach of thousands who live in crowded industrial towns.

No higher praise is needed of the old Derbyshire bridges than that they are worthy of the rivers they span. Among the outstanding bridges are the two at Ashford-in-the-Water (one of them the old Sheepwash Bridge whose sheep pen is still used for its original purpose), two at Bakewell, those of Baslow, Beeley, Rowsley, and Cromford, Conksbury Bridge over the Lathkill, the Monks' Bridge at

Egginton, and the romantic and partly mediaeval Swarkestone Bridge which crosses the Trent and strides for most of a mile over meadows like the Field of the Cloth of Gold in spring. The Young Pretender's advance guard came to this bridge in 1745, but instead of crossing it went back to Derby to join in the retreat which ended at Culloden. At Froggatt, Haddon, and over the Bradford near Youlgreave are three of the little pack-horse bridges still left in the county, and another is one of those at Bakewell.

From the point of view of industry and business it is the eastern mineral belt of Derbyshire and the agriculture of the south, with the influence of Derby, that in the main makes the county prosperous; but it is the call of northern Derbyshire to lovers of nature that appeals most strongly. Next to the Lake District, it is the part of England that has attracted the greatest number of enthusiastic ramblers. Sheffield, on the one hand, built on the spurs from the Pennine range, and Manchester and its neighbouring towns on the other hand, pour them forth in thousands.

For those who want caves, Derbyshire has some genuine ones, such as Peak Cavern at Castleton and the Blue John and Treak Cliff Caverns at the head of the dale, where the unique "blue john" mineral is found. Here, too, are glittering arrays of stalactites and crystals, all skilfully shown; and there are mines well worth a visit, such as the Speedwell Mine near the foot of the rugged Winnats Pass, with miles of underground recesses inviting variations from the breezy moorlands.

There are bare grey hilltop villages, like Taddington and Over Haddon, which are keys to beauty close at hand; villages which are delightful green oases such as Hassop and Snelston, and Alport where the Lathkill and the Bradford Rivers join hands. There are villages which have come into history. At Whittington the Glorious Revolution was born; here the Whigs got together and decided that the Stuarts must go and that William of Orange should rule in their stead. Pentrich has its pitiful story of the rioters after Waterloo. At Dethick was born a boy who grew up to lose his handsome head for plotting against a queen. In an attic at Blackwell an invention was perfected which revolutionised the hosiery trade. Alabaster from Chellaston, now a suburb of Derby, has found its way into many a fine hall and church, and stone from Darley Dale has helped to make the Thames Embankment. Near Matlock and Wirksworth, at Hope, and in Peak Dale near Buxton are some of the largest limestone quarries in the world.

Derby, the county town, has lost much that was old, but makes up for it in enterprise. It was the home of the first silk mill in England, and has set up the fine iron gates of the old mill, typical of a noted county craft, by its library. Now artificial silk is made on its doorstep, at Spondon. Derby makes some of our loveliest porcelain and our most famous aeroplane engines; and it has the largest locomotive and railway carriage workshops in Britain. Dr Johnson was married in one of its churches; All Saints, now the cathedral church, has one of the finest towers in the land, and shelters the great monument to Derbyshire's great builder, Bess of Hardwick.

In 1771, Sir Richard Arkwright built the first mill to be operated by water-power, at Cromford; at Riddings the petroleum industry was born, mother of our great oil industries. Glossop, the northern gateway of the Peak, is the county's textile town today, with paper mills as well as cotton mills. Ashbourne, the gateway to green hills and dales, has a factory turning out millions of tins of milk a week, much of it going abroad; it comes, of course, from the rich pasture lands, which support many dairies of repute. Buxton, famous for its warm springs, is the highest town in England, in a glorious situation, and has the biggest dome in the world in its hospital.

The story of Derbyshire's churches is one of fine architecture of all the great building centuries, of beauty and many treasures, of rare and unique things. Chesterfield has a stately 14th century church with a famous twisted spire. Wilne has one of the oldest fonts in the land. Youlgreave's Norman font is unique. Lovely Repton, with its fine school, is the site of the first Christian church of the converted Saxons in the Midlands, and has in its church a crypt which has been described as "the most perfect example of Anglo-Saxon architecture on a small scale now extant". Melbourne has one of our finest Norman churches, and modest Steetley has what many believe to be the loveliest example of a small Norman church in England. Bakewell has one of the finest collections of ancient coffin stones, and groups of faded funeral garlands (rare pathetic relics) are to be seen at Matlock and Trusley and Ashford-in-the-Water.

There is beautiful woodwork old and new, and much old glass at Morley and Norbury. There are brasses of knights and priests and civilians, and fine monuments in alabaster and stone. There is no

7

daintier tomb than that with the figure of Thomas Cokayne in Youlgreave church; no lovelier figure than Penelope Boothby, who is buried in Ashbourne church, below the soaring spire known as the Pride of the Peak. Kedleston's old church is a textbook of sculpture, with a rich modern chapel where the sculptured figures of the Marquess Curzon and his first wife lie on their tomb. Tideswell church is magnificent and beautiful enough to be called the Cathedral of the Peak. Dale church, one of the smallest in the land, shares its roof with an old farmhouse.

Some of the loveliest trees in the country are in the churchyards. Darley Dale has one of England's oldest yews, and Doveridge has another ancient veteran. Rowsley has a grand old elm, and Ashbourne a cedar it would be hard to beat.

Into Derbyshire's roll of honour for men who won national distinction come John Flamsteed, our first Astronomer Royal; Samuel Richardson the novelist; William Howitt the poet and traveller; Herbert Spencer the philosopher; Joseph Wright the painter; Sir Francis Chantrey the sculptor (who will always belong to Derbyshire though Sheffield has seized his native village); Jedediah Strutt who invented the ribbed stocking frame; Benjamin Outram the engineer, and his son Sir James Outram, the Bayard of India; William Bagshawe, Apostle of the Peak; William Newton, the Peak Minstrel; Anthony Fitzherbert, the great judge; William Hutton, historian; Thomas Linacre, physician; Aston Cokayne, the poet; and Sir John Chandos of Radbourne, who saved the Black Prince at Poitiers. Here lies Erasmus Darwin, born in Nottinghamshire but buried at Breadsall; and at Ault Hucknall is buried Thomas Hobbes, closely connected with the county as tutor in the Cavendish family. George Stephenson lies at Chesterfield, where he settled down when his work was done; the town owes its industrial rise very largely to him. Florence Nightingale belongs to the county, too, for though she was born in Florence, it was her childhood home at Holloway that came to her mind in the quiet hours when she was far away.

Take it for all in all, the traveller who has seen his last of Derbyshire will never see its like again, for it is unique in its beauty, as changing as the flowers in spring, with a freshness and a tenderness which seem to hang about its hills and dales, and a haunting loveliness which rises to enchantment at its greatest heights and in its deepest solitudes.

Abney. It stands with Abney Grange, two hamlets a mile apart, set in a solitary world of moor and hill and wooded vale. From 1000 feet above sea-level, Abney looks out to Shatton Moor nearly half as high again, and to that proud knight of Derbyshire, Sir William Hill, over 1400 feet high on Eyam Moor. On the moor are the remains of the Wet Withens, one of the county's several pre-historic stone circles.

A lovely green hill is Abney Low, with two brooks flowing round it on their way to join the Derwent through rocky woodland and a charming glen. Whether we come to Abney or leave it the road is sheer delight. One way we come by deep plantations to where the 16th century Highlow Hall stands near the road, a battlemented manor house now a farm, with a ball-topped gateway and a stone dovecot.

Alderwasley. It lies in a hollow, high above fine woodland slopes rising from the lovely valley of the Derwent. With a glorious hill all aglow in rhododendron time, and flowers abounding everywhere, it has views as fair as eye could wish to see in a landscape full of story.

From the surrounding uplands, we see Crich's lighthouse monument, the woods of Lea Hurst, home of Florence Nightingale, and the limestone ravine through which the Derwent flows past Matlock Bath. Less than two miles away to the south-west rises Alport Height, the loftiest ground in the south of the county, over 1000 feet high and commanding a magnificent prospect. Here the upstanding monolith called the Alport Stone challenges climbers.

The great 18th century house of Alderwasley Hall (now a Roman Catholic school) has been the home of the Lowes and the Hurts. It was Thomas Lowe who built the old church, when Henry VIII was king, and Francis Hurt who built the new one on the middle of the last century. A simple building, the Tudor church has a doorway carved in somewhat crazy fashion under a hood-mould with stone heads. Francis Hurt's church of 1850 is just within the gates of the beautiful park. A splendid cedar throws its shadow on the walls,

B

while just below a sparkling stream runs with little waterfalls and clear pools.

Alfreton. It was mining coal in Chaucer's day, and it now has knitwear, hosiery, and other manufactures, but it has kept some beauty and much interest. The broad King Street climbs the hill to the busy marketplace, with the 18th century George Hotel, and in the High Street to the right is a well-preserved Elizabethan house, now council offices. Close to the stir of the marketplace, but peacefully set at the end of a road which opens out to a path across the park of the old Hall, is the large church, with a story going back to the last days of the Normans when Robert FitzRanulph gave it to Beauchief Abbey. Its oldest fragment is the lofty pointed tower arch of about 1200, with cable and nail-head in its capitals, the rest of the tower being 200 years younger. As old as the tower arch is part of a coffin-lid carved with the head of a cross that may have marked the grave of the first priest of this place.

The fine 14th century porch is guarded by a modern figure of St Martin in an elaborate niche, below which projects a cornice carved with flowers and shields. The doorway through which we enter the church is as old as the porch. So too are the nave arcades, though each was given an east-end bay in 1868, when the north arcade was rebuilt stone for stone. From the 15th century comes the vestry with its stone-vaulted roof. In the north aisle is the delicately sculptured memorial of George Morewood, who died in 1792.

The Morewood family lived at Alfreton Hall, near by, until 1963, when it was taken over by the county council. The fine house, built in 1750 and much enlarged in the 19th century, was reduced to manageable proportions and opened as an adult education centre in 1968, and a fine new swimming pool has been built in the grounds.

In a wayside garden at the foot of the hill is a Methodist chapel and a manse, with a school across the way. They are the gift to the town of an Alfreton pit-boy who went to America, made a fortune and reached high administrative office. He was Robert Watchorn, who came back to his birthplace, laid out this garden, built the chapel on the site of his old home, and opened it on the day his mother would have been 100 years old.

At Alfreton is buried a brave old parson whom none could stop preaching, with a story well worth remembering. Born near Chesterfield in 1627, and educated at Bromfield grammar school, Cumberland, John Oldfield was appointed, when 22, rector of Carsington. Although his parishioners were difficult to please, he refused a much richer living to serve them.

For 15 years he conducted the meetings of church elders held at Wirksworth, and it was at their instigation that he preached a series of sermons against the errors of the Socinians, disciples of two 16th century Italians who held that unless a doctrine was reasonable it should be rejected. The Act of Uniformity of 1662 drove him from his parish, and for the last 20 years of his life he was mainly a wanderer.

He was caught up in the toils of a system which made it a criminal offence for more than five people, in addition to the members of the family, to meet for worship not according to the Church. From that age of persecution came a shoemaker's man named George Fox and a tinker named John Bunyan, and Oldfield, sound mathematician and scholar, quietly plodded on through it all, risking fine, penal servitude, and transportation, always in peril, and once in grave danger from the false testimony of perjurers, who were afterwards pilloried for swearing what was untrue.

His closing years were passed here, and he ventured, in spite of threat of pains and penalties, to hold fortnightly services at the house of a friend. He died in 1682, leaving four clergyman sons, of whom Joshua Oldfield was a notable Presbyterian minister who won a considerable reputation at Oxford University, where scoffing undergraduates found him a man of high character and great ability.

Alkmonton. We find it at the end of a straight five-mile stretch of Roman road that is all up and down, with wide views reaching into Staffordshire. Its church, with lancet windows and a bell-turret with a leaded spire, is of the mid 19th century, a neat and trim little place unusual in the neighbourhood for its outside walls of flint and stone. It has one old possession, a fine Norman font like part of a massive pillar. This is all that is left of an ancient chapel, and after being lost for three centuries was dug up on a farm.

Bentley Hall, to the west on the Cubley road, is a charming early 17th century brick house with a later 17th century wing.

Allestree. It is now the most favoured of Derby's residential suburbs, with large new housing estates, but it keeps its fine view over the valley of the Derwent, and what is old clings to its little hilltop in company with the church, the old cross-shaft set on a wall between the churchyard and the vicarage, and two fine old yews, one of which is as old as the story of the church. Its gnarled and twisted trunk seems as if it had grown out of a fairy tale. Very fine it looks from the lychgate, and the lychgate itself, with its shingled roof, fits into a charming picture seen from under the yew, with a splendid (if restored) Norman doorway inside the timber porch.

It is this doorway with its curious carvings which is the chief possession of a church made almost new in 1866. It retains its 13th century tower and part of the east wall of the chancel built at the same time; and under a 14th century founder's arch is a stone engraved with a cross which may have covered the grave of the builder of the first church here.

Here are many memorials of the families of Allestree Hall, a house of about 1830 in a fine public park with a golf course. The oak stalls in the church, the altar in the lady chapel and oak seats in the nave were all made by a village craftsman just before World War II.

Alport. Derbyshire delight, with grey limestone houses in gay gardens, and a mill by the bridge where stream runs into stream and dale meets dale. We may come to it along the dale that bears its name, the river flowing with many little waterfalls over a rocky bed, and the road fair with flowers; or we may come from Youlgreave, glorying in the sight of two of Derbyshire's loveliest valleys drawing closer to each other until their waters, the Lathkill River and the Bradford River, meet at the foot of the hill.

The Bradford River made a stir last century by disappearing and running six miles underground and into the Derwent at Darley Dale, instead of joining the Lathkill at Alport as usual. It seems that heavy floods and disused mines were responsbile for its adventure, but later it found its way home again.

On a slope of Priest's Hill, a mile away to the south, is a farmhouse with a gable of Old Harthill Hall, the home of Edmund Cokayne, whose figure lies with his father's in such a noble setting in Ashbourne church. It was probably from the old house that he rode out to fight at Shrewsbury against Hotspur. He was knighted on the field and died that morning, a knight for an hour. In the fine view from the old Hall across the valley, a queer mass of rock called Tuppenny Loaf stands out conspicuously.

Alsop-en-le-Dale. Set in the lovely limestone country, a mile from the River Dove and the Staffordshire border, is this cluster of homes, an old church and a great house with gables and windows telling us it is from the 17th century.

To this secluded spot a wanderer found his way 400 years ago. He was Thomas Becon, chaplain to Archbishop Cranmer and Protector Somerset, a preacher who preached himself from Canterbury Cathedral into the Tower of London. Free once more, he sought obscurity in travel and found shelter here for a year with John Alsop, writing of his welcome:

"Coming into a little village called Alsop-en-le-Dale I chanced upon a certain gentleman named Alsop, lord of the village, a man not only ancient in years but also ripe in the knowledge of Christ's doctrine. After we had saluted one another, and taken a sufficient repast, he showed me certain books which he called his jewels. I found there very good wits and apt unto learning."

The Alsops were lords of the manor for 500 years until 1688, and until 200 years later their descendants were again in the old home. The small church, with a tower of 1883, has a Norman doorway with unusual moulding like two rows of zigzag and a little Norman window in the south wall. The sides of the pointed chancel arch, and the crudely shaped piscina niche, are perhaps Norman too.

Alvaston. Though almost lost in Derby's 20th century fringe, its history goes back a thousand years. A few of its old houses are older than the church, yet the church has something in it which men would look at curiously before the days of Agincourt, before Magna Carta.

The church has a 14th century piscina, and a font rather oddly given as a thankoffering for the capture of Sebastopol in the Crimean War; but it is notable for three other things in iron and stone. One is a piece of beaten ironwork, now against a wall, with an angel trumpeting the song of the Shepherds. Once a reredos and now preserved as a fine piece of craftsmanship, it may have been the work of the famous Nottingham blacksmith, Huntingdon Shaw, who

13

DERBYSHIRE

made for William III the fine gates which used to be at Hampton
Court.

The oldest things in Alvaston are two coffin stones, old friends indeed if stones are friends. They were together for centuries in the
Norman church which once stood here; they were buried for centuries under the old tower, and were found together in 1856 when
the church was made new. Now they are companions in the porch,
a greeting from the ancient world as we come into this modern place.
One from the 12th century has a cross with a round head; the other,
perhaps from Saxon England, is a truly remarkable tapering stone
(the lower end missing) which has a cross of unusual design with 11
rings about it.

Ambergate. A fine stretch of road brings us from Belper to this
gateway of the romantic country of the Peak, now a workaday village where roads, rivers and railways meet, keeping the lovely setting
nature gave it in the sweeping valley of the Derwent, with the
splendid woods of Shining Cliff and the slopes of Crich Chase rising
on each side. Here the Amber joins the Derwent, flowing with it
under an old bridge to a bower of trees.

The church was rebuilt in the late 19th century, but in two small
windows of the porch is old glass found in a box in a cottage, some
of it English and some Flemish; some quarries are 500 years old, a
panel of the Ascension is of the 16th century, one of the Crucifixion
is of the 18th century, and a small roundel came from Shrewsbury
Abbey. The marble figure of an angel protecting a child from a serpent is the work of a Belgian sculptor who sought refuge here during the Great War.

Ashbourne. All roads find this old market town among green
hills and lovely dales, and a famous company of people all these
roads have seen. King Charles I himself and Prince Charles Edward Stuart, and men with fame outlasting kings and princes; James
Boswell and Samuel Johnson, the poet Thomas Moore and the
novelist George Eliot, the 'compleat' angler Izaak Walton, Congreve
the dramatist, Canning the statesman, and that most astounding
Frenchman, Jean Jacques Rousseau—all these knew the lovely roads
to Ashbourne, for all of them lived or stayed here, and these authors
wrote here or put this country in their books.

14

Ashbourne Hall, where Prince Charles Edward stayed on his journey that was arrested at Derby, has lost its greatness; only part of it still stands, and that is now a public library. But below the steep marketplace is the old inn, the Green Man and Black's Head, visited by Dr Johnson's Boswell. Here the landlady, "a mighty civil gentlewoman", gave the Scot a low curtsy and an engraved sign of her house; and a sign still swings on a beam stretching right across the road.

In Church Street, one of the finest streets in Derbyshire, are groups of old almshouses, and the Elizabethan grammar school, founded in 1585, is unaltered as we see it, its gables all in a row, its windows with their leaded panes. Facing it (and now the head-master's house) is the 17th century brick house to which Dr Johnson came for many a holiday with his old schoolfellow John Taylor. Dr Taylor was rector of Market Bosworth and of St Margaret's at Westminster, and was also a prebendary of Westminster Abbey, but he loved his farm and his garden here, and, though winter found him in London, summer brought him home again. Boswell tells us that he was like a hearty English squire with the parson added. We have a peep of the gabled south front of Dr Taylor's house, with its projecting room (added by the brothers Adam) from the bridge over the Henmore Brook flowing at the bottom of the garden. The grounds have changed very much since the days when the Duke of Devonshire arrived to dine with the doctor, and the coachman was ordered to drive twice round to give him a good impression of their size.

Of the two friends Dr Johnson was the first to die, two months after leaving Ashbourne in 1784, and it was Dr Taylor who read his burial service in the Abbey. Four years later they laid Dr Taylor to rest in the famous church of Ashbourne, where he is buried in a vault in the south transept, far below the magnificent steeple which abundantly deserves its title of the Pride of the Peak. It is a noble spectacle rising above a churchyard magnificent with yews and cypresses, and with a splendid avenue of 50 trimmed limes on each side. One of these cedars spreads its branches over a patch of ground 80 yards round.

Thousands come to Ashbourne for its monuments, but even without them it would be a place of pilgrimage. It has a few Norman stones, but the church as we see it is the work of our three great mediaeval building centuries, a place of gracious charm without and within. A tiny brass plate in the south transept chapel records its consecration in 1241. A large and luminous place indeed it is, as Boswell tells us in his *Life of Samuel Johnson*. It is built in the shape of a cross, with chancel, transepts, nave, and aisle gathered about its central tower, and it has magnificent arcades of lofty bays.

The glorious tower with its spire, rising 212 feet, has been looking down on the old town since the 14th century. The tower has fine belfry windows and an open parapet; the elegant spire has 20 windows in five tiers, and strings of ballflower running up its eight angles; there must be about 1700 flowers in all. The turret staircase at one angle of the tower is crowned by a pinnacle and although now filled in still has its doorway with a sculptured head. In this doorway hangs a fine 14th century door, cut from a solid block of oak and black with age; it is divided lengthways into two panels and has wrought-iron bands and hinges. The fine arcades are of the 14th century, their pointed arches resting on clustered pillars, and some of their capitals finely carved. The font is of the 13th century.

In the chancel is a recessed tomb said to be that of Robert de Kniveton, who died in 1471; and near it is a tomb with sculptures in memory of Christopher Harland, who died in 1839 and was the last representative of the Knivetons. Battered and worse for much moving about are the 15th century figures of John Bradbourne and his wife, who must have known Robert Kniveton; they lie in the north transept with the great array of monuments to the Cokaynes and the Boothbys. Enclosing them all is a lofty screen with open tracery about 500 years old, but the splendour of all this sculpture, one of the most remarkable mediaeval exhibitions in the country, is not improved by its overcrowding.

High on an alabaster tomb lies Sir Humphrey Bradbourne with his wife, he in armour of the days before the Armada, with his sword and dagger, ruffs at his neck and on his wrists, feet on a lion, gauntlets close by and a double chain round his neck. She has a short cloak over a long gown and wears a ruff and a close-fitting cap. The tomb is adorned with heraldic display and the figures of 16 children, three in christening robes.

The monuments of the Cokaynes are with one exception com-

16

plete with the heads of the family from 1372 to 1592. John of 1372 wears a short tunic and long hose with a purse hanging from his belt, his long mantle reaching to the lion at his feet. His son Edmund is with him, clad as a knight. Edmund's son Sir John lies in armour with the SS collar of the Lancastrians, his wife in a mantle held with a cord and tassels. Sir John's son John has but a piece of alabaster stone for his memorial, and the next of the line has a beautiful alabaster tomb at Youlgreave. Sir Thomas of 1537 is here at Ashbourne with his wife Dame Barbara, their figures engraved in Purbeck marble; he was with King Henry VIII on the Field of the Cloth of Gold. His son Francis has his portrait in brass with that of his wife in a long gown with a jewelled girdle, but the brasses were renewed last century. Their son Thomas, who died in 1592, has a fine marble monument on the wall outside the screen, showing him kneeling with his wife at a desk, their children, and a display of arms.

But it is not for these great folk we come to this great place; it is rather for a little child, Penelope Boothby. Who that has seen her can forget her, the little white figure of a child of six summers set here in marble so that we wait for her to wake from sleep? Her figure, which won for Thomas Banks lasting fame among sculptors, shows Penelope lying on a mattress in a simple frock with a sash, her hands clasped, her feet one upon another. Her delicate and fragile form has never ceased to be counted among the gems of English art.

Penelope was the only child of Sir Brooke Boothby and Lady Susannah, and it is said that her stricken parents parted at her grave, a little tragedy which perhaps explains the epitaph:

> *She was in form and intellect most exquisite*
> *The unfortunate parents ventured their all on*
> *this frail bark, and the wreck was total.*

There are other inscriptions in three languages, one telling of her curling locks of shining gold and the lightning of her smile, which made a paradise on earth. She was painted by Sir Joshua Reynolds in his old age, and her figure here inspired Sir Francis Chantrey's famous sculpture of the Sleeping Children in Lichfield Cathedral.

The church has beautiful glass, old and new. About 20 shields of ancient heraldic glass fill the tracery of the east window, and in the

17

clerestory of the north transept are what is left of various coats-of-arms of old Ashbourne families. Old glass from Fenny Bentley church forms a broad band of shields and odd fragments across a window in this transept with a fragment above it of the Crucifixion, but the priceless treasure of the windows is the 13th century glass filling the lancet in the same transept. As old as the church and perhaps the earliest glass in the county, it is in five medallions, filled with groups of small figures in scenes from Bethlehem.

Among the 19th century glass is the story of David and Goliath, which John Ruskin rightly described as a disgrace to a penny edition of Jack the Giant Killer. The seven lights of the east window, under the old glass in the tracery, have stained glass by C. E. Kempe; it is sometimes called the Mary window because the money for it was collected from the Marys of Ashbourne by Mary Corbet, who gave the figure of Christ on the pulpit as a thankoffering for the recovery of her sight. She is buried in the shade of the majestic cedar in the churchyard. In the south aisle is a window by Christopher Whall, in memory of two sisters, Monica and Dorothea Turnbull. They were 19 and 21, and they died in 1901 from burns received when the frock of one sister caught fire and the other rushed to her help.

In the church is preserved, its paint remarkably fresh, a fragment of a 14th century triptych of Calvary; it is on wood and was found under the plaster. By the tower is a tablet in memory of Dean Langton who is buried here; he was riding his horse up a steep track from Dovedale to Tissington when the horse missed its footing and rolled down the bank, killing its master. With him was a lady who was saved through her long hair catching in the branch of a tree.

In the lovely country round about Thomas Moore lived for about four years. In a cottage at Mayfield, beyond the Dove, in Staffordshire, he wrote his famous *Lalla Rookh*, a fantasy of oriental splendour, and the bells of Ashbourne church inspired his lovely lines:

> *Those evening bells! Those evening bells!*
> *How many a tale their music tells*
> *Of youth and home and that sweet time*
> *When last I heard their soothing chime.*
>
> *Those joyous hours are passed away:*
> *And many a heart that then was gay*

Within the tomb now darkly dwells
And hears no more those evening bells.

And so 'twill be when I am gone:
That tuneful peal will still ring on
While other bards shall walk these dells,
And sing your praise, sweet evening bells.

Ashbourne is famous for its traditional game of football, played in the streets and around the town on Shrove Tuesday and Ash Wednesday. The game, in which the ball can be kicked, carried, or otherwise transported by human agency, is played between the "Up'ards" and the "Down'ards", those living on either side of the Henmore Brook, which runs through the town. The ball, which is filled with cork, is thrown up each day at the start of the game (usually by a sporting or other celebrity) on an open space behind the Green Man and Black's Head, and a goal is scored by one team or the other by touching the wall of one of two mills, three miles apart on the Henmore Brook. Play usually continues until a goal is scored or until darkness falls, which in fact sometimes occurs without a goal being registered.

Ashford-in-the-Water. It lies in a lovely valley where the River Wye flows by mill and weir and under fine old bridges, wooded hills and rocky heights rising all around. Of all its joys there is nothing more delightful than the 17th century Sheepwash Bridge and its fold (still used in washing sheep), spanning the tree-shaded stream with three low arches where lusty trout and grayling sport in sparkling shallows. We see from the bridge Great Shacklow Wood, below which the river has come from Monsal Dale; we see the rough and rugged Kirk Dale begin its steep climb to windblown heights, and a lovely bit of the village with the old pump in its shelter, the old stone dwellings, and the church.

Ashford is an ancient place where old customs linger in the ringing of the Curfew every day and the Pancake Bell on Shrove Tuesday, and where a Well-Dressing ceremony (like that of Tissington) takes place on Trinity Sunday or the first Sunday after. In the church still hang four paper garlands which speak to us with infinite pathos of the past. For the custom was to carry these garlands in the funeral processions of betrothed maidens who had died before their wedding days, and to leave them in the church; sometimes a kerchief, a glove, or a collar would be tucked away among the flowers, and an inscription.

One of the garlands treasured here was made for Ann Swindel, who was 22 when they brought her here in 1798, and the inscription they left on her grave, now faded away, was a prayer that she who had lost her youth might find great joy to come. Garlands are to be seen also at Matlock and Trusley in Derbyshire, but not in many other churches in England; they are pathetic because they bring the touching thought of Shakespeare's Ophelia to mind, for it was these tributes of love, these "virgin crants" as Shakespeare called them, to which the churlish priest objected at Ophelia's burial.

Ashford has lost the great house near the church, once the home of the Plantagenets, the Hollands, and the Nevilles, but some of the old church they knew is in the building which has for company a fine old yew and remains of an ancient cross. It was almost all made new in 1870, though the tower is mainly 700 years old. Over the south door is the oldest possession of Ashford, a Norman tympanum with two wild creatures, one like a wolf under a tree. The north arcade of the nave and the tower archway are of the 14th century.

The chancel roof has old stone corbels, one with a head and hands. There are two chairs and a chest of the 17th century, and a Jacobean pulpit with carved panels. The font is 14th century, with the head and tail of a dragon on opposite sides of the bowl (as if the creature is creeping through the bowl).

It is good to find here a memorial to Henry Watson of Bakewell, discoverer of the treasures of the village, who not only discovered them but sent them up and down England. His father was Samuel Watson of Heanor, who was responsible for the splendid carving at Chatsworth, and Henry invented a machine for cutting and polishing marble. He opened the quarry of Ashford black marble at Sheldon, near by, in 1748, and was the first to make ornaments of the marble, lovely things treasured in many homes. How many imposing halls, how many magnificent tombs, owe their glory to this village we do not know, but it is not a few.

Lovely are all the ways about this village. We can climb the delightful road in company with the river as it goes towards Monsal

Dale, and then uphill through the beautiful woods of Taddington Dale. We go to Little Longstone for the glorious view from Monsal Head, or with the river downstream through Ashford Dale to Bakewell, enjoying from the bridge at the eastern end of the village a peep of the 18th century Ashford Hall in a lovely setting.

Ashover. We are in the peaceful valley of the Amber, a land of rocky hills enriching the village with their varied beauty and the wonderful views from their tops, hills that have given abundantly of their riches since the Romans worked them for lead, and that are now quarried for their sandstone. For long Ashover has lain in their shelter.

Across the valley there is the Fabric's massive rock-strewn ridge with its magnificent panorama (oddly named Fabric, they say, because it yielded stone for churches). There is Ashover Hay, the rounded hill beyond Milltown hamlet; there are the tree-clothed slopes of Raven's Nest and the height of Cocking Tor, and Overton Hall (now an old people's home), which was once the home of Sir Joseph Banks, who went round the world with Captain Cook and persuaded Australia to become a nation.

And there is much charm about the village, in the happy grouping of the mediaeval church with its graceful spire soaring from a bower of trees. The picturesque stone school and old inn have something left of the day when Thomas Babington and his Ashover men came home from Agincourt; and the old men drinking ale in the Crispin Inn will tell you how in 1646 the soldiers of the king turned the landlord out while they drank all his ale, and forgot the king and Cromwell too. The Babingtons of Dethick built the tower and spire of Ashover church; they are of the early 15th century and rise 128 feet high, the tower with embattled parapet and three long gargoyles, the spire elegant and lofty, with eight windows.

Of the church which the Normans built, nothing remains unless it be the tiny piscina projecting from the chancel wall. But there is a lovely Norman relic we would come far to see, for here is a lead font with 20 figures of men in flowing drapery, all holding books and standing under arches raised on tiny pillars. Below these rows of little men is a band of fleurs-de-lys. The font was made about half-way through the 12th century; it is one of only about 30 in England, but it is especially interesting in being made from local lead. The south doorway, with three quaint heads, is of the 13th century; the north arcade is of the 14th, as is a fine little doorway with open tracery in the north aisle, and most of the church is of the 15th century.

The great stone in the chancel floor has the brass portrait of a priest in richly embroidered robes. His head is uncovered, his hands are folded in prayer; he is perhaps Philip Eyre, a 15th century rector. Another chancel brass has portraits of James Rolleston and his wife; he is in Tudor armour with sword and dagger, she has a flowing robe with tight-fitting bodice, a wide belt from which hangs a pendant, and a headdress with embroidered lappets. With them are their 13 children, girls dressed like the mother and boys in long tunics.

On a fine alabaster tomb lies Thomas Babington of 1518 with his wife, both elaborately carved and painted. He has a long gown with a purse hanging from his girdle, a double chain round his neck and a ring on each hand, his head on a pillow held by an angel each side; her dress is fastened by a tasselled cord, and she has a ring on each hand. The sides of the tomb are carved with handsome canopies under which are little figures of the 15 children and their marriages.

Above this tomb is a brass plate to this same Thomas Babington, interesting for being a palimpsest, with an inscription on the other side to some Robertus Prykke, sergeant of a queen's pantry. Above the fine open tracery in the bays of the chancel screen Thomas Babington erected is an embattled cresting over a band of quatrefoils. A tablet in the nave to William Dakeyn, who died in 1630, is interesting because it is thought to be one of the many forgeries of his notorious grandson, whose forgeries of arms and pedigrees sent him to the pillory and lost him an ear.

In the chancel is a tribute to Obadiah Bourne which brings to mind the story of his father Immanuel Bourne, whom he succeeded as rector in 1669, and the fate of their old home, Eastwood Old Hall, whose ivied ruins of a few rooms and part of the tower still stand. On the outbreak of the Civil War Immanuel Bourne tried to keep out of the struggle by leaning to neither side, but first one party assailed him and then the other. Even when he openly avowed himself on the side of Parliament they did not trust him, but left him with a ruined house and a broken heart. Immanuel found it vain to plead that he was in their service, and when the Parliamentarians found they could not bring down his house with cannon they set a barrel of gunpowder in the tower, destroying half the Hall and leaving the rest in ruins.

There are two carved chairs in the sanctuary said to have come from the Old Hall, and an odd tablet on the wall has a quaint memory of David Wall, "whose superior performance on the bassoon endeared him to an extensive musical acquaintance, and whose social life closed in 1796". A small brass plate pays tribute to George Eastwood, who lived for years in the village and did much of the woodcarving in the church. He carved the panelled reredos over the altar in the north aisle with a wealth of vine leaf and grape, and adorned the ends of the fine benches with fine and varied tracery, dying in 1903, just before they were completed. One of the eight bells in the tower is of the 18th century and has lovely scrollwork round its rim, and another boasts that it "rung the downfall of Bonaparte and broke April 1814".

Here is buried, as we gather from the register, a bad woman who has found a sure place in our literature. She is Dorothy Matley, who died here in 1660, and she is known because she comes into John Bunyan's *Life and Death of Mr Badman*, her story being told as an example of sudden judgment:

"Take that dreadful story of Dorothy Matley of Ashover, a liar and thief that washed the rubbish that came from the lead mines. Her usual way of asserting things was with imprecations such as, I would I might sink into the earth.

"On the 23rd of April she was washing on a hill and was there taxed by a lad for taking twopence out of his pocket. She denied it, wishing the ground might swallow her if she had them. Now a man of good report came by and saw her with her tub and sieve twisting round and sinking into the ground, and a great stone fell upon her head, the earth fell in upon her, and she was afterwards found four yards within the ground, the boy's twopence in her pocket."

Aston-on-Trent. Clustering by the wayside in this attractive brick-built village is a fine group: the old church, the rectory, the Hall, partly of the 18th century (now a hospital), and the massive oak lychgate, richly carved, with a fine roof of grey stones from the sea, in memory of a rector who was here for 47 years.

The church, one of the loveliest old shrines in Derbyshire, has a tower begun by the last of the Normans and finished in the 15th century, and 13th century nave and chancel arcades. It is a light and spacious place with fine arches, a 500-year-old clerestory, and charming windows, most of them of the 14th and 15th century. One is especially beautiful with canopied niches in the sides, and at the foot of one niche is a sleeping figure with branches growing from him as in a Tree of Jesse.

On an alabaster tomb lie a man and his wife of five centuries ago, hand in hand, he in a gown and a round cap, she in a dress fastened with a buckle, a veil falling over her fine headdress. They may belong to the Hunt family, one of whom gave the altar table in the time of Charles I. There is part of an old coffin stone built into a pillar near the chancel, but the oldest stone here is one wonderfully carved by a Saxon mason, now set in an outside wall near the tower. A village carpenter of the present century made the carved stalls in the chancel, and they are not unworthy of the stout oak benches of Elizabethan days.

Ault Hucknall. He lies in the quiet church on its green hilltop, the poor parson's son whose portrait hangs with those of kings and queens and nobles in Hardwick Hall near by; who had among his friends Ben Jonson and Galileo. He was Thomas Hobbes, who died with a name ringing through Europe.

Much of his early manhood was spent at the Hall as tutor, and in his later years he made his home at Hardwick and Chatsworth. He lived to be nearly 92, his mind vigorous to the last, fond of his dozen pipes of tobacco ready filled in front of him, hating the thought of death for all his philosophy, and afraid to be left in the dark. So much did he dread being left alone that he insisted on coming with the family from Chatsworth to Hardwick even though his end was near, and he had to be carried on his feather bed in a coach.

When he knew he could not recover he said, "I shall be glad, then, to find a hole to creep out of the world at." This he found at Hardwick Hall, dying in 1679 soon after he had expressed his wish that his epitaph should be simply *The Philosopher's Stone*. But the black marble gravestone in the floor of the Hardwick chapel tells of his service to learning. In the chapel, too, is a great tomb to Anne Keighley, wife of the first Earl of Devonshire, who died in 1627. On the edge of the tomb, perhaps designed by John Smithson, the architect, stand five draped alabaster figures.

It is a fine little church in which they lie, with a charming effect given to the interior by the tower which comes between the nave and chancel. It opens from the nave with a Norman archway, strangely ornamented with beak-heads and curious faces. It opens again to the chancel with a smaller arch which some think Saxon. Other Norman remains are the base of the tower, two round arches of the north arcade, a small west window, and some stones set in a blocked doorway in the west wall. One of the stones is crudely carved with strange figures: on one side is a tall four-legged animal with a long neck and beaked head; it has clawed feet, and its tail curls between its legs; behind it is a tiny quadruped. On the other side is a figure, half man, half animal, holding a cross. Below this is a second stone, oblong in shape and carved with a man holding a sword and a winged dragon with a protruding tongue. A third stone carved with zigzags is over the little Norman window.

A 13th century piscina projects from the chancel wall. The three-light west window and the arches of the south arcade are of the 14th century. The nave roof keeps much 14th century work with bosses and corbels at the ends of the beams. A massive old font, probably Norman, is kept in honour, but it is a modern one that is used.

There is much old stained glass. In the east window of the chapel are remains of glass inserted in 1527 by Sir John Savage. In the upper part of each of the four lights are remains of a figure; they show saints, Christ, and the Madonna. In the lower part are Elizabeth Savage and her daughter kneeling at desks, wearing cloaks embroidered with coats-of-arms; the Hardwick shield of the father of the famous Bess; a man in a blue cloak, and kneeling figures of the two sons of John and Elizabeth, in cloaks of rich blue.

The churchyard has a distant peep of Bolsover Castle; and near one of its many yews is a fine new cross on an old stone. Wooded hills and lovely lanes are all about this place, on the edge of Hardwick's fine park.

Thomas Hobbes was born at Malmesbury in 1588, son of a vicar who sent him to Oxford and got him appointed tutor in the Cavendish family. He enjoyed the friendship of Ben Jonson, Francis Bacon (who dictated some of his essays to him), Galileo, Descartes, and other illustrious men.

His first literary effort was a poem on the Wonders of the Peak of Derbyshire, followed by a translation of Thucydides, which he thought would be a warning to his countrymen, then in the throes of civil ferment. In 1640 he wrote a defence of the royal prerogative, and fled the country fearing the wrath of Parliament. During the next ten years he wrote two other works on his theory of government, and in 1651 issued his masterpiece, *Leviathan*, a work which caused Charles II, who had been his pupil, to refuse to see him. The book made him hated by the Royalists because they thought it implied obedience to Cromwell, and by the Church because it made the ruler head of ecclesiastical affairs.

At 65 Hobbes received a life pension from the Cavendishes, supplemented by £100 a year from the Crown. When over 80 he wrote his autobiography in Latin verse, and translated Homer. He died at Hardwick in 1679.

Bakewell. We must all come to this old Peakland market town if we would know Derbyshire and feel the thrill of it. It is a piece of rare delight, with green pasture and upland breeze, a running silver river and the shade of lovely lanes; a group of charming villages about it, exquisite dales, and two of England's famous houses, Haddon Hall and Chatsworth.

Bakewell is well known for its agricultural show, held on a Thursday early in August. The most important in the North Midlands, it is now claimed to be the largest one-day show in England. The town lies on the banks of the Wye and has two fine old bridges, one of the 15th century with five arches and huge cut-waters where the river is charming with a mill and a weir; and a little packhorse bridge of 1664, hardly four feet wide with a string of arches, on the very edge of the town. Near by is the embattled Holme Hall, built in 1626.

The wells the Romans may have known are of no importance now, but in a wayside garden in the heart of the town is the old ivied bath house the Duke of Rutland built in 1697. There are charming gabled buildings and old inns in the town, a 17th century market-house refashioned and keeping much of its old charm, a delightful row of almshouses as old as Queen Elizabeth I, and the Rutland Arms Hotel where Bakewell's famous tarts (called "puddings" locally) were first made in about 1859, accidentally, it is said, by a kitchen-maid who misunderstood her instructions.

But among all its ancient sights and its old cottages gay with gardens, this fine old place has no more beautiful picture than its church in the shape of a cross with its elegant spire rising from the trees. It is the glory of the town. Its churchyard has lovely views over the valley, quaint epitaphs, and the shaft of one of the finest Saxon crosses in the land. It is about eight feet high and probably of the late 8th century; it was found long ago on the moors with its top part worn away. Richly carved with knot-work and elegant scrolls, the Saxon mason sculptured on it a little animal nibbling foliage, five scenes from the life of Christ (fading away with the centuries), and a recognisable scene of Christ riding on an ass into Jerusalem.

There are only two churches in Derbyshire mentioned in Domesday Book that had two priests, and Bakewell is one of them. Its importance in the old days is shown by what is believed to be the finest collection in England (for number and variety) of ancient coffin stones, carved with all kinds of crosses and other devices—shears, keys, horns, swords, chalices, a bow and arrow, and the curious type showing parts of a figure as if through openings in a coffin-lid. About 60 of them, some of Saxon and Norman date, are in the porch, others are at the west end and some of them are built into the walls as masonry.

The Normans built the noble west doorway with its rich carving of grotesques, beak-heads, and animals; over it is their interlaced arcading, broken by a 15th century window. A massive oblong pillar at the west end of each nave arcade (to support two towers that were never built), the round arches in the west walls of the aisles and traces of the old corbel table in the chancel, are all Norman.

The central tower (an octagon on a low square base) and its spire were mainly rebuilt last century in their mediaeval style. The chancel is fine 13th century work; the porch is of the 14th century, the battlements and clerestory are of the 15th. There is woodwork old and new, the old including the door still swinging on its hinges, a chest made before the Reformation, and a traceried screen nine feet high which has seen over 500 years, but has a modern cornice. The new oak is the chancel screen, the open benches with carved ends, and the 20 stalls with carved misericords, not unworthy of three old ones that remain. New also is the great reredos reaching nearly to the roof, but it embodies wood carving of the figures on Calvary, said to be German work of about 1500. The gem of the mediaeval relics of this church is the octagonal 14th century font with figures of Christ and saints under canopies.

It is a touch of romance, however, that brings so many travellers to the church, for here is the Vernon chapel (made new last century) in which is buried the famous Dorothy Vernon of Haddon Hall. Her monument is a ponderous thing with much heraldic display, on which she kneels with her husband Sir John Manners, he in armour with a beard, and she in a long robe, a close-fitting cap, and a little ruff. At the foot are tiny figures of four children on cushions. They laid the mother here in the reign of Elizabeth, four years before the Armada came, and her husband followed her a few years before Shakespeare died.

Facing them on the chapel wall is another pretentious monument on which kneels their son George. He is at prayer with his wife, and above them are the words nobody believes: *The day of man's death is better than his birth.* Below them are nine children, each one under an arch with a Bible text. One is in swaddling clothes with the words, *Mine age is nothing in respect of thee;* another, said to have been weak-minded, has for his text, *By the grace of God I am what I am.*

The oldest of the Vernon monuments is the small table tomb of finely veined alabaster of John Vernon of 1477; it has angels at the ends and seated figures at the sides. Dorothy's father, Sir George, called the King of the Peak, lies in alabaster with his two wives. His hair is straight, he is in armour with a sword, and he has a double chain round his neck. Both wives have long robes and small caps. But older still is a knight now lying on a modern tomb, Sir Thomas Wendesley, who fell at the battle of Shrewsbury in 1403. He is rich indeed with skirt of chain mail, SS collar, and a richly decorated belt, and his head is on a cushion supported by angels. On the wall of one of the aisles is an exquisite little sculpture of Sir Godfrey Foljambe and his wife, both at prayer under a double canopy, he wearing armour and helmet, she in a lovely headdress. It will soon be 600 years since they were buried here.

Near Church Lane, above the church, is an interesting 15th century house, once called the Priest's House and perhaps a chantry house connected with the church. It has been converted into a folk museum, with relics and antiquities of old Bakewell.

Ballidon. It has a few cottages and farms sheltering under White Edge and Blackstone's Low, with its huge limestone quarry, and a lonely chapel away in the fields. Much restored, this has a nave and chancel under one roof, and keeps a Norman chancel arch and a Norman doorway, some 15th century windows, and a 15th century font crudely carved with varied patterns.

Bamford. On a hillside above the Derwent Valley lies this Peakland village near the Yorkshire border. On one side is the long gritstone outcrop of Bamford Edge; on the other, it looks out to the great height of Win Hill, which rises over 1520 feet above sea-level and looks down into five dales. Ebenezer Elliott sang of it in his *Corn Law Rhymes*:

> *The might of man may triumph or may fail,*
> *But, Eldest Brother of the air and light,*
> *Firm shalt thou stand when demi-gods turn pale:*
> *For thou, ere science dawned on reason's night*
> *Wast, and wilt be when mind shall rule all other might.*

Bamford's people live in gritstone houses with gay gardens, and they go to a church built in 1861 by William Butterfield, with a slender steeple over 100 feet high. Sheep-dog trials are held at Bamford each year on Spring Bank Holiday Monday.

Barlborough. Almost on the Yorkshire boundary, it is a charming village of old stone houses and colourful red roofs. Within a stone's throw it has the old cross with three sundials, two fine 18th century houses, a charming almshouse of 1752, and the church. The Normans thought it important enough to mark its name with a red line in the Conqueror's Domesday Book, and of their church there still remain four round arches between the nave and the north aisle, resting on pillars of the late 12th century. As old as the pillars is the chancel arch on foliage corbels, and part of the base of the tower with a small window. The south arcade, with the south aisle, was rebuilt in 1899.

On a great stone in the north aisle is the battered sculptured figure of a woman wearing a long mantle over a close-fitting gown; she is Lady Joan Furnival, and her monument has come here from the chancel of Worksop Priory, where they laid her about 1395. A brass tablet in the north chapel tells of Margaret and Mary Pole, two maiden sisters who died within two months in 1755, after restoring part of the church and giving the village its almshouse. The old home of the Poles was Park Hall, still a substantial house some two miles from the village. In the chancel is a small 14th century painting of the crucifixion, brought from Italy.

A mile from the church is the fine Barlborough Hall, with projecting bays and embattled turrets, built in 1583, probably by Robert Smythson, the great Elizabethan architect of Hardwick Hall, for Francis Rodes, who was born a few miles away at Staveley Woodthorpe and was one of the judges who tried Mary, Queen of Scots. One of its great possessions is a magnificent stone chimneypiece with the figures of the judge and his two wives. The house, with its glorious approach along an avenue of limes planted at the end of the 17th century, became the home of the judge's son, Sir John Rodes, and of many generations of his descendants, but is now a Roman Catholic preparatory school.

Barlow. It looks across a green valley to the slopes of Monk Wood, and has a little aisleless church both old and new. It has been here over eight centuries, and has Norman work in the lofty doorway within the porch, sheltering an old oak door, and in a deeply splayed window in the north wall of the nave. A rare possession is the tiny Norman piscina found last century and now built into an east wall. The 14th century builders made the porch, near which is an outside stairway which once led to a gallery over the little chapel, and two of their windows still remain. The 19th century chancel was intended to be in keeping with the ancient church.

A fine 13th century coffin stone carved with a raised cross, with foliage springing from the stem, is a memorial to Julia, wife of Adam Frauncies. Against a wall is an alabaster stone engraved with portraits of Robert Barley and his wife; he wears 15th century armour and a helmet, his sword by his side, and is holding the hand of his wife who wears a cloak fastened by a cord. Another of the family buried here was Robert Barlow, who died in 1532 not long after he married Bess of Hardwick when he was very young and she only 14. He was the first of her four husbands and left her large estates.

A Well Dressing Festival (resembling that at Tissington) is held at Barlow every year in August, and the ceremony here is said to be over 200 years old.

Barrow-on-Trent. The church of this lowland village and an old timbered house near by look across the Trent meadows where floods sweep down at times and lap the garden walls. Within a a stone's throw of one another are a long row of attractive brick cottages and a fine cross. Made after the fashion of 1000 years ago, from a block of stone weighing 12 tons, it came to this small place after being offered in 1916 to the Derbyshire village which sent the greatest number of men to the Great War in proportion to its population.

Nothing is left of the Norman church given to the Knights Hospitallers whose house and chapel are thought to have been at Arleston not far away, where ancient stone foundations are in a farmhouse. The earliest work in the bright church is the 13th century group of pillars with unusual clustered shafts in the north arcade; most of the rest is of the 14th century, including the charming windows. The tower was given its belfry in the 15th century; the font is 500 years old. Between the chancel and south aisle is a great peephole, and on the opposite side is a passage which probably served the same purpose. In a recess of the south aisle, which he perhaps rebuilt, lies the battered alabaster figure of a 14th century priest, his head on a cushion and his feet on a dog. In the chancel is a tomb with inscription to William Sale of 1665, one of the figures in the family group in the church at Weston-on-Trent.

Barton Blount. At the end of a lane which becomes an open road through the park, it lies in undulating pastoral country with

31

a tiny church in the grounds of the great house, grown out of the old home of the Blounts who were here from the 14th to the 16th century. An old manor house at the time of the Civil War, it was partly fortified to watch the movements of the Cavaliers at Tutbury, and perhaps the sorry plight of the old church at the end of the 17th century was due to that war. On a terrace is fine wrought ironwork by Robert Bakewell, brought from St Mary's Bridge in Derby.

Neat and trim with its bell turret and lancet windows, the church keeps two relics in the massive 14th century font and the 13th century figure of a woman holding a heart in her hands. She belonged perhaps to the Bakepuze family who sold the estate to Sir Walter Blount, the famous warrior. The arms of Bakepuze and Blount are in the windows.

Sir Walter Blount lives as the Blunt of Shakespeare's *Henry the Fourth*. He was standard-bearer for Henry at Shrewsbury, and was killed there, it is said, through being mistaken for the king. The most famous of the Blounts was another Sir Walter who was Lord High Treasurer in 1464 and became the first Lord Mountjoy. Another was made Earl of Devonshire in the year Elizabeth died. He was one of the handsomest men of her court, and was not more than 20 when he fought a duel with the Earl of Essex, who had been envious of him because the queen gave him a gold brooch for his skill in a tilting match. He was with Sir Philip Sidney at the Battle of Zutphen, and in Armada year he built ships at his own expense and sent them against the Spaniards. He is buried in Westminster Abbey.

Baslow. It is delightful, set in a valley of rich meadows where hills and woods and rocks climb up to rolling moors, where the Derwent comes sweeping grandly down on its way to the glory of Chatsworth. For a magnificent view we climb Baslow Edge to the lonely Eagle Stone; and for something altogether charming we go down to the old bridge, with three lofty arches spanning the stream and still with the little stone shelter built for the toll collector.

A younger bridge carries most of the burden for the old. Venerable grey houses gather round the bridge they have kept company with so long. A lane leads to the stone-gabled Bubnell Hall, built in the 17th century on the site of a homestead of the Bassets for many generations, a family ever on the side of justice and liberty. One put his name to Magna Carta, another went on the Crusades with Richard Lionheart, a third sat in our first Parliament.

Between the new bridge and the old is the church, in a churchyard a joy to see, with trimmed yews here and there and great elms round the edge, some of them reflected in the river. There is an 18th century sundial on an older flight of steps. The oldest story of the church is told by fragments of stone knotwork thought to be part of a Saxon cross, now in the porch. Built into the porch is a coffin stone perhaps 700 years old, with a carved cross and two keys. Engraved coffin stones are built into the lintels of the clerestory windows. The low tower and its spire are 700 years old, and from the 14th century come the nave arcades, and a doorway in which a stout old door still hangs. The chancel was made new in 1853 and restored again in 1911.

Near the door by which we enter are a whip which was used for driving dogs out of church and a pitch-pipe used for retuning the organ after it was installed in 1856. There is elaborately carved modern oak in the chancel screen, in the altar, the reredos, and the stalls, and two reading-desks with figures of the Evangelists. Among the windows is one with a figure of St Martin to a doctor who served the village for half a century and died in 1912. A tablet tells of two vicars, father and son, who were both here for 30 years, and another tells of the third generation, Frederick Barker, who followed for a year before he went to Australia to become Bishop of Sydney. For 28 years he served the Dominion Church with great success, built a noble cathedral, and founded a college. He loved his kingdom overseas, but when he died he was brought to this village where he was born. The story is told of this Barker family that when the Duke of Cambridge came to Baslow church he saw four young men seated near him all over 6 feet 3 inches, and on hearing that they were sons of the vicar said one of them must be a soldier. Within a week a commission in the army was sent to the vicarage, and one of the sons accepted it.

Beeley. Near the gate of Chatsworth's glorious park and set among the hills, Beeley has wonderful views whichever way we turn. Sheltered on the east by Beeley Moor, it looks down the Derwent Valley to fine wooded slopes rising to Stanton Moor, a panorama all the lovelier when the heather is in bloom.

The village has joys of its own, hidden from those who hurry by to Chatsworth. Its roads go up and down and twist and turn as they take us by houses of old grey stone, by cottage and school and the 17th century grey hall (still proud above the wayside though a farmhouse now), by a little green with a splendid lime, to an ancient church with sturdy tower close to the gabled vicarage.

There are limes round the churchyard, too, and a gnarled yew which was once a massive tree is said to be as old as the oldest part of the church, the Norman doorway within the porch it shelters. With three heads carved on its hood, but with new marble pillars in place of the old shafts, this doorway is all that is left of the Norman church except for a corbel in a corner of the aisle and the font so altered that its ancient character is lost. The yew has looked on many changes as its glory has waxed and waned. It saw the coming of the 13th century builders whose masonry is in the north wall of the chancel. It saw the 14th century add to the tower, and the 15th crown it with battlements and pinnacles.

In the chancel is a Jacobean chair and on the wall is a brass not quite nine inches square in memory of a man who was born while Shakespeare was still at Stratford, and lived to be 95. He was John Calvert who died in 1710, and the interest of his brass is in the engraved figure below the inscription, clad in a shroud but showing face and hands. A 17th century sanctus bell once here now hangs over the school.

There are memorials to the Saviles, and a stone in the baptistry to John Greaves of 1694, the last of the Greaves of Beeley. With these two families the story of the village was linked for five and a half centuries, and their memory clings to a 17th century gabled farmhouse nearly a mile away.

Beighton. Its church, bordering on Sheffield, was in such a sorry plight before its restoration that the chancel walls were taken down, and on the plaster being removed from the pointed arch there was found above it the splendid arch the Normans built 800 years ago. It was a delightful surprise, but unhappily the arch was so decayed that it could not be saved. Its old proportions have been kept in the new chancel arch, however, and also the zigzag design.

The tower is of the 15th century, with earlier work in the capitals of the arch opening to the nave, these being carved with nail-head ornament and curious heads. A mediaeval stone with a pair of shears by the stem of a cross forms the sill of one of the windows in the north aisle. The church has lost its Norman arch but has found some of its mediaeval treasures. The restoration brought to light fragments of 15th century glass now in the windows of the aisles, and an altar stone with five consecration crosses which is in use again, set in an oak frame. This was once part of the roof, over 500 years old.

Beighton has been transferred to the City of Sheffield for administrative purposes, but remains in the diocese of Derby.

Belper. The Derwent has made it into a busy town, for its water power decided Jedediah Strutt in 1776 to build his cotton mills here. Part of the old mills (rebuilt in 1797) survives among the newer buildings (now making sewing-thread), and in the shadow of their great walls some of Belper's beauty lies, delightful gardens where the water mirrors the wooded hillside. Just beyond the mills the river is spanned by a fine stone bridge of 1795, replacing the older one washed away by a flood. Here, in a lovely natural setting, the river makes a crescent waterfall on its way to the valley beyond the bridge. In the river here original timbers were discovered from the foundations of the only viaduct constructed by George Stephenson, as good as new after 94 years immersion in the river bed.

It is thought that Edmund Crouchback, Earl of Lancaster, who had a seat here and called the village Beau Repaire, built the 13th century chapel of St John the Baptist, which has become a sacred place again after being a school. It is a simple nave and chancel with a single roof on five old beams. There are two stone seats for priests and a piscina niche, and the church has a rare possession in a stone altar table still in its original position, with one of the five consecration crosses still visible. Back in the church is the 15th century font, whose bowl was at the vicarage while the base was buried in the churchyard.

St Peter's Church was completed in 1824, a fine building outside which has a great tower with turrets and battlements, though inside it looks as if it has turned nonconformist. It has two fine avenues of limes in its churchyard. At The Fleet, some distance south of the marketplace, a Well-Dressing Festival is held in July.

Outside the town to the north, at the top of a lovely hillside graveyard with fine trees, is buried Jedediah Strutt, high above the valley where the river flows which turned his mill-wheel to fortune. He was born at South Normanton in 1726, the son of a farmer. Distinguishing himself by a faculty for mechanics, revealed by his making water-wheels and improving his father's ploughs, he was apprenticed to a Findern wheelwright. He followed his trade for seven years after his apprenticeship, and then, inheriting a farm from a Blackwell uncle, married Elizabeth Woollatt, with whose family he had lodged at Findern, where her brother William was a hosiery manufacturer.

At the suggestion of Woollatt, Strutt invented (in 1756) a machine with turning-needles which, applied to the stocking-frame, produced, as desired, either ribbed stockings or unribbed stockings. Adapted to other machines it furnished a variety of fabrics such as manufacture had not previously known. With factories at Derby and Nottingham to utilise it, the firm of Strutt and Woollatt, with a third partner, named Need, prospered greatly. When Arkwright appeared at Nottingham and the bankers, doubtful of the feasibility of his cotton-spinning machine, declined to finance him, Strutt came to his aid and is said to have suggested improvements in the machine which was to revolutionise the industrial world. A new firm (Arkwright, Strutt, and Need) was formed, and in 1769 opened in Nottingham the first cotton-spinning factory.

The factory had horses as motive power for the machinery, but after two years a move was made to Cromford, where water-power was available, and there in 1773 the first calico was produced. Many lesser contrivances stand to the credit of Jedediah Strutt, who, dying in 1797, left sons who inherited his inventive capacity, enabling them to contribute in turn to the wealth of their generation.

Birchover. Its old stone houses cling to the hilly road which climbs to Stanton Moor, with its stone circle, monoliths, and burial mounds, and brings us to a glorious panorama of wooded hill and valley. At the foot of the village are the Rowtor Rocks, an outcrop of millstone grit rising in places to 150 feet.

36

This massive pile of rocks, which has vague connections with the Druids, was shaped according to the whim of a parson who lived in a Tudor manor house at their foot, since made new. Thomas Eyre, who died in 1717, one of a famous Derbyshire family, built himself a study in the rocks, and had the seats hewn out for the entertainment of his friends, so that they might sit and enjoy the glorious prospect of the valley far below giving way to beautiful hills. He built a new chapel in the shadow of the rocks near his house, and by the porch there are architectural fragments from the Norman church.

Near enough to be neighbours are the fine rocks of Cratcliffe Tor and Robin Hood's Stride. Cratcliffe Tor has a shallow cave at the foot in which a hermit of 600 years ago has carved a crucifix and hewn out a seat and a niche for a lamp. The other pile of rocks has been given its queer name because the distance between two upstanding pinnacles (about 22 yards) is supposed to measure the length of Robin Hood's stride.

Blackwell. A rural oasis in a countryside of collieries is the old part of the village, with fine views from its hilltop, and a cross in its church porch taking us back a thousand years. It is the lower part of a Saxon cross, five feet above the base, two sides carved with interlacing knotwork and two with braid work. It was marking time when the Saxons worshipped on this spot, perhaps before the first church was built. The church was rebuilt in 1826 and enlarged in 1870, and all that is left of its olden days is a round pillar and capital of a lost arcade of about 1200, built into the new nave wall.

Not far away is a farmhouse which has come into England's story, for its attic, whose little window looks out to the church, saw the working out of an invention which was to revolutionise the hosiery trade. Here came Jedediah Strutt when his uncle died and left him all his stock. It was here that he brought his bride in 1755, and here he turned from his farming to follow his bent for mechanics. Under this old gabled roof he brought his ribbed stocking frame to perfection, and here his first child was born, the oak cradle he made for it being one of the cherished possessions of the Strutts today.

Bolsover. It glories in its situation, its old remains, and its story. It had a market 700 years ago. Once it was famous for making spurs and brilliant buckles which had to stand the test of a loaded

37

cart passing over them, and stone from its quarries helped to build the Houses of Parliament.

Bolsover came into the Conqueror's Domesday Book as part of the vast possessions of William Peveril. It was he who built a fortress on the rocky spur where Bolsover Castle stands now, a lofty pile, partly in ruins, crowning the fine ridge nearly 600 feet above sea-level, a splendid landmark from the valley below.

Nothing is left today of the Norman structure, which had fallen into ruin by the time Sir Charles Cavendish came into possession in 1612. True to the tradition of his mother, Bess of Hardwick, he set about rebuilding the Castle as we see it, employing John Smithson (the son of Robert Smythson, builder of Hardwick Hall) as architect. He preserved the site of the Norman keep in the square and lofty house with corner turrets and tower, and a domed lantern rising from the roof. He preserved the site of the Norman bailey in the massive wall enclosing an old-world garden.

Over the main entrance of the house a great figure of Hercules supports a balcony and the Cavendish shield. Some of the 30 rooms are notable for their vaulted ceilings, fine chimneypieces, their panelling and decorations; the finest and largest room, the Star Chamber, has a ceiling of blue and gold. Sir William of the next generation carried on the work, building the magnificent range stretching along a natural terrace outside the precincts of the old keep, their great rooms and long gallery now roofless ruins. He also built the splendid Riding School adjoining the stables, probably to the designs of Huntingdon Smithson, the son of John.

Three times did Sir William Cavendish receive Charles I here with lavish expense. In 1634 he provided a "stupendous entertainment" for the King and Henrietta Maria, at a cost of £15,000, an enormous sum for those times. It included a masque, *Love's Welcome*, written by Ben Jonson, the friend of Shakespeare. Sir William garrisoned the Castle for the king and was made general of the northern army. He was on the losing side at Marston Moor and fled to the Continent, where he lived (often in great poverty) till the Restoration. He accompanied Charles II to London, the poorer, it is said, by a million pounds for his loyalty, with his Castle more or less in ruin. In 1665 he was made Duke of Newcastle and is buried in Westminster Abbey.

The church is said to have been begun by William Peveril, but nearly all that remained of the mediaeval church was destroyed by fires in 1898 and again in 1960, which left the 13th century tower and spire, the Cavendish chapel of 1618, and a few interesting relics. Fragments of coffin-lids in the porch are carved with a sickle, shears, and a hatchet as well as a cross. A tympanum over the south door of the chancel, carved with figures of Mary and John by the Cross, badly weathered, is of the 13th century. A great battered sculpture in the north chapel was found face downward in use as a step at the door: it is thought to have been the altarpiece of the 13th century church, and is richly carved with the Wise Men adoring the Child on Mary's lap, two curious animals in the background.

Made new again after the second fire, the church is spacious with high roofs and bold arcades, and has much fine new woodwork.

Two elaborate monuments in the Cavendish chapel are to Sir Charles who built the Castle and died in 1617, and to Henry Cavendish (second Duke of Newcastle), who died in 1691. Sir Charles lies under a canopy, wearing armour; his wife is on the tomb below, on the side of which kneel their daughter and two sons. To them the father addresses a quaint poem. The monument to Henry Cavendish has a pediment on four massive columns, and sculptured figures of Fame and History. The architects of the castle, John and Huntingdon Smithson, were also probably buried in the church. Huntingdon's grave-slab, with a curious epitaph, full of praise, now stands in the south aisle, but John's burial (1634) is recorded only in the parish register.

Bonsall. Once famous for its lead mines, it is tucked away in a deep cleft of the hillside, with the lovely Via Gellia far below and Masson towering above, a hill well worth climbing for its glorious panorama and its view of the Matlocks in the valley of the Derwent. Charming is the grouping of old stone houses and the 17th century inn round the picturesque old market-cross, a slender ball-topped pillar on a great flight of 13 steps.

The fine church above the housetops has a 14th century tower and spire, the tower low and sturdy, with embattled parapet, pinnacles, and gargoyles, and the lovely spire with three encircling bands of quatrefoils, flowers, shields, and fleur-de-lys. Of the same time are the porch and the doorway through which we enter the church, and the pillars and capitals of the north arcade, with a curious animal carved at the foot of one pillar. The oldest remains are of the 13th century, including the clustered pillars of the south arcade, a tiny piscina, and fragments of coffin-stones. The font is of the 15th century, and a small headstone cross with crude carving, now in the church, may be 600 years old. There is a brass inscription to an honest 17th century lawyer, Henry Hopkinson of Lincoln's Inn.

A Well-Dressing Festival (like that at Tissington) is held at Bonsall early in August.

Boulton. It is almost swallowed up by Derby, but its church, though made new in the 19th century, and restored in the present century, has something left of Norman days. It stands in a pleasant churchyard, its porch sheltering a Norman doorway with shafts and capitals and zigzag moulding. A holy-water stoup of curious shape, with four outer ribs, has had its adventure after a life of 800 years, for this Norman treasure was found in a farmyard.

Near the pulpit (made from an alabaster gravestone in the sanctuary, and inlaid with marble) are old tiles set in the floor, one with the unusual pattern of two keys on a cross, while on two others are the heads of a king and a queen, perhaps Edward I and Queen Eleanor.

Boylestone. Little happens to it now, for it is a quiet place, yet it had its hour of drama long ago. Here came a little company of Cromwell's men in the night, dismounting from their horses and silently surrounding the church that stands so high above the sunken lane. They waited for the peep of dawn to call upon the enemy to surrender. Indoors were 200 Cavaliers sheltering for the night on their way to the relief of Wingfield Manor. They had kept no watch outside the church and so were caught in a trap of their own setting. One by one as they came through the priest's doorway they were taken and stripped of their arms, "men, colours, and all, without the loss of one man on either side".

An avenue of stately limes has grown along the way the soldiers must have trod, bringing us to the church whose tower with odd peaked roof is little more than a century old. The oldest stones of the church are in the 13th century buttresses of the chancel, the rest of it having been made new in the 14th century, perhaps by Walter de Waldeshef who was chief butler to the king, and Governor of the Castle and Honour of the Peak; but the east window is a century later, and some of the windows are new, as is the chancel arch. The font is 600 years old. Here still is the priest's doorway through which the Cavaliers walked out to meet their captors; and there are still oak tie-beams and bosses in the roofs which looked down on that dramatic day.

Brackenfield. Tucked in a steep hillside high above the road to Ashover, looking out on a fine panorama where distance lends enchantment to the patchwork fields, the towers, spires, and distant chimneys of an industrial countryside, is a little grey ruin, roofless and alone, hidden from view by the chestnut trees around it, and glorying in the bracken which gives the place its name.

A soft green carpet grows within its walls, and wild flowers have rooted in the crevices, but the windows, the bell turret, and the two stone seats of what was once a porch tell the tale of an ancient chapel made new in the 16th century, and abandoned in the 19th when a new church was built.

The new church is about a mile from the ruin, down in the hamlet of winding lanes and fine trees. It shelters a few oak benches and the 15th century screen from the old chapel, the screen now against the west wall of the nave, with tracery in its bays. To the north is the attractive Ogston Reservoir, completed in 1958 and now a favourite venue for sailing. The River Amber, flowing from it, bounds the park of Ogston Hall, an interesting building of many periods, from the early 16th to the 19th century.

Bradbourne. In a charming setting on its peaceful hilltop, it feels the blast of the north winds from the limestone uplands, but sees the kindly green of Haven Hill on the other side. Down below, the Havenhill Dale Brook flows past to the wheel of an old corn-mill, still working, by the Ashbourne road.

A charming group is the vicarage, the old church, and the fine Hall which has come through the years. A stone house with many gables in an old-world garden, it is said to have something yet of the

D

old place built here for a few monks of Dunstable Priory looking
after great flocks of sheep on these rich pastures. It was enlarged
and given its fine oak staircase early in the 17th century by the
Buckstons, who have memorials in the church. One is to Thomas
Buckston, who fought at Culloden in 1746 and was 87 when he died
a few years after Trafalgar, one of the oldest officers in the army.

The churchyard has in its keeping the oldest possession of the
village, all that is left of an 8th century Saxon cross, carved with
foliage and crude figures. Part of it stands about three feet high,
and to this are now attached two other pieces which have been used
as posts for a stile and a gate. The fine tower stands almost as the
Normans left it, massive, like most of their structures. It has a turret
stairway, and a Norman corbel table of tiny heads below a 15th
century parapet, but the glory of the tower is its charming south
doorway with three orders of moulding, one of beak-heads, the other
two of birds and animals. The doorway of the porch and the one
through which we enter the church are also Norman.

The nave arcade with clustered pillars is over 650 years old, and
the windows are of the three later mediaeval centuries. There is an
old stone coffin and two fonts; the fine square one in use is 700
years old, the round one is older still. The arms of Edensor are
among old glass fragments. Four pieces of wood, carved with
quaint heads, leaves, and flowers, are about 400 years old, and may
have belonged to the pew of the Bradbournes who held the manor
from the 13th century until the end of Tudor days. Their old home,
Lea Hall, to the west, beyond the valley of the Bradbourne Brook, is
now a farmhouse.

Bradley. With its beautiful bowers of trees and winding lanes, it
knows the stillness of the dreaming countryside. Its wayside church
by the open fields, with the great house over the way, is a bright
place with chancel and nave under one fine old roof. It was made
new in the 14th century, the east window and those in the nave
being of this time. Stone faces adorn their hoods outside. Two
14th century brackets in the chancel have carvings of men with
beards and curly hair, and in the south wall of the nave is an ancient
stone with crude figures under a tree, perhaps Adam and Eve. The
13th century font has a round bowl enriched with arcading. Fine

carving of our own century is in the oak pulpit, and the altar table with eight spandrels in eight patterns.

The Hall opposite the church was converted out of stables which had been built in advance for another house. It was here that Dr Johnson used to visit Mrs Meynell and her daughters when staying at Ashbourne with his friend Dr Taylor, and here he began his friendship with Miss Hill Boothby. Their friendship was one of the fine things of his life. A gracious woman with many accomplishments, she encouraged Johnson when he needed encouragement most, and his letters show how greatly he valued her friendship. Her death in 1756 robbed him of the precious thing he found here. Long afterwards, when his great Dictionary had made him famous, he looked back with thankfulness to the happy times this small village gave him.

Two other men who made their name in the world have known this place: John Bingham the Nonconformist, who lived here for three years after being ejected from the living of Marston-on-Dove in 1662, and Thomas Bancroft, known as the small poet, and long remembered for his epigrams.

Bradwell. Relatively plain amid much loveliness, encircled by lofty hills and sheltering under the fine height of Bradwell Edge, it is all very old, lying near the Batham Gate, the Roman road which ran from Brough to Buxton. In its busy lead-mining days it found the Bagshaw Cavern, with fine crystalline formations. A flight of 130 steps leads us down to grottoes of singular beauty.

Reached through a short avenue of limes is the plain little 19th century church, with good modern oak in the chancel. At the south end of Bradwell Dale, the mile-long gorge with towering cliffs sheer on each side, is Hazlebadge Hall, a 16th century farmhouse, one of the oldest in Derbyshire, with the arms of the Vernons on a gable. It was part of the dowry Dorothy Vernon of Haddon Hall brought to her husband Sir John Manners. A Well-Dressing Festival (as at Tissington) takes place at Bradwell early in August.

Brailsford. Trim and pleasant, midway between Derby and Ashbourne, is this old village which belonged to one of the few Saxon families who kept their lands through the days of Norman England. It has still one thing that its Saxon owner knew, the

43

remains of the 11th century churchyard cross. Long buried under its old base, the shaft has been set up on a new stone, leaving its old foundation a few feet away. There are fine 19th century benches in the church, so that we are able here to see the work of craftsmen separated by a thousand years.

The old church stands with great limes and a splendid yew in the fields between the village and Ednaston, for it was built to serve both places. Of the church the Normans built when the cross was young only three things remain, an arch at the end of the aisle, the great pillar adjoining it (helping to support the tower), and a sturdy column and capital holding up one side of the chancel arch. The rest of the pillars of the arcade are of the 14th century, but their arches and the clerestory over them are at least three centuries younger. The chancel with its sedilia and piscina and an arched recess is also of the 14th century. The fine embattled tower was built about 1500 in the western bay of the nave, leaving the aisle longer than the nave, and shortening two of its own buttresses which end in hideous gargoyles.

The mediaeval porch, made new in the 17th century, shelters a massive 400-year-old door with heavy ironwork, the great lock and key-plate bordered with chevrons and flowers. An old chest is about six feet long, and on a wall is a piece of panelling from a 17th century pew on which we read that somebody paid 22s. for this seat to Mr Barnabas Pool, rector. Several sturdy benches are all that is left of the fine seating which filled the church in Elizabeth 1's day. The font is of the 15th century, its base carved with the Tudor rose. Built into the outer wall is part of a coffin lid engraved with a cross and a pair of shears, in memory of a mediaeval wool merchant or sheep farmer.

In the hamlet of Ednaston, lovely with trees on the other side of the Brailsford Brook, was born in 1790 Thomas Beighton, one of the bravest missionaries, who went to the Malay Straits. Soon after his ordination at Derby and his marriage with another earnest evange-list, Abigail Tobitt, he left England in 1818, giving the rest of his life to mission work in Malaya where he was the best-loved white man. He not only went about preaching and teaching, but set up his own printing press at Penang, so that he could publish books in the Malay language. Every year he issued thousands of copies of books and tracts, the crown of his labours being his own translation of *Pilgrim's Progress*.

Brassington. This grey limestone village on a green hill has 17th century houses and an old church set high above the wayside. Its tower comes from Norman days, except for the embattled parapet, the tops of the old buttresses, and a 13th century window over a much later doorway. From Norman times also is the plain bowl of the font and a fine nave arcade of round arches on massive pillars with bold capitals. The two small bays between the chancel and the chapel are of about 1200, the porch is of the 13th century, the lofty chancel arch is of the 14th century, the clerestory and a chancel window are of the 15th.

We may spare a thought for a 17th century Yorkshire rector who died on a journey and was buried here; he was Michael Adams of Treton, and this is what we read of him:

"Pause, Traveller, for a while and drop at least a passing tear for the lamentable death of a certain traveller, whom perchance travelling hence, when a fierce winter was raging without, the more raging heat of an inextinguishable fever seized him within, and carried him without a doubt to the mansions of the Lord in a chariot of fire like unto Elijah."

High up in the wall of the tower, only seen with much difficulty, is a stone 12 inches by 10 inches, carved with the quaint figure of a man with one hand on his heart. Its story is unknown, but it is probably the work of a Saxon sculptor found by the Normans and built into their tower. He is the oldest inhabitant of the village, and the one most rarely seen.

On a steep hill about 800 feet above sea-level, Brassington is famous for the scenery and the ancient remains around. We can trace a Roman road and find the graves of prehistoric men; near by are the jagged Rainster Rocks and Hipley Hill with its caves, Hoe Grange Quarry where remains of some of the first animals in England have been found, and Harborough Rocks, with the strange fantastic shapes of weathered limestone outcrops, and a cave occupied during the Early Iron Age. A wide view opens from this hill, over 1200 feet above sea-level.

Little more than two miles away to the north-west rises the

distinctive hill of Minning Low, crossed by the Roman road that ran from Buxton to Derby. On its summit, a ring of beeches surrounds the rock-chambered graves of the New Stone Age. Here we are alone on the top of the world, looking out to a mighty panorama of limestone hills, in the solitude of the earth with the wonder of the past.

Breadsall. It lies on the hillside above the Derwent, with a treasure it lost and found, and memories of a strange man who is buried in the church. A charming road under the trees brings us to Breadsall Priory, a 17th century house with tower and turrets (modernised in the 19th century) on the site of an Augustinian priory of 700 years ago. Many families have lived here since the monks were turned out and the estate became the property of Henry Grey, who married a daughter of Mary Tudor. Here the Darwins lived from 1799 to 1858, and here Erasmus Darwin died in 1802. He was a physician, poet, and philosopher, and there is a memorial to him in the old church on the hill.

The massive 13th century tower with a 14th century spire is a fine landmark, and its churchyard has charming views over the Derwent. All that is left of the Norman church is the fine south doorway, in which swings a modern door on beautiful iron hinges, at least 500 years old, some of the curves forming graceful necks and heads of birds. The church was set on fire by Suffragettes in 1914 and was carefully restored two years later by W. D. Caröe.

It was in 1877 that Breadsall found a rare and beautiful thing it had forgotten, an exquisite carving in alabaster of Our Lady of Pity. The artist has depicted a wonderful pathos on her face as she holds the Crucified Christ on her knee. The sculpture was found under the floor; it is thought to be 600 years old, and probably of German origin.

The chancel has a 13th century lancet. From the 14th century come the nave arcade, the south walls of nave and chancel, and the porch. The east window and the great embattled font are of the 15th century. The nave roof has beautiful bosses, and angels support the richly moulded beams.

One of Breadsall's rectors was the scholar, John Heiron. He used the mediaeval Old Hall near the church as a vicarage, a building of stone and timber, once the manor house. The old scholar was one of the ejected Nonconformists at the Restoration. It is quaintly recorded of him that he had many Providential Deliverances when he was but a child. He was tossed by a cow; he fell out of a window; he fell into the Trent and yet received no harm. He was carried down the river in a boat alone when the wind was high, and he would probably have been drowned in a whirlpit if one that saw him had not taken the private boat and stopped him. He survived all these excitements to preach in 66 churches in Derbyshire and in 30 churches in other counties.

As Scott thought his poet's fame would suffer if he acknowledged the authorship of the Waverley Novels, so Erasmus Darwin feared his standing as a physician would be compromised if he permitted his name to appear on the poems which have kept his fame alive.

By his first marriage he was the grandfather of Charles Darwin, and by his second he was grandfather of Sir Francis Galton, a title indeed to renown, but Erasmus stands broad-based and secure in the opinion of posterity, apart from the celebrity of his descendants. Trained at Edinburgh, he established a lucrative practice and a delightful circle of friends at Lichfield, stronghold of Dr Johnson. Diametrically opposed in all that matters in politics and philosophy, the two men met, admired, and disliked each other.

But Darwin, who was not only the best physician of his age but a man of deep learning and original thought, was king of the Lunatics, as they called themselves, friends who met in turn at each other's houses: Anna Seward, who wished to marry him; Richard Lovell Edgeworth, father of Maria; Thomas Day, author of *Sandford and Merton*; Josiah Wedgwood, the potter; Samuel Galton; the inventors James Watt and Matthew Boulton; and the discoverer of oxygen, Joseph Priestley.

Erasmus Darwin lives for us today mainly because of one work which in effect was two. He published first the *Loves of the Plants*, but this was really the second part of his *Botanic Garden*, which followed. The first poem teems with wit and fancy no less than with extravagant absurdity; the Botanic Garden is rich with foresight and prophecy. His mind ranged over an immense field, and, however dimly, he foreshadowed a host of things which were to come, ideas which incurred the ridicule of his own age in England but now prove him to have been of the true fellowship of the prophets.

Breaston. Its trim houses and gardens have views of the meadow-lands where the Trent and Derwent meet. Four fine limes lead to its church, most of which was made new 600 years ago, though the tower and the spire are 700 years old, and a blocked-up doorway was used in the time of King John. It is remarkable for the unusual carvings of the arch stones (now very worn), no two of the patterns being alike.

The interior is bright with pointed arches and windows, and has a fine roof. There is a rich oak reredos with four figures under canopies, an unused Jacobean altar table, three old oak chairs, and a graceful alabaster font of 1720. For six centuries the wide-open eyes of a chubby-cheeked boy have been looking on the happenings in this place. He came into being during the rebuilding of the church and has held up the end arch of the nave arcade ever since. He saw the raising of the walls and the lowering of the roof when he was a hundred years old. A good place for long life Breaston would seem to be, for a weatherworn stone on an outside wall is to Sarah Dyche, who died a centenarian before the Victorian Era had begun.

Bretby. This quiet spot has seen the glory of a castle wax and wane; it has seen the destruction of a wonderful house said to have been built by Inigo Jones, and the passing of an ancient church. It is said that the stones of the old castle were used for the building of the great house, a magnificent place, full of treasures of art and set in gardens with lakes and fountains. Its chapel, richly adorned and lined with cedar wood, was finished in 1696, and it was here that John Heiron, the great Nonconformist, used to preach for the Countess of Chesterfield. In the Civil War the house was fortified for the king and plundered by the Parliamentarians. The wife of the second earl was one of the famous beauties of the court of Charles II, and lived here often. The splendid pile was destroyed in the 18th century, owing, it is said, to a mistaken idea that it was unsafe, and the present hall, now a hospital, was built in 1813 by Sir Jeffry Wyatville, who made the large addition to Chatsworth.

The 13th century church, over half a mile away, was pulled down when the new one was built on its site in 1878; all that remains of it is masonry in the west wall. The reredos Crucifixion was once a picture in the Hall. It is strange to find in this little church, so hidden from the busy world, an inscription to Lord Beaconsfield. We understand why it is here when we remember that one of the joys of Disraeli's life was to leave his troubles in London to spend a few quiet days as the guest of Lady Chesterfield. The memorial was put here by the countess, one of the two beautiful sisters Disraeli loved, and we read that it is in memory of the foremost man of his age, a record of a much-prized friendship and a lasting regret. Lord Beaconsfield used to say of Bretby that it scattered flowers and fruit over his whole existence.

In the years after the death of his wife Disraeli found great consolation in the friendship of Lady Chesterfield and her sister Lady Bradford. He made them members of a little group he had playfully formed of his woman friends; he called it the Order of the Bee and he gave his members a brooch with a bee on it. Lady Chesterfield's house was always open to him, and his table was regularly furnished from its gardens, its dairies, its coverts, and its poultry runs. One of his letters to her says that once, at a dinner, the servant came in perpetually, announcing, "Fruit from Bretby, Flowers from Bretby, Butter from Bretby; Blessed Bretby!"

Once he wrote from Bretby to Lady Bradford expressing his great concern at the burden he was imposing on her remaining there as an invalid. The dear angel, he said, was more than kindness to him as he sat in silence, quite unable to read, musing over the past.

Buxton. Set amid great natural glory on the River Wye, it is the highest market-town in England, over 1000 feet above the sea, like a cup in the everlasting hills of the Peak. The rude hamlet of long ago became a great spa through the fame of a warm spring known down the ages for its healing virtues, unfailing and unchanging in all seasons at a temperature of 82 degrees Fahrenheit. It was the Aquae Arnemetiae of the Romans, who brought roads here from some of their military stations.

In the Middle Ages, in spite of its remoteness and its poor accommodation, pilgrims flocked to the well at the foot of the cliff, and the walls of the old well chapel of St Anne close by were hung with the sticks and crutches they were able to discard. Under Henry VIII the relics were removed and the well and the chapel locked up and sealed, but in the time of Elizabeth I the waters were again in good repute. Mary, Queen of Scots, was brought here for the benefit of her health; she stayed at the Old Hall, which was rebuilt in 1670, but has some remains of the older house, including the pillared entrance. It is now a hotel and stands at the end of the Crescent.

The town is old and new, Higher and Lower Buxton. Higher Buxton is the older part beyond The Slopes, where the village green has become a busy market square, but keeps its old stone cross. Here Buxton's oldest church stands in a secluded corner of the busy road. It was built in 1625 after the well chapel had been abandoned. It has a stone roof and a bell gable, and is lighted by small square-headed windows. Fine stout old tiebeams support the roof. The Jacobean font is oblong, carved with a shield, a cross, and a Greek letter. There is a 17th century oak reading-desk handsomely carved. In the little churchyard is the grave of John Kane, the 18th century comedian, restored by J. T. Toole a hundred years later.

Lower Buxton is the newer part, with fine houses and buildings, lovely gardens and walks. It has the fine Pump Room where the waters are drunk from the flowing source, and the splendid Crescent built by the fifth Duke of Devonshire in 1780–86. Designed by John Carr of York and said to have cost £120,000, it is built in the classical style of architecture with three storeys and a fine arcade. The curve is 200 feet long with wings 58 feet, and there are 380 windows. It looks across to the Pump Room and the terraced gardens of The Slopes. Behind the Crescent is the Devonshire Royal Hospital, also designed by Carr of York, converted from the old stables and riding school, with a clock tower and a great dome said to be the biggest in the world, covering a round floor 50 yards across.

The classical church of St John, built in 1811 by Sir Jeffry Wyatville, has an imposing portico and a cupola for one bell. Bright and spacious within, it has a massive pulpit of marble and alabaster and a pleasing font. One of the windows has fine glass of rich colour with figures of St Michael and St George, and two windows have glass by C. E. Kempe.

The Duke's Drive, made in 1795, runs from the Bakewell to the Ashbourne road; it rides for a while above the Ashwood Dale and has a fine peep of the Lovers' Leap. At its foot the delightful ferny Sherbrook Dell comes to the dale, with a profusion of wild flowers and plants and a stream flowing to the Wye.

From a tower crowning the wooded slopes of Grin Low, a mile south of the town, is a wonderful view 1400 feet above sea-level. The tower has replaced the old Solomon's Temple which once stood near a tumulus here. Under the slopes of Grin Plantation is Poole's Cavern, where a brigand stored his treasure long ago and nature has stored treasures longer than men have lived. Thomas Hobbes counted it one of his Seven Wonders of the Peak, and Charles Cotton sang the praises of this cave, one of the sources of the River Wye, which we can explore for 700 yards, with masses of rocks of strange shape and formation, and a great wealth of stalagmites and stalactites.

To the north are the Corbar Woods, with winding walks about the great hillside, a transformation from old quarries and shattered rocks to a glory of trees, ferns, and wild flowers. From the top of Corbar Hill is a magnificent view of Buxton close at hand, and away to Kinder Scout, Mam Tor, and Axe Edge.

A Well-Dressing Festival (resembling that at Tissington) is held each year in July at Buxton, in the marketplace and at the fountain (from which the natural spring water gushes) outside the Pump Room. From this fine town we may best enjoy the beauty of much of the Peak: Axe Edge, the Goyt Valley, and glorious moorland drives. Axe Edge is a gritstone ridge of heath and moss and bog, looking out from 1810 feet high to a glorious panorama over three counties, and giving birth to five rivers, the Dane, the Goyt, the Dove, the Manifold, and the Wye. The wildly romantic Goyt Valley begins as a wooded ravine enclosing the new Errwood Reservoir. Above this we have a view of Errwood Hall on the hillside, noted for its rhododendrons. A fine moorland walk of five miles from Buxton takes us to the Cat and Fiddle in Cheshire, the second highest inn in England, 1690 feet above sea-level, with views over the great plain of Cheshire to the Mersey on the horizon, into Staffordshire and Lancashire, and to the Welsh Hills.

Buxton was a home of man 100 centuries ago, when the Ice Age was retreating in the Peak; its museum is one of the most suitable places in which we can study the things our prehistoric ancestors left behind them in the caves and gravel-beds. Here also we may compare their legacies to the Peak with things found all over England, for in the library is the collection of reference books kept by that intrepid discoverer of our past, Sir William Boyd Dawkins. We may see his many informing notes on the margins of these books which are kept under a window given by Lady Boyd Dawkins.

Hereabouts great discoveries have been made of historic and pre-historic time. Dr Dawkins found an amazing number of bones and teeth of extinct animals, the very oldest collection from caves that had been found at that time. He discovered them at the Victory Quarry, Dove Holes. They included bones of the mastodon, sabre-toothed tiger, rhinoceros, and the elephant; here they are in this museum, the marks of the hyena's teeth plainly visible on the bones of these great animals.

Here also have been found flints and pebbles worked by the Stone Age men, jaws and teeth of men and animals, stones and flints from the Arbor Low circle nine miles away. With all these we may compare the fine and comprehensive collection of implements from all over the world given to the museum by F. A. Holmes, a tireless friend of the Peak and one of its first advocates as a National Park. With it all is a collection of things from the Roman period, coins, brooches, vases, altars, quern stones; and a milestone which told the Roman traveller the number of miles to Brough, near Castleton.

Caldwell. This quiet place of a few homes, an old Hall, partly of the 17th and 18th centuries, and a small church made almost new, was old over 600 years ago when a king and his earls halted here. The king was Edward II and he was in pursuit of Thomas, Earl of Lancaster, who was at Burton five miles away. They met soon afterwards at Boroughbridge, in Yorkshire, where the earl was taken and beheaded.

One touch of beauty older even than that touch of war has this little place, for here is something from the church the Normans made: three tiny lights, two in the nave and one in the chancel. From earlier in the present century this little light of a thousand years in the chancel has had as company a reredos of translucent alabaster, with traceried panels and handsome carving of vine and grape, crowned by two angels.

Among echoes of other wars found here are two alabaster stones to the parents of Colonel Thomas Sanders, who fought for Parliament against Charles I in the Civil War. In the west window are two medallions of stained glass, probably of about 1400, from Nuremberg.

Calke. Its story goes back to an Augustinian priory founded about 1130, whose site was acquired by Henry Harpur in 1621. He made it his home, and the family home it has been since. Sheltered by the rising ground about it, and hidden from the road, it was rebuilt on a grand scale in 1703 (by an unknown architect) and given the name of Calke Abbey, keeping some of the old masonry in walls six feet thick. Also in the beautiful wooded deer park is the church, rebuilt in 1826 and containing the fine monument of Sir John Harpur, who died in 1741, and of his wife.

A glorious drive from Melbourne leads to this quiet place with a handful of dwellings beside the great park. Two miles we go up and down among the rolling hills of the Leicestershire border, above a valley where a new reservoir has been made into a beauty spot, with fine woods for a background.

Carsington. The charming small village nestles in a valley, sheltered by a steep wooded hillside to which its tiny church seems to cling for life. This is a simple place 50 feet long and 20 feet wide, with something of the 14th century left in the east window and part of another in the vestry, and in the font carved with four small heads at the base. Old oak pews now line the walls, and there is a sundial of 1648, when the church was "re-edified", a remarkable survival of the late Gothic style. The west gallery was added in 1704, and in the north aisle is a coat-of-arms of 1706. Two interesting windows are in memory of the Gells of Hopton close by, one with the names of all their women from 1452 to 1862, the other with the names of all their men from 1404 to 1926.

Two odd items are in the church register here, one of the planting of the yew tree in the churchyard in 1638 and another of Sarah Tissington, who was born here in 1664 without arms but who learned to knit with her feet. One of Carsington's rectors was John Oldfield, who was driven from the church in 1662, and here was born his son Joshua. Both have found their way into our national roll of fame, and we meet them at Alfreton, where the father is buried.

Castleton. It nestles snugly in the heart of Peakland, in the gentle loveliness of the Hope Valley and looking up to wild and romantic scenes. It is an old, old place where rocks are riddled with wonderful caves and the earth with old mines. It knew the men of prehistory, who left their fortress on the top of its highest hill. It knew the Romans, who worked its mines. It saw the splendour of the proud Peverils or Peverels who had these lands from the Norman Conqueror among their vast estates. Time has left us something of these proud folk, in the castle they built at the top of a precipice, and the church down in the valley is perhaps even older.

Crowning the top of Castle Hill is Peveril Castle, or the Castle of the Peak, like a tireless watcher over the valley, one of the most interesting survivals of a Norman fortress, almost invulnerable except on one side where a winding path climbs to the summit. It frowns above a precipice dropping down to the grim and narrow Cave Dale, and towers above the entrance to the Peak Cavern in the sheer face of the rock.

The castle wall which still remains, with ruins of a gateway, is the work of William Peveril of the Conqueror's day, but the keep, whose roofless shell still stands, was rebuilt in 1176; its walls are 8 feet thick and nearly 60 feet high, enclosing about 400 square feet. Sir Walter Scott made the castle famous by his *Peveril of the Peak*, but the book has little foundation in historic fact.

At the foot of the hill is the charming village to which the castle gave a name, stone-built, all twists and turns, with a little three-corner green. Close by is the church, in a churchyard of trim lawn and sycamores. Through all its many changes it has kept one thing perhaps of the days before William Peveril; it is the handsome chancel arch with chevrons. The 15th century tower has long been associated with the festivities of the Garlanding Ceremony, when the whole village does honour to the old custom observed in the evening of Oak Apple Day (May 29). The merrymaking begins with a procession of dancers and musicians in attendance on a king and queen in fine array. The king wears a massive bell-shaped garland,

and at sunset rides to the tower, where the garland is hoisted by a rope to one of the eight pinnacles and left until the flowers wither.

The church has an old font, 17th and 18th century box-pews with the names and initials of those who once sat in them, and a small 15th century oil painting of the Adoration of the Magi, attributed to Jan Van Eyck. In the vestry beside the chancel is a library of hundreds of books left in 1817 by a vicar, among them a Cranmer's Bible of 1539 and a Breeches Bible of 1611.

John Mawe, a mineralogist who was buried in London in 1829, has here a marble tablet according to his wish. It was at Castleton that he acquired his love of geology, and for many years he came here every autumn. He toured England and Scotland in search of mineral specimens for the King of Spain, was in Cadiz when war broke out between the two countries, and was arrested as a spy. He visited the diamond mines of Brazil and wrote many books about rocks and precious stones.

If we would fathom the secrets of the hills and of the earth there are wonderful caves to explore at Castleton. The magnificent natural entrance arch of the great Peak Cavern, once known as the Devil's Hole, rises for nearly 60 feet in the wooded face of the cliff on which the castle stands, opening into the yawning mouth of the cave, 114 feet wide, where a ropemaker still plies his craft, an old craftsman of 84 weaving ropes by hand, as has been done here for over 400 years. From the entrance winding passages lead to chamber after chamber, galleries and halls, for a mile into the heart of the hill, while all the time the sound of hidden waters add weirdness to the place. Almost at the mouth of the cavern the Peakshole Water bursts into life from the rock and hastens through the village to join the Noe beyond Hope church.

This remarkable cavern was described as one of the Seven Wonders of the Peak in a Latin poem by Thomas Hobbes. At one place the roof shelves down nearly to the floor, though blasting of the rock has given more space here than of old. At one time visitors to the cavern had to lie flat in a punt which the guide pushed along the surface of a stream. Byron came here in those days with Mary Chaworth, and wrote of his strange adventure:

"I had to cross in a boat a stream which flows under a rock so close upon the water as to admit the boat only to be pushed on by

55

the ferryman, a sort of Charon, who wades at the stern, stooping all the time. The Companion of my transit was M.A.C., with whom I had long been in love and never told it, though she had discovered it without. I recollect my sensations but cannot describe them, and it is as well."

The Speedwell Cavern farther up the valley is made partly by nature and partly by man, and is reached by a disused mine-shaft abandoned after a vain search for lead. A long flight of steps and a voyage down a subterranean canal ends where the sound of waters becomes a roar as they fall with eddy and whirl into the abyss of the Bottomless Pit, of immeasurable depth, and the great cavern rises above to an immense height into the heart of the mountain.

The Blue John Mine is famous for a spar coloured like amethyst and topaz, a lovely product of the limestone which is made into ornaments and jewellery. Here we have a feast of spectacular beauty, where spacious vaulted chambers, reached by labyrinths of passages, reveal magnificent scenes of glistening fairylike formations of stalactites and stalagmites. The Romans probably worked this mine; two vases found at Pompeii are said to have been made from its spar—treasures from the heart of an English mountain buried for 18 centuries under the ashes of an Italian volcano. In the Treak Cliff Cavern, another series of caves with "blue john", discovered only in 1926, on the other side of the same hill, the stalactites and stalagmites are even more beautiful.

One of the glories of Castleton is the magnificent scene from its heights: from its own Castle Hill, from Mam Tor, another of the Seven Wonders of the Peak, nearly 1700 feet above sea-level and crowned with an Iron Age camp (its curious crumbling of shale has given the hill the name of Shivering Mountain), and the sudden vision of the Hope Valley as we come from the steep, wild, romantic gorge of the Winnats, whose very name (Wind Gates) is eloquent of the fury of the winds that haunt this winding mile. At the head of the Winnats is the cavern of Windy Knoll, where have been found the bones of the rhinoceros, the bear, and the wolf.

Chaddesden. It is now entirely swallowed up by Derby's large new housing estates, but it retains its very interesting old church. The great house once lending beauty to this scene has gone, but the

The stone circle at Arbor Low.

The Grammar School, Ashbourne.

Bakewell Bridge.

Bolsover Castle.

name of the Wilmots, an old family with a thane at the court of Edward the Confessor, will not soon be forgotten. Robert Wilmot founded almshouses here, now demolished. Sir Edward Wilmot, who was 93 years old when they buried him at Monkton, was physician to two of the Georges; his wife was Sarah Mead, daughter of a famous physician through whom inoculation came to be adopted in England. He spent his last years giving his service to the poor of Derbyshire.

The linenfold panelling of the sanctuary and the oak and alabaster reredos are in memory of Sir Henry Wilmot who won the V.C. with two of his men for a shining deed at Lucknow. He and four others found themselves opposed to a great number, and one of the men was shot through both legs. He was lifted up and carried away under fire, while Captain Wilmot covered the retreat of the party by firing with the men's rifles. By what was like a miracle he managed to keep a clear course for his companions and the four men with their wounded comrade were able to get back.

The old church was rebuilt about 1357 by Henry Chaddesden, Archdeacon of Leicester, and from that time come the nave and aisles, the chancel, fine sedilia and piscinae, and a stone lectern of the unique Derbyshire type. A great treasure of the church is the 15th century chancel screen, which has modern vaulting on the western side and beautiful old tracery in the bays. Two massive stall-ends at the entrance are richly carved, their enormous crockets climbing to the tracery in the screen and having two charming figures as poppyheads.

Chapel-en-le-Frith. Industry has come creeping into this little stone town on the slope of a fertile valley, but it keeps its old-world marketplace and its stocks for ne'er-do-wells, and it rings a "pudding" bell on Shrove Tuesday at 11 in the morning.

All round are Peakland heights: Combs Moss, dark and threatening; Brown Knoll, rising to over 1860 feet above sea-level; South Head and Mount Famine; Chinley Churn's bold mass; and the conical hill of Eccles Pike.

Of the chapel founded over 700 years ago by the foresters and keepers of the old Forest of the Peak, little is left in the church, which was largely made new in the 18th century. The chancel arch and

E

the nave arcades are of the 14th century; some of the capitals have nail-head ornament, and one has a quaint face. In the oak-lined tower stands the 15th century font, and across the tower arch are the altar rails carved by a vicar in Cromwell's century. A stone coffin now indoors has been a coping stone in the churchyard wall. A brass candelabrum by a Flemish craftsman has been here 200 years.

The mediaeval chapel was consecrated in 1226 by the 41st Bishop of Lichfield, and we read on the back of the pews at the west end of the nave that at its 700th anniversary a sermon was preached by the 93rd Bishop of the same cathedral. Two other things the pews have to tell: the names and dates of the vicars from 1339 onward, and the record of three centuries of service as sextons and churchwardens by the Bramwells.

In the chancel is buried William Bagshawe, a much-loved Nonconformist minister known as the Apostle of the Peak, and his coloured arms are on the wall. He was ejected from the living of Glossop in 1662 and spent the rest of his life working in the wildest parts of the Peak. Several chapels were built for him, and, though warrants for his arrest were often issued, they were never enforced.

It was at Ford Hall, a 17th century house much changed since his day, that the Apostle of the Peak lived after his ejection from the church. It is one of about a dozen old houses that have stood for centuries near the town. Some survive as farms, some have only a wing or a gable left; and many of them have grown out of the old homes of the foresters who lived here and built the mediaeval chapel. Of the Ridge, the home of the Bagshawes, part of an original gable remains in the modern house; Slack Hall's twin gables can still be seen; Marsh Hall has still a wing known to 18 generations of the Brownes, guardians of the Forest six centuries ago.

On the steep slopes of Eccles Pike is Bradshaw Hall, now two farmhouses, with an ancient gable of the home of the Bradshaws and the fine 17th century gateway with their crest and the name of Francis, the last of his line to live at the house, which has old beams and panelling. John Bradshaw, President of the Court which sent Charles I to the scaffold, belonged to a branch of this family.

The church stands on a site which has become known as Derbyshire's Black Hole. In 1648 the Scots under the Duke of Hamilton marched in to England to help Charles I. They were defeated at Preston, and 1500 of them were brought as prisoners to this little town. With a brutality that amazes us, they were crowded into the small church here, though there was hardly room for half the number. Unable to lie down, pressing one against another in the chancel and nave, with not enough air to breathe, the poor wretches were imprisoned 16 days. Over 40 of them died before the door was opened and the miserable prisoners, more dead than alive, were allowed to stagger out to begin the fearful march northwards. Ten of them fell down before they reached Cheshire, and with the others they were buried in the churchyard, a pitiful company far from the land they loved.

Chatsworth. It was said long ago of this great house of the Cavendish family, Dukes of Devonshire, that it was the noblest private house in England commanding influence with the Whigs who set William of Orange on the throne; and we can well believe it, for it is perfect still. Built in the late 17th century in the Palladian style, no house has a finer setting than this majestic pile on a rising slope above the River Derwent.

It stands in a deer park ten miles round, laid out by "Capability" Brown in the 18th century, with hills and woods, and with gardens and lawns, far-reaching vistas, cascades and terraces within its vast enclosure. The beautiful three-arched bridge across the river was built to give the house the best approach and seems a part of the creative scheme; the wild moorland behind the wooded hillside above the house is another. The picture is perfect, a worthy setting even for our Dukes of Devonshire.

The house was built for the fourth Earl of Devonshire, who became the first Duke for the part he played in making William III king. It was begun in 1687 by William Talman, the king's architect, who built the south and east wings, and completed in 1707 by Thomas Archer, another leading architect, who built the west wing (the grand main front) and the bowed north wing. It is a vast block of great dignity, with a decorated balustrade and finely spaced windows. The duke gave twenty years of his life to the development of this great house on the site of the large mansion begun in 1552 by his grandmother, Bess of Hardwick and her second husband, Sir

59

William Cavendish, in which Mary, Queen of Scots, was imprisoned five times with the Earl of Shrewsbury, Bess's fourth husband, as her guardian. The Duke of Devonshire called in the greatest artists of the day to decorate it, carvers in wood and stone, craftsmen in iron. The court artists, Louis Laguerre and Antonio Verrio, painted the walls and ceilings; in the ironwork we see the master hand of Tijou, and in the wreaths and festoons of flowers, the carvings of fishes and birds, and the delicate profusion of ornament everywhere, the inspiration of Grinling Gibbons, though the work was done by a Derbyshire carver named Samuel Watson from Heanor.

Where every room is fit for a king we may take it for granted that all is magnificent, but even amid this splendour some things of interest stand out. The chapel has a magnificent altarpiece of Derbyshire alabaster and marble, designed by Caius Gabriel Cibber, the Danish sculptor who worked on St Paul's Cathedral and who carved two figures here. The rest of the altarpiece, like the wood carving around the walls, is the work of Samuel Watson and his helpers. Everybody has heard of the fiddle painted on the back of the door in the Music Room which so many people have taken to be real. It was brought from the Duke of Devonshire's house in Piccadilly, London, when that was demolished. In the State Bedroom is the bed in which George II died in 1760; it was given to the fourth Duke, who was the Lord Chamberlain, as one of his perquisites.

The long north wing at Chatsworth was added to the house from 1820 on by Sir Jeffry Wyatville, the court architect under George IV, for the sixth Duke of Devonshire, who also altered the great Painted Hall and other apartments. In the sculpture gallery of the north wing is Canova's marble of Napoleon's mother, and many other fine classical sculptures, and in the dining-room and elsewhere are paintings by Rembrandt, Van Dyck, Sir Joshua Reynolds, and many other masters.

The collection of original drawings of old masters at Chatsworth is unrivalled, and the library has a precious collection of manuscripts and rare books. There are beautiful collections of furniture and porcelain, and in the sculpture gallery are fine miniatures and Henry VII's illuminated Prayer Book and many other treasures.

We may imagine how beautiful everything has always been at Chatsworth from the accounts which exist showing the lavish spending on it; there is an item somewhere for over a mile of fringes and lace, and work in silver and gold.

No word will serve for the gardens, which are beyond all our imagining. They were laid out for the sixth Duke of Devonshire by Sir Joseph Paxton, whose great conservatory (since demolished) served as a model for his Crystal Palace at the Great Exhibition of 1851. In the gardens is the Emperor Fountain, sending its water 290 feet high (the highest yet anywhere), and a wonderful cascade falling 60 feet and running down steps for 200 yards before the water sinks into the earth and disappears. The temple of the cascade has sculptured dolphins and symbolic figures, and in the gardens are stone sphinxes on the piers, statues and relief panels, and the Willow Tree Fountain, which was once a popular attraction. There are lovely iron gates, delightful walks, and stately avenues, and we do not wonder that this princely house in its kingly situation attracts a crowd of visitors numbering many thousands every year.

Chellaston. Now practically a suburb of Derby, it had for centuries a great share in the beauty of England, for the alabaster quarried in its hillside has added to the glory of a thousand homes and churches. Here was one of the chief quarries of the Middle Ages. Its deep deposit of alabaster (a kind of sandstone containing lime) covered a wide area and was much worked. Some of the most gorgeous alabaster tombs in the country came from these quarries, and flourishing schools of carvers grew up at Nottingham and Burton-on-Trent. It was here that the practice began of putting on tombs small angel weepers holding shields. These first appear about 1390, and are characteristic of the Trent valley workers.

All that is left of the 12th century church here is the great bowl of a Norman font set on a new base 600 years ago. The chancel arch, the nave arcade, the doorway and windows of the nave and aisles are of the late 13th century. The chancel was made new in the 15th century and enlarged last century; the tower was rebuilt in 1842.

It is said that many memorials from the old church were used by a churchwarden to make a stable floor, but two 16th century mutilated

61

floorstones remain. They are in memory of the Bancroft family, who gave the neighbouring village of Swarkestone its 17th century poet, Thomas Bancroft.

Chelmorton. One of the highest villages in England, it stretches along the steep slope which goes on climbing to the summit of Chelmorton Low, a limestone height crowned with two great burial mounds, looking out west to the long ridge of Axe Edge and north across Wye Dale towards the lofty moorlands of Kinder Scout.

The little church at the head of the village clings to the hillside, and its 15th century stone-roofed porch tells us the story of its past. Its walls are lined with ancient coffin stones and its floor is laid with them, a round dozen of them carved with crosses, swords, and shields, two fine ones known to be of the 12th century, another carved with a pair of scissors and a cross 700 years ago, others from Norman days. Even the two stone seats for the priest in the chancel wall are made from an ancient cross-stone.

A rare possession of the church is the stone chancel screen; it is of the 15th century, and stands between 5 and 6 feet high, with an embattled parapet above traceried panels. The 15th century font is unusual for having mysterious letters and signs on its eight sides, nobody knowing what they mean.

The south arcade was built before 1200; the base of the tower and the north arcade are of the 13th century. The top of the tower, the spire, and the clerestory are of the 15th century. The chancel roof has a few old bosses, and the old chest is 300 years old. The churchyard has a shapely yew and the broken shaft of its old cross.

Chesterfield. It stands in the Rother Valley among the clustering hills, set in the heart of Derbyshire's coal and iron, but within reach of some of its most famous beauty spots.

An old market-town, for centuries it has been famous for its twisted spire; for more than a hundred years its wealth has come along the straight lines planned by George Stephenson, to whom in the first place the town owes its present prosperity. He came here to supervise the construction of the Midland line, and he lived and died at Tapton House, built on the crest of a wooded hill and now a school. He is buried in Holy Trinity Church, built in 1838, where his grave is under the altar and there is a memorial east window to him, as well as new communion rails and a stone in the sanctuary. The Memorial Hall (which has a civic repertory theatre) keeps his name alive, as it should be kept, for he led Chesterfield along the straight way to industrial prosperity.

This busy town is not too busy to be concerned for its appearance; it finds its recreation in attractive parks, and has reclothed itself in some of its busiest haunts in Tudor dress of timber and gables. It has given itself a classical Town Hall, opened in 1938, set on a green slope looking over the town to the Derbyshire hills, and below this is the Court House, built in 1965 and one of the finest examples of modern architecture in the county. To the south of this are the large buildings of the Accountant General's Department of the Post Office, moved here in 1964.

Chesterfield has nothing else so old or fine as its church of All Saints, with its crooked spire, rising 228 feet, as singular a curiosity as any church has. It is eight-sided, built of timber and covered with lead plates set in zigzag fashion, so that in addition to its decided twist, nearly eight feet out of the perpendicular, the spire has the unusual appearance of being ridged and channelled. The twist which has made it famous is due to the lack of adequate cross supports, accentuated by the warping of the wood under the expansion of the lead in the heat of the sun. It was only the town's affection for the old spire which saved it last century, when experts declared it unsafe and urged that a new one should be built, and again in 1961, when it came near to being destroyed by fire.

Like the tower, the spire is of the 14th century, and it crowns a stately 14th century church built in the shape of a cross. Under the tower are four lofty pointed arches on clustered pillars, all resting on the foundation of a Norman church which William Rufus gave. Of this church there remains the font, the round bowl carved with crude foliage and stem-work. There are traces of the 13th century in the crossing piers, in the north and south transepts, and in a piscina in the northernmost of the four eastern chapels (originally the chapels of mediaeval trade guilds). Most of the rest of the church is of the 14th century, but the clerestory is of the 15th. The handsome 14th century porch has a gable cross and a recess over the entrance with a modern Madonna; a projecting stair turret to the roof ends in a pinnacle like a pyramid.

The church has a lovely interior with fine arches and much screenwork. The nave is light and lofty, contrasting strongly with the chancel, though this has been improved by new stained glass of 1947 by Christopher Webb. The nave arcades of six bays on each side have clustered pillars. Of the four chapels at the east end, the chancel opens to two on each side with 14th century archways, one with a peephole to the altar.

The church is rich in old screenwork. In the north transept is part of the 15th century chancel screen with six angels below the cornice. A slightly later and loftier screen runs the length of the south transept, with delicate tracery in its transomed bays and a wide cornice coved on both sides. The old Foljambe screen behind the choir stalls under the tower, however, was destroyed in the fire of 1961 and has been replaced by a new rood-beam and figures. The 19th century screen across the chancel has traceried bays and a coved cornice.

The Jacobean pulpit is of black oak, ornately carved, standing on a single pillar. In the south transept is an oak chest with a mass of ironwork which includes 16 bands, two locks, and six padlocks: so much ironwork is there that little of the oak can be seen, yet for all its seeming security a reward of 40 guineas was offered for information about thieves who robbed it in 1808. Here also is a smaller chest, likewise heavily banded with iron. In a handsome canopied recess in the south aisle lies an unknown priest in simple robes, his feet on a lion and his head supported by weathered angels. He is perhaps from the first half of the 14th century.

The monuments of the Foljambes are huddled together in the south chancel chapel. On a fine alabaster tomb of 1510 are the brass portraits of Henry Foljambe and his wife, both at prayer, he in armour with sword and dagger, his feet on a dog, she with a girdled cloak and a headdress with lappets. Under richly carved canopies are figures of knights and ladies representing their 14 children. On this tomb is the kneeling figure of a knight in richly chased armour with hands in prayer and four-roped chain round his neck. His helmet has quaint spy-holes like stars. He does not belong to the tomb, and may be Sir Thomas Foljambe, who died in 1604.

Henry's son Sir Godfrey and his wife have brass portraits on a floorstone, with three sons, five daughters, and four shields. Sir

Godfrey is in armour, his head on a helmet and his feet on a stag; his lady has a long mantle and a girdle held at the waist by a clasp of three roses. She has a headdress with lappets and a chain round her neck; his coat and her mantle are decorated with arms. A wall monument shows Sir Godfrey's son James, who died in 1558, kneeling in armour with a helmet and gauntlets at his feet. Below him kneel his two wives and a dozen grown-up children with a baby among them. A gruesome wall monument, perhaps to his brother Godfrey, shows a figure tied up in a bag on a stretcher; above it is a fearful figure of Death with an arrow and a spade and a foot on a skull, with a fat little boy at one side of Death and at the other an old man hobbling along.

A fine Renaissance alabaster monument is in memory of Sir Godfrey Foljambe of 1585 and his wife. He lies in elaborate armour with sword and dagger, his wife in fine Elizabethan dress with a ruff. Their only son Godfrey lies in armour with his wife on plaited matting; his wife has a fine gown with buttoned bodice and slashed sleeves, and a charming ruff. An alabaster floorstone has the engraved portrait in armour of George Foljambe, who died in the year of the Armada.

In the day of his triumph, rich and admired, with his engines thundering over railways that he and his son had laid in Europe as well as at home, George Stephenson came here for rest and happiness. A Northumbrian, born at Wylam in 1781, he passed from poverty and squalor through a superb triumph of invention to the luxury of Tapton House with its flowers, fruits, and agricultural experiments, the greatest mechanical genius of the age turned country squire.

He grew up in a cottage which had only one room to house the family of six; he earned twopence a day among the turnips, and thought himself made for life with 12s. a week, plus extras won from cobbling and the repair of clocks and watches. On those terms he married the country girl who was to become the mother of Robert, yet he managed to support a mother and father brought to poverty, and to raise £6 to buy himself out of the draft in which he was drawn to go to France and fight against Napoleon.

His work in gassy mines led him to hazardous experiments resulting in the invention of his famous safety lamp, for which, when he was 37, he received £1000. While working in a colliery he mastered the principle of the steam engine by taking one to pieces, repairing and rebuilding it, but as he could not read until manhood (his son Robert then taught him) he wasted time and effort on schemes already in existence. Nevertheless he built a complete engine that began to draw the coal of Killingworth Colliery in 1814, and a year later, with the steam blast added, produced two more of greatly increased power.

The first railway in the open, running from Stockton to Darlington, was laid for horse-drawn vehicles, but Stephenson, with his infectious courage and confidence, induced the owners to try a locomotive, and on September 27, 1825, George drove the first steam train in the world, six wagons with coal and flour, and one coachful of passengers, with a mounted flagman patrolling ahead until the engine developed a speed that put him to flight.

This success did not persuade sceptics or disarm opponents, and the triumph of the 4-ton Rocket, with her 30 miles an hour, had become history before Stephenson could establish his right to enrich the country with the greatest improvement in locomotion that had been achieved by man. It was his fortune to see his work crowned with rich and abundant success, but he remained unspoiled, a born philosopher who loved laughter and played as hard as he worked.

Church Broughton. It has nothing more beautiful than its fine avenue of limes and the old church to which they lead, a gracious place of lovely stone all splashed with streaks of amber, with something left of Norman days and much of 600 years ago when the old church was made new.

The legacy of the Normans is the font (with an unusual pattern of angles and circles), a half-pillar with a capital near the chancel, and perhaps the round pillars of the nave. Two oval pillars at the west end are of the 14th century, their capitals having extraordinary figures which seem to be grimacing at each other. As old as these pillars is the embattled tower with a stair turret and a low spire, the chancel with three stone seats and a piscina niche, a small priest's doorway, an outside recess with a curious little window in the wall, and the capitals of the arcades.

On each side of the beautiful east window (of the 14th century like many others) is an old bracket, one carved with a head. The glass of 1905, by Hardman of Birmingham, shows the Resurrection and figures of St Michael and St Gabriel, with minstrel angels in the tracery.

Worked into the modern reredos is the tracery of screenwork perhaps 600 years old. The clerestory and the oak roof of the nave, with carved spandrels, is largely of 1506. The oak pulpit is of the 18th century; though altered since his day, it was the gift of one of the Woolleys of Sapperton a mile or so away to the west, where the gabled 16th or 17th century manor house still stands with its fine farm buildings at the foot of a shady lane. William Woolley's manuscript history of Derbyshire, over 200 years old, is in the British Museum. Here it may have been written, but nowhere was it ever published.

In a 17th century chest with three locks is the old village bassoon, the most curious possession of the church. An interesting possession is the winged figure of St George and the Dragon, on a bracket in the chancel, carved in Oberammergau in the early years of this century. A stone in the floor at the west end of the church marks the spot where Francis Fearn used to stand to wind up the old clock in the tower. For 32 years he was parish clerk, and when at last he knew he was winding himself down he chose to be buried near this spot.

Church Gresley. It has miners now instead of monks, but here and there are things to remind us of its vanished glory, and it remembers the great family of the Gresleys, said to have been the only Derbyshire family to have kept their lands from Domesday Book to the 20th century. Nothing is left of the castle they built except the grassy mound on which it stood, still known as Castle Knob, a mile to the west, near Castle Gresley. Later, they lived at Drakelow Hall, farther north-west, near the Trent, but their fine house has been replaced by a huge power-station.

Though today it keeps company with a pit-head instead of its small 12th century priory of Augustinian canons, the church still has links with the past. The chancel and the priory buildings were pulled down in Tudor days, and the church remained more or less a ruin until about 1820. A new chancel was built on the site of the old in 1872. Remains of the priory have been found, fragments of

67

painted glass, mediaeval tiles, and stone coffins. All that is left of the old church now is the sturdy 15th century tower and two 14th century arches leading to the north aisle.

On a great alabaster monument is the figure of Sir Thomas Gresley kneeling under an arch. He has a curly wig, as was usual in the 17th century, and a gown of rich brocade. Round the arch are arms showing the marriages of his ancestors from the time of William the Conqueror. But the pride of the church are 10 massive and handsomely carved stalls with misericords brought from Drakelow Hall before it was demolished; it is thought they may have belonged to the church in its great days.

Clay Cross. This unprepossessing small town stands on a ridge between the Rother Valley, with its collieries, and the pleasant Amber Valley, and commands a wide view over East Derbyshire. Though iron smelting had been carried on in the neighbourhood for centuries, the present town has grown up only since the first collieries were opened in 1837 by George Stephenson, the famous railway engineer, who is buried at Chesterfield. He discovered coal and iron while driving a railway tunnel through the hill on which the town stands, and founded the Clay Cross Company which established the first ironworks here. It was in the workshops of the company that William Howe, Stephenson's engineer, made an invention, known to engineers as Link-motion, that revolutionised the internal combustion engine. The collieries in the district are now on the decline, and Clay Cross is today dependent mainly on its ironworks and engineering works.

The church, whose spire is a prominent landmark in the surrounding country, was built in 1851 by H. I. Stevens of Derby, and is in the 13th century style of architecture. Near the entrance is the base of the ancient preaching cross from which the town was named.

Clowne. Many things it has from our ancient past, the old cross crowned by a ball in the middle of the village, and a church of 800 years ago with a variety of old possessions.

The aisleless church, though much renewed, has fragments of Norman England, including the doorway in the porch and the chancel arch (both with carved capitals), the priest's doorway, and the font. On a window-sill is a moulded stone which was the drain of the piscina used by Norman priests. The roof has some of its 14th century beams, a century older than the embattled tower.

Two extraordinary buttresses support the north wall, projecting ten feet at the base and climbing in steps until they reach the roof. On the chancel floor (now boarded over) is a stone to William Inskip, a parson for 54 years buried here just before the Armada. He must have been here through the troubled period of the church in the reigns of four Tudors.

The road passing the church goes on to the delightful wooded dell of Markland Grips, with a stream running through the bottom. Farther down this skirts the remains of an unusual promontory fort, probably dating from the century before the Romans.

Codnor. The ruins at its doorstep, set in billowy fields and woods, make it easy to forget the coal and iron which have made this part of Derbyshire famous. Once it was a great park of nearly 2000 acres, and the ruins were a mighty castle, the feudal home of the Greys. Richard Grey was one of Henry III's loyal barons; another Richard was visited here by Edward II after fighting the rebels at Burton-on-Trent; another was sent by Henry V to bring Hotspur's son from Scotland; Henry, the last of them, busied himself in trying to change base metals into gold.

It is thought that the Greys built their castle on the site of one which had William Peveril for its lord, making it a great and deeply moated place with two courts, four massive round towers, and a great gateway. It was when the Zouch family sold it 300 years ago that it began to decay. Today all that survives is a length of the great boundary wall of the upper court, portions of the dividing wall and of the defending towers, and here and there a doorway, a window, and a fireplace, all standing proudly high and looking over the Erewash Valley into Nottinghamshire.

Farmsteads have been built from the ruins, one the next-door neighbour of the castle since the 17th century. Near it stands a round stone dovecot, tall and slightly conical, and crowned by a square wood turret, but now in decay. The lords of Codnor have said goodbye. The great park has changed, much of it was taken up by the ironworks of the Butterley Company, who laid out some acres as a park on a hill above the ruins. But the park has changed hands again, the roads are private, and visitors are not welcomed.

Cressbrook. The stream of its delightful dale comes down to join the Wye as it leaves Millers Dale for Monsal Dale, flowing through a chain of lovely limestone ravines.

It has a fine stone Hall and pleasant houses built here and there on steep and densely wooded slopes. Its woods are a glory of lilies of the valley in spring, and all its ways are rich in lovely views.

We find it at one end of a most charming mile where the Wye winds like the letter M, deep down in a narrow gorge shut in by rocks and woods, a mile of beauty which comes suddenly to earth with the textile mills at each end.

An intrusion of industry into romance were these mills, and it is odd that the Cressbrook Mills were owned by one who could make them prosper and be a poet too. He was William Newton, the carpenter-poet whom Anna Seward, the Swan of Lichfield, christened the Minstrel of the Peak. Perhaps it was the poet in him that gave his little apprentices more kindly treatment than most boys suffered in the cotton mills then.

Burial mounds on the hills around tell the story of long ago. In a barrow on Hay Cop above the dale was found the skeleton of a child.

Creswell. It is a mining village, but it has beauty at its doorstep. It has given its name to Creswell Crags, a tiny ravine of richly wooded magnesian-limestone rocks rising each side of the road towards Sherwood Forest. One side of the Crags is in Derbyshire, the other in Nottinghamshire. In their sides are the famous caves where remarkable implements and works of art made by the earliest men in Britain have been found. These caves have names of their own, Robin Hood's Cave, Church Hole (named from its narrow tapering entrance), Mother Grundy's Parlour, and the Pin Hole.

Nearly 80 years ago Sir William Boyd Dawkins began to dig in these caves, and among many treasures he found the earliest example of pictorial art discovered in our land, a piece of smooth bone three inches long and an inch deep, on which had been scratched the head and shoulders of a horse. The mane of the horse is remarkable, as the hair stands up straight; drooping manes were seldom shown in drawings by the cave men.

Inch by inch the soil from these caves was removed and sifted, down to the white sand in which there were no remains. Above the white sand and red sand were bones, and one or two rude implements of quartzite which were also found in a layer of red clay above. The remarkable thing about these bones is that they belonged to the hippopotamus and the rhinoceros, animals which needed a far warmer climate than ours. Hyenas shared the cave with them, the marks of their teeth being on the larger bones. The hippopotamus is a survivor of the Pliocene into the early Pleistocene age, and the man who made these quartzite implements before the ice ages descended on the land must have had a hot meal from the flesh of these beasts, for signs of fire remain on the bones.

Above the clay we come to the mottled and light-coloured cave earth with implements in a higher stage of manufacture. The hare was the chief food of these men. On a higher layer still is a red cave earth in which charcoal fragments and blocks of limestone occur with the bones, with implements made of flint brought from a distance. The men who made these were the artists, and used implements of bone as well as of flint. The top layer of all consisted of stalagmite material and other worked flints. These objects are in the British Museum and the Manchester Museum.

The Pin Hole Cave proved the richest of all, and from it we have evidence that at least two glacial periods have passed over Creswell Crags, driving men from it. Thousands of years separate the periods of its habitation. The remains extend over a depth of 15 feet, and one of the most thrilling finds was the bone of a mammoth which a cave man split to obtain the marrow and then threw aside, leaving his flint knife embedded in the joint. Another amazing find was the egg-shell of some kind of goose. At its narrow end was a hole through which the cave man had sucked its contents.

A rare find was a pendant of mammoth ivory, oval in shape and no thicker than a postcard. A round hole cleverly pierced at one end suggests that it was a charm worn by a lady of the caves. Here also was the skull of a huge bear as big as any at Whipsnade Zoo, and the strange thing was that all its teeth had been extracted, doubtless to make a necklace for the queen of the cave. But the gem of Pin Hole was an engraving of a masked man or woman on the bone of a

71

reindeer. The figure is standing erect, apparently engaged in a ceremonial dance.

Other engravings worked on ivory, and the beautiful flint tools with which they worked and hunted and fished 20,000 years before the birth of Christ, were found in the upper part of this cave which has proved one of the most valuable records we have of the men of the Old Stone Age over a period of nearly 500 centuries.

Crich. The village stands high up on an exposed ridge, a prominent landmark from half Derbyshire, and it stretches along the ridge towards Crich Stand, a hill nearly 1000 feet high, interesting to geologists and notable for the rich lead mines that were about it. The outlook, especially across the Derwent Valley, is as fair as any in a county of wonderful views.

Crich Stand has something which draws all eyes, a lighthouse tower rebuilt in 1923, with a beacon light seen from five counties. It is a tribute to 11,400 men of the Sherwood Foresters (the former Notts and Derby Regiment) who lost their lives in the Great War. A memorial service is held each year on the first Sunday in July. In a disused limestone quarry in the side of the hill, a fascinating museum of old trams and tramway equipment has been laid out. It is the only one in Britain, and it has vehicles ranging from a horse-car of 1873 (brought from Portugal, but made in Birkenhead) to a modern all-electric tram of 1953, from Leeds.

Of the old church begun in the mid 12th century there still remain the nave arcades, with square capitals on one side and round ones on the other, and the font with heavy cable moulding is also Norman. But most of the church is of the 14th century—the tower and spire, the chancel with a priest's doorway and beautiful tracery in its windows, three stone seats under trefoiled arches, a piscina drain in the sill of an east window, and a stone lectern built into the chancel wall in the Derbyshire fashion. The modern roof of the chancel rests on 10 stone heads 600 years old; the nave roof is a century younger than this.

The oak screen across the chancel arch had an adventure towards the end of its 500 years. Turned out of the church in 1861, it was found in a timber yard and taken to St Peter's in Derby, but was later returned to Crich. From the 14th century also is a finely carved

Bretby Park.

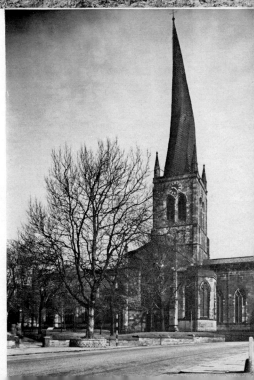

Chesterfield Church.

Chatsworth
(a) The west front.

(b) The south front, seen from the lake.

oak seat with poppyheads of human faces. Very quaint they are, one looking rather astonished, another smiling at us with a good humour 500 years old.

William de Wakebridge lies in a long gown buttoned from neck to waist under an aisle recess. He has long hair and a beard, and his hands are on his breast, his feet on a dog, and a tiny angel is holding a Catherine wheel to his ear. Sir William sat in the Parliaments of Edward III, but after the Black Death had bereft him of his wife, his father, his three brothers, and two sisters, he gave himself to religion rather than to worldly affairs, and founded two chantries here. In one they laid him in 1369. In the chancel is the stone of a tomb with the figures of German Pole and his wife, both in Tudor dress and ruffs. His widow married John Claye of Crich, who has a tomb in the chancel showing himself and his first wife, with their five children round them.

Another alabaster tomb has the engraved portrait of Godfrey Beresford in 16th century armour, and a brass tablet tells of Robert Marshall and his wife, who lived happily in the village for more than 50 years 500 years ago. A tiny brass on the chancel wall has a quaint inscription to the baby whose little shrouded figure is engraved on it, the child of Thomas Shelmerdine, vicar here in Stuart days. In an arched recess is a stone to Thomas England, vicar 200 years ago. On the other side of the stone is engraved a chalice, and it is perhaps the stone which covered the grave of the first chantry priest, Richard Davy, nearly six centuries ago.

Cromford. It is set in a great natural glory, in the midst of some of Derbyshire's most majestic scenery. We come from the Matlocks down by the Derwent, or up a delightful stretch of the vale from Whatstandwell, or through the Via Gellia's sylvan glades. We come from Wirksworth over the hills, with a feast of splendid views that become a superb panorama if we climb the frowning Black Rocks on our right. Great masses of millstone grit they are, rising 80 feet from the crest of the hill and backed by dark pine woods, piled-up crags like great bastions of varying size and shapes, now a favourite rock-climbing ground. Into the glorious scene from the top come Wirksworth, the Middleton quarries, and the dip of the Via Gellia; the rock-bound Derwent is winding through Matlock Dale, with

Masson and the Heights of Abraham looking across to High Tor and Riber's "castle" on its great hill; and through the wooded valley is seen the lighthouse-tower on Crich Stand.

Down in the hollow nestles Cromford with its great house, its church, and its mills, the story of them all closely woven with that of the man who turned this secluded hamlet into a busy industrial village, the man who, born the 13th child of a working man and starting life as a barber, was able to give every one of his ten children a Christmas box of £10,000. He was Sir Richard Arkwright, the genius of the cotton world, whose inventions revolutionised the industry by removing what had been its greatest stumbling block, the difficulty of spinning cotton fine and strong enough for warp.

In this lovely corner the first cotton mill in Derbyshire was built in 1771, when Arkwright was in partnership with Jedediah Strutt. Some of the mill remains in the gaunt works (now a colour factory) whose grim severity suggests the troublous days when machinery was coming into the world. The Arkwrights spent much of their wealth on the countryside in building, making roads and planting trees. It was the inventor's son Richard who opened a new gateway into Matlock Dale by blasting through the rock, near the place where Arkwright had built his second mill, in 1783.

It was Sir Richard himself who started the great house of Willersley Castle, but it was burned down before it was finished and he died before he could rebuild it. He began his castle and did not see it; he began the church and did not see it: it was left for his son Richard to finish both. Willersley Castle, now a Methodist guest house, has a background of fine woods, and lawns down to the Derwent. The church, completed in 1859, stands at the foot of the grounds, and in it the great Arkwright was laid to rest. There is a memorial tablet to him and to the family, and one to his son's wife and her three children.

Cromford's beauty spot is at the fine old bridge which spans the river, with three pointed arches on one side, and three round ones on the other. Next to it are the ruins of a 15th century chapel, and beside this an 18th century fishing pavilion (restored in 1968), with the inscription, *Piscatoribus Sacrum*. On the other side of the main road, around the Greyhound Inn, is Arkwright's industrial village, now fitting as well into the landscape as the older part. Beside the pond here is a waterwheel, nearly 200 years old, built by Arkwright to help provide power for his cotton processing.

Sir Richard Arkwright, the creator of the cotton trade on mass production lines, was nearly 40 and a made man when he arrived here in 1771 to build the first cotton mill in Derbyshire, and to find his last resting-place within sound of his mill 21 years later. Born at Preston, he was a barber at Bolton and tramping wig-maker with a secret dye before he applied himself to invention.

James Hargreaves had just invented a spinning jenny multiplying the number of spindles for each operator, but the product was a yarn too soft for use without other material as strengthening warps. Arkwright one day saw red-hot iron drawn between rollers, and with great difficulty he got a spinning frame constructed on the same principle, the cleaned and carded cotton being drawn between two pairs of rollers, the second pair moving more quickly than the first.

Testing the machine in secret, the inventor was accused of witchcraft, the hum and clack of the mechanism being ascribed to Satan tuning his bagpipes and Arkwright dancing to them. Fearing the Lancashire machine-wreckers, he went to Nottingham, where he erected his first mill in 1769, the mechanism driven by horses. It was the necessity for water power and lower costs that brought him to Cromford.

So fierce was the opposition of Lancashire that he was driven out of spinning until by indomitable will he secured the repeal of an old Act of Parliament that made his oppression possible. Then this illiterate genius invented the most wonderful contrivance textile manufacturers had known, a machine embracing the entire process of carding, drawing, roving, and spinning.

At one stride he was able to multiply output a thousandfold, but a mob smashed the machines he erected at Chorley, and infringements of his patents involved him in costly litigation. But in the end, in spite of the malevolence of ignorance and the rascality of manufacturers, he succeeded in establishing an immense trade which made Lancashire supreme in cotton, yielded him a fortune of half a million, and founded our industrial system. He bought the manor of Cromford, obtained the grant of a market for his new village, and died immortal.

Cubley. It consists of Great and Little Cubley, hamlets on a green hillside encircling a valley where streams unite, a quiet spot with memories of the great days of the Montgomerys whose four centuries here ended more than four centuries ago. Their old home stood near the church where some of them are buried, set in quiet isolation with the rectory and an ancient yew. On the outer walls of the Tudor tower are ten of their shields, while within the church are some of their tombs.

On his alabaster tomb in the chancel lies the battered figure of Sir Nicholas Montgomery of 1435, wearing plate armour with a collar of roses, and a hip belt engraved with flowers; a helmet is under his head, and at his feet a dog with bells on its collar. The brass portraits of Sir Nicholas of 1494 and his wife are gone, and of their tomb itself only the front panel is left (projecting from the chancel wall), with sculptured figures of a man with a book, a knight, and his lady, a man in a long robe, and a knight with his shield. The figure of a lady, carved in high relief on a stone in the floor, may be their daughter, Catherine Montgomery.

From Norman days come the round arches and pillars of the nave, the pillars and capitals of the chancel arch, and the great round font. The priest's doorway and five lancets in the chancel are 700 years old, and two of the windows are filled with 14th century glass. One shows St Catherine with her wheel, the other a kneeling saint. Two other windows have an effective medley of old fragments, and the east window is lovely for its 14th century stonework.

Montgomery was the great name of this place, but there was a humbler name that will not be forgotten. It was Johnson, and one of them left this place to be a Lichfield bookseller and became the father of Samuel Johnson, the greatest talker in the world, who not only talked but put all our words into our first great dictionary.

Curbar. A village of rugged charm, it climbs the hillside between the winding River Derwent and the moors above, from a church of 1868 at the foot to a quaint house near the top with a round stepped-roof set cleverly on square walls. An odd little building, it was once a shelter for prisoners on the way to distant gaols.

Has any village in Derbyshire a finer outlook? It is lovely where the old moorland road comes down past the church, where valleys meet and a three-arch bridge crosses the stream which swings round the foot of Calver Sough; but from the windswept Curbar and Baslow Edges above, 1000 feet above sea level, the panorama of hills and dales is superb. We look down beyond the village and the river, with Calver village in the hollow, to a glory of swelling hills rich in pasture and woodland. We get a peep of Chatsworth House and Edensor's graceful spire. We look from Stoney Middleton's rocky ravine to Eyam Moor, and up the valley towards Grindleford Bridge.

In the churchyard is a stone marking the grave of one whom all fishermen loved. He was George Butcher, known as the Izaak Walton of the Peak, and he died in 1875. To him the river and the countryside were as an open book, and he was a carpenter and a preacher as well as a fisherman. By the river, near the bridge, is Calver Mill, a huge, gaunt stone-walled spinning mill, built in 1786 and operated by water-power. It was still in service as a cotton mill until recent years, but is now used for making stainless-steel sinks.

Dalbury. It consists of two widely scattered hamlets, Dalbury and Dalbury Lees. More than a mile from the Lees is the remote church, with a cluster of dwellings for company and the Radbourne Brook not far away, and with a fine treasure 700 years old. This is a small figure of St Michael, with mitre and bare feet, in 13th century glass, filling a lancet as old as itself in the nave.

Nothing is left of the church which came into Domesday Book, but of the 13th century there is another lancet in the nave and a little bell-tower with later battlements, resting inside on an enriched arch which makes a fine frame for the west window.

Pleasing today, the church tells of the love of a rector of last century who gave the unusual woodwork. Two sturdy roof timbers carved on both sides, window adornments like pelmets of wood, borders around the organ pipes, and a very elaborate panel on a wall with a bracket from which hangs a splendid font cover, were all the work of Charles Evelyn Cotton, who restored the church.

Other treasures are a fine oak chair of 1689, a reredos of five ancient wood carvings of two winged angels on each side of a panel of scroll-work, a 19th century alabaster font, and a very rare thing, a beautiful communion chalice of wood.

77

DERBYSHIRE

Dale Abbey. It has a hermit's cave, an unusual church sharing
a roof with a dwelling-house, and the majestic arch of a window
which was once the glory of a large abbey, all set in a green valley
near the busy industrial district, and all coming into a story over
800 years old.

It was between 1130 and 1140, according to tradition, that a
Derby baker found his way to Depedale, a wild and marshy place,
and made it his home, cutting out of the sandstone rock a dwelling and
a little oratory where he lived. One day, when Ralph FitzGeremund
had come from Normandy to hunt in his English woods, he found
the hermit, and, touched with pity for his poverty, gave him not only
the site of the hermitage but a tithe of his mill at Borrowash, towards
Derby. Then the hermit built himself a more pretentious oratory
and a cottage in which to end his days. After 1149 Depedale passed
to the Augustinian canons of Calke, who founded a small priory
here. In 1197 the estate passed to William de Grendon, who replaced
the canons with monks of the Premonstratensian order from
Lincolnshire.

The hermit's cave is here, hewn out of the rock and measuring six
yards by three, with a doorway, two windows, a peephole, and a
niche for a light. The division which made it into two compartments
for the dwelling-place and the oratory has gone. The hermit's well
is said to be that in the orchard, now the water supply for the house.

The curious little church which shares a roof with the old house
must surely be one of the smallest in the land, yet, while it measures
only 26 feet by 25 feet, it is really two churches thrown into one, for
it is said that the south aisle is on the site of the hermit's second oratory, and that the nave and chancel are the chapel built by the
Augustinian canons. In about 1198 the aisle we see took the place
of the original oratory and new windows were put in the walls,
but these were altered in the 15th century.

For more than 200 years two gabled buildings stood side by side,
but about 1480 the church was altered to its present form. The roof
was given gables north and south, a wooden partition took the place
of the stone wall between the chapels, and a screen was erected
across the nave which, with the wooden partition, was made to
support the gallery. This gallery covers all the church except the
chancel and is entered by an outside flight of steps. It is believed

that the old church was made into an infirmary and infirmary chapel for the new abbey.

In an interior in which all things seem askew, held up by props and posts, the oak pulpit is leaning sideways as if with the weight of over 300 years, perched up in a corner of the chancel and level with a window top. The chancel screen and the partition are those put up in the 15th century, though the old solid panels of the partition have been cut open. There are numerous 17th century box-pews, but the only seating in the nave is the four benches. There is a great uncomfortable-looking chair, the one massive thing we see in this tiny church. It was given in 1824 by an Earl Stanhope who loved this place and called it in affection his little cathedral. So the chair became the Bishop's Throne, and the whimsical title has crept into the inscription on the tablet to his memory, where he is called Lay Bishop of this church.

By a strange chance this tiniest of churches has one of the biggest things of its kind in the land, a chalice of 1701 measuring 9 inches high and 15 inches round. The 15th century abbey font is here with worn carvings of the Madonna and Child and the Crucifixion; it was long used as a flower vase in the garden of Stanton Hall. Fragments of 15th century glass are in two windows. Traces of wall paintings have been found, the finest showing the Visitation, with good line and colour from about 1300; the figures of Mary and Elizabeth are in black.

The farmhouse with the church has had a varied life. At first presumably the hermit's hut and separate from the church, it was rebuilt in about 1480 and attached to it. For some time before 1820 it was an inn, the bar being used as a vestry, with a door into the aisle, but it was rebuilt in 1883.

Of the abbey itself, which was completed in the late 13th century, and grew in importance and wealth until its dissolution, there remains the splendid arch of what must have been a glorious east window with fine tracery. The tracery has gone, but the arch stands proudly, 40 feet up to its keystone and 16 feet wide. The sites of part of the nave, the choir, the transepts, two chapels, and the chapter house have been discovered, while some remains of the kitchen, the refectory, and a gateway are in buildings round about.

Some fine relics of the abbey have been used in the enriching of other Derbyshire churches. Radbourne has some splendid old wood-work, and Morley church has the old stone framework of the abbey windows and much rich 15th century glass.

Darley Abbey. This stone-walled village, with the noise of Derby barely a mile away and in sight of its towers and spires, stands at the gate of a great estate which is now a fine public park where we may wander at will—along the drive with beautiful rhododendrons and great trees, above the winding River Derwent, in and out of glass-houses fragrant with scents and ablaze with colour.

The great house, also known as Darley Abbey, after the 12th century Augustinian priory which was once the biggest and most important in Derbyshire, has gone, and the scanty remains of the priory, down in the hollow, are built up into dwellings. Near them is a great cotton mill on the Derwent built in 1783, and it is a fine sight to see the mighty rush of water through the sluice gates when the mill is still.

Crowning a hilltop above the village is the church, built in 1818, its walls rising from a churchyard of lawn and great trees. In the churchyard is buried a man whose voice was often heard within a stone's-throw of London's Fleet Street, for he was Alfred Ainger, who was born in the first year of the Victorian Era and known all over England as a preacher and lecturer. He was known best of all for the sermons he preached in the Temple Church. He was at school with the sons of Charles Dickens, and the novelist taught him to act and recite. He was a friend of Tennyson and of George du Maurier, to whom he suggested many of the subjects for his *Punch* drawings. He wrote the life of Charles Lamb and some favourite hymns, and he loved beauty all his life.

To the south of the park was discovered in recent years the remains of an early Roman fort, older than that at Little Chester, on the other side of the river, but the site is covered by housing.

Darley Dale. Its famous quarries have sent stone to Hyde Park Corner and the Thames Embankment and to a hundred great places, but it is for the stones that remain in Darley Dale that we come to this open valley of the Derwent.

It is where Churchtown gathers about an old road off the beaten track that we step into the past, finding something of Norman and

Saxon and perhaps Roman days. Here still lives the famous Darley Yew, almost without a rival in the land if we think of its years and its condition. No man can guess its age, but it may be old enough to have seen the coming of the Norman church when the Saxon church came down, and it still stands firm and grand and green with a trunk about 32 feet round.

Perhaps we find more interesting a round stone near the chancel door in the churchyard. It is four inches thick and nearly four feet wide and it was found buried a century ago with a twin stone which fell to pieces when they moved it. On top of each stone were charcoal ashes and the earth was burned about them and below. It is thought the stones may have been used by Romans to cover human ashes buried here.

Out of the far-off past also have come three stone coffins lying in the churchyard, the smallest of them found under a pillar in the nave; it had a child in it, and its discovery reminds us of the pagan tradition of sacrificing a child and laying the body under a foundation stone. About us in the churchyard are many 17th century tombs, some carved with roses, one with a heart pierced with darts, and one with the handloom and shuttles of a weaver.

From Roman to Saxon and Saxon to Norman, on to our great English building centuries, the stones of Darley Dale come. One Saxon relic remains in the walls between the porch and the tower, a dark stone carved with knotwork and showing the heads and legs of two figures whose bodies are worn away. From the Norman days there have survived for us two doorways in the chancel, the bowl of a small font, the capital of a Norman shaft built into the outside chancel wall, a stone outside the tower carved with grotesques, and stones in the porch with the head of a cross and a three-toed animal. From the 13th and 14th centuries come the chancel arch and the arcades, and from the 15th century come the clerestory and the pinnacled tower. By the entrance to the turret staircase inside the tower is a corbel carved into a terrifying fellow with hair on end, sharp teeth, and hands like claws.

These old walls house old monuments. Sir John de Darley, lord of the manor over 600 years ago, is in a suit of mail with his legs crossed, his hair curled, and a heart in his hands. Thomas Columbell is here in a fur-trimmed gown such as he wore over 400 years ago, his wife in a dress with a girdle. In the chancel kneel John Milward and his wife with their 11 children; they lived at Snitterton Hall, a charming stone-gabled Elizabethan house two miles from the church, beyond the Derwent, and John was a colonel for the king in the Civil War. A fragment of alabaster in the vestry has on it the eight children of Elizabeth Needham, buried here in Tudor days, and a tiny brass in the chancel is engraved with four faces and a death's head in memory of Mary Potts, a rector's wife of 1654.

Finely kept in the north transept are two engraved stones. One of 1513 has the portraits of John Rollesley and his wife, he with eight sons, she with four daughters. John has a chain round his neck, she has an embroidered girdle, their heads are on cushions, and over them are elaborate canopies. On the second stone is the eldest son John, with his wife and tiny figures of their 12 children. John's gown comes just below his knees and his shoes are fastened with straps; his wife's dainty dress has a girdle. A remarkable possession is this pair of stones with 28 Rollesleys of two generations.

Darley's Elizabethan ship came home with the discovery of a wall painting of a vessel thought to be one of a series of the banners of the 12 patriarchs once adorning the walls. It is older than the Spanish Armada. In the south transept is a window with vivid colours in its 12 panels, illustrating the Song of Solomon, the work of Burne-Jones and William Morris. The roof of the nave is 400 years old, with carvings on its massive beams and faces on the corbels; and ancient stone screenwork has been built round a pew in one of the aisles.

From the peaceful meadows of Darley Bridge, beyond the river, the charming village of Wensley climbs the steep hillside, with a small church of 1843 in the Norman style, and Oaker Hill close by.

On Oaker Hill is a solitary tree which has long been a landmark for miles around. It is one of two sycamores planted on the top of the hill by two brothers who parted here to go separate ways into the world to seek their fortune. One of the trees has gone, but the other lives, and round it has been woven the story which Wordsworth made into this sonnet:

> *Tis said that to the brow of yon fair hill*
> *Two brothers clumb, and turning face from face*

Nor one more look exchanging, grief to still
Or feed, each planted on that lofty place
A chosen tree: then eager to fulfil
Their course, like two new-born rivers, they
In opposite direction urged their way
Down from the far-seen mount. No blast might kill
Or blight that fond memorial: the trees grew
And now entwine their arms: but ne'er again
Embraced those brothers upon earth's wide plain:
Nor aught of mutual joy or sorrow knew
Until their spirits mingled in the sea
That to itself takes all—Eternity.

At Darley Dale is buried the man who mechanised half the world, Sir Joseph Whitworth. His motto was Let us Try. Constantly confronted by new problems in mechanics, he grappled with his difficulties and mastered them. In his way he was as true a genius as a poet or an artist; in his life he embodied the principle of self-help.

Born at Stockport in 1803, he finished his schooling at 14 and entered the cotton mill of his uncle, where soon he was managing the whole business, and then, because the machinery was so inefficient and primitive, he ran away to Manchester and worked for four years to improve his knowledge. Still dissatisfied, he went to London and entered the service of the great Maudslay, who found in him a kindred spirit and employed him in his private workshop. Living frugally, young Whitworth worked by night at home and there completed his first astounding invention, the true plane, basis of a host of machines that have since covered the cities of the earth.

It was the beginning of Whitworth's astonishing succession of creations. Steam-power was being applied to machinery, and there was no exactitude in the making; nothing was true or standard; everything was haphazard. Whitworth revolutionised it all. Establishing himself in Manchester, he introduced the first series of instruments for refined measurement; standard gauges, taps and dies, true screws precise in thread, power lathes, planing machines, drills, and so on, with machines that would measure to a millionth of an inch. He made a fortune, gave vast sums to education, bought an estate at Darley Dale, converted a quarry into an un-rivalled winter garden, enriched the place with its hospital and institute, and was buried here.

Denby. Coal and iron and pottery have made its name, and its Elizabethan Hall is a farm, keeping company with a colliery, recently closed. But its pottery works, founded in 1809, are still thriving, and its old ways are unspoiled.

It is in the old part, a mile away, that we find its little church, in a churchyard lovely with trees. It is charming without and within, save for a gallery which it pleased the 19th century to build in place of a 15th century arcade! The round arches and pillars of the south arcade come from the late 12th century. The chancel with its sedilia, piscina, and aumbry, is of the 14th century, and of this century also are the tower and the spire, the fine porch with its stone roof, and the font, looking like the capital of an eight-sided pillar. The altar table is of the 17th century.

The richly ornamented bell given by Patrick Lowe in Shakespeare's time still rings in the tower, and in the chancel Patrick and his wife kneel under canopies. He is in armour, she in cap and ruff with a triple chain round her neck. Behind them are a boy and a girl, and two other children with their heads covered by one hood, an odd way of showing that they died before their parents.

Here lies Sir Drury Drury-Lowe, who was buried here in 1908. He fought at Sebastopol, saw the closing scenes of the Indian Mutiny, and in the Egyptian War of 1882 made a daring moonlight cavalry charge which saved Cairo from destruction. Here also was born in 1646 John Flamsteed, a poor boy who became the first Astronomer-Royal, starting his great career among the stars, at a salary of £100 a year, in the new Observatory at Greenwich.

Derby. It is seated at a gateway of the Midlands on the threshold of the North. The Derwent, bringing a tale of hills and dales and rippling shallows, flows here past wall and mill and garden, its swiftness tempered, and something of its romance forgotten. So with the town, which, though steeped in memories of Romans who came and went, of the Saxons and Danes who followed them, resumed after each irruption its placid course, adapting every change to good advantage and retaining always that sobriety of outlook which is the

Midland gift. It is not without significance that here the Young Pretender turned back from his rash incursion into settled England, and that here the last hopes of the Stuarts faltered, to founder eventually at Culloden.

Its earliest records bear witness to a recognised stability. Saxon kings gave it the privilege of its own mint, where coins of Athelstan and Edgar were struck, and under the Vikings it became one of the "Danelaw" capitals. The Normans plundered house and mill, but the town found its feet again. It became an important trading centre and received a market charter in 1154. King John gave it the right of dyeing cloth, and it kept the trade for centuries. A charter of 1553 speaks of three fulling-mills, and Full Street, near the market-place, was the street of the fullers. The first successful silk-mill in England was established here by George Sorocold in about 1717, and it was the earliest factory in England to have looms operated by power. To it John Lombe brought the secret of the machinery which he stole from Piedmont in Italy.

Long after that trade had fled it established almost at the door of the town one of the largest firms for the manufacture of artificial silk. The transaction is typical of the town, which, borne forward on the wheels of the Industrial Revolution, now has numerous other in-dustries. It still keeps the china factory taken over by William Duesbury in the 18th century, and prides itself on the fine Royal Crown Derby porcelain, sent all over the world. It is the manu-facturing and research centre of the Midland Region of British Railways, with the largest locomotive and carriage works in Britain. It makes the famous Rolls-Royce aero-engines, and it has large foundries and other metal works, engineering and chemical works, and nuclear engineering research plant. As a town it is as ancient as any in England, but it lives in the present.

Derby is not unmindful of its past, however, and a new spirit for its preservation has arisen. Many of its fine old houses are gone, though some of them remain about the Market Place, now turned into shops, and in the Cornmarket and the narrow Sadler Gate near by. It was in a house in the marketplace that Charles I stayed for three days on his march to Shrewsbury, borrowing £300 from the Corporation. Of Exeter House in Full Street, where Prince Charles Edward stayed, nothing remains but the oak panelling of the room

where he held his last council of war, and that lines the walls of a
room in the public library. Old houses of note include a fine Jacobean
mansion in the Wardwick and the Dolphin Inn in Queen Street,
gabled, half-timbered, and dated 1530; but the best street in Derby
is Friar Gate, which has many houses showing the affluence of the
18th century.

An older building is to be found alongside St Mary's Bridge over
the Derwent, rebuilt in 1788. On the mediaeval bridge, of which a
buttress survives, pious men of the 14th century built a tiny chapel.
Less pious ages let it fall into disrepair and it became a carpenter's
shop and a storeroom. It might well have been swept away altogether had not the new spirit come to its aid to make it a house of
prayer once more. From inside its stone walls we can see the great
timbers supporting the roof, or can examine the place on the floor
where a way to the river could be found in times of danger.

From the banks of the Derwent, where the oldest settlement stood,
we can read a great deal of the town's history, ancient and modern.
The Derwent Bridge, where the stepped embankment follows the
curve of the river, has four bronze medallions of four of the town's
famous sons: John Lombe, of the silk mill; Erasmus Darwin, grandfather of the greater Charles; the historian William Hutton, and
Herbert Spencer, the philosopher. The embankment on one side of
the river has now been completed with charming flower gardens and
a sunken lily pool; and at each end of the pool, standing on a pedestal
just out of the water, is a giant bronze tortoise. To this garden has
come the bronze boy with his pipe who used to stand in the marketplace and now plays his soundless music by a fountain in a ring of
flowers.

Most of the churches gather about the old ways of the town, and
are within a few minutes' walk of one another. There were six of
high renown in the Conqueror's day, and four of them, recorded in
Domesday Book, remain, though they have been so much rebuilt
that apart from the cathedral tower only one, St Peter's, retains any
mediaeval remains in its fabric. All Saints, made the cathedral
church in 1927, was one of the two collegiate churches in the time of
the Confessor. Its great glory, and indeed the architectural glory of
the town, is the majestic tower, a legacy of the early 16th century.
It rises high above the surrounding buildings, but its stature of 210

feet from base to lofty pinnacle impresses us less than the beauty of
the structure, which is one of the finest examples of Gothic architecture in England. The rich buttresses, with their niches and
pinnacles, rise above ornamented battlements, and the three stages,
with fine traceried panels and windows, are divided by bands of
ornamental tracery. After Boston Stump it is the highest parish
church tower in England, and seen from the river or the neighbouring
hills, its great size and graceful form are alike impressive.

The church itself was rebuilt in the classical style in 1725 by James
Gibbs, the architect of St Martin-in-the-Fields in London and the
Radcliffe Library at Oxford. The builder was Francis Smith of
Warwick, who designed the splendid Sutton Scarsdale Hall and
added the rooms to Melbourne Hall; but the chancel is now being
extended, to the designs of Sebastian Comper, with new vestries and
other offices underneath. Across the church runs a magnificent ironwork screen, extending on either side of the chancel to the side
chapels, its delicate scrolls and foliage as beautiful as anything made
by the Derby ironsmith, Robert Bakewell, who is buried here.

It is a monument of fine craftsmanship, but the church has many
others of another kind, saved from the older fabric, and repeating
some of the history it preserved. The most striking of them all is the
elaborate alabaster tomb in the south chapel, which the autocratic
Bess of Hardwick, Countess of Shrewsbury, had designed for herself
by John Smithson (the architect of Bolsover Castle) during her lifetime. She spent a little fortune on it, and often came to admire the
huge projecting tomb with pillars reaching now to the roof and
supporting a great canopy adorned with stags and shields. Her
stately figure lies on it, apparelled in costly dress. Over her embroidered black gown flows a crimson mantle lined with gold, a small
ruff is about her neck, a coronet about the proud brow resting on a
cushion. Full of pride she was, and seems so here, though her hands
are meekly clasped in prayer.

She came to look on her monument for the last time in 1607, and
must have observed with satisfaction the long Latin inscription
telling of her four husbands and her great houses. She was the
ancestor of the Cavendishes, and to this church more than one followed her: Charles Cavendish who was killed at Gainsborough in
1643, and Henry Cavendish, one of the greatest of the great chemists

of the University of Cambridge, where he spent a secluded lifetime in research, and was found dying alone in his room in 1810.

There are other monuments of men and women who left no such name or fame, yet have a place in the annals of the town, and one at least with an interest all its own. This is a unique wooden figure, lifesize, of a canon of the church who has rested thus on his wooden table-tomb with his hands folded in prayer, his vestments about him in graceful folds, for nearly 500 years. A hound looks up alertly from his feet, and on the front of the tomb is an odd gallery of 13 little monks, some with beads, some with a book or staff, all standing patiently as if they were waiting for the sleeper to wake. Below are the remains of a grisly skeleton or cadaver.

The oldest monument of all is the figure, engraved in alabaster, of John Lawe, who preached his last sermon here in the 15th century. Also in alabaster we come upon Richard Crowshaw, kneeling in long black robe at a prayer-desk; he was born in Derby, made money in London, and was a benefactor of his town. Near the imposing monument of Bess of Hardwick is the 18th century white figure of Caroline, Countess of Bessborough, and near to her the bust of her husband William Ponsonby.

Next in order of the churches, and even earlier in time, was St Alkmund's, built on the shrine of the saint, who was a Saxon Bishop of Hexham and was apparently killed in a battle with the Danes in about 819. The old church made way in 1844 for a new church which was itself pulled down in 1967 to provide room for a new road under-pass. During the demolition, the foundations of the original Saxon church were discovered, together with a richly carved sarcophagus, presumed to be that of the saint himself, though when opened it was found to be filled with rubble. The church furnishings to be moved to a new church in Kedleston Road, not far away, include the fine 14th century font at which John Cotton, the curate of the Pilgrim Fathers, was baptised, and carved Saxon stones which came to light when the ancient church was replaced. A huge coffin stone which stood in an outside recess may have been carved by a Norman sculptor, and others are fragments of a cross with carvings of the Madonna holding some unrecognisable instrument, and two other figures in short skirts. A plaque commemorating Joseph Wright of Derby, the painter, who was buried here, is to be moved to

All Saints Cathedral, Derby.

The County Hall, Derby.

Dovedale, looking down the River Dove.

the new church, as is the table-tomb of John Bullock, who lived at Darley Abbey and died in 1607. His monument, one of the strangest in Derbyshire, is richly panelled, and on it he lies, an immensely elongated alabaster figure in mantle and ruff. Though six feet long the head is so small that we can cover it with one hand.

Facing the site of St Alkmund's is the Roman Catholic church built in 1839 by Augustus Pugin, who was justly proud of it. It is notable for its fine tower, with the Madonna looking down from it on the thousands who pass by.

St Werburgh's church has had a very harassed life beside the once unruly Markeaton Brook. Domesday Book records it, but the church we see was mostly rebuilt in 1894 by Sir Arthur Blomfield, though it keeps an older tower and a chancel which is now a chapel. The 15th century tower collapsed in a gale in 1601, weakened by the many floods it had survived, but was rebuilt with some of its old stone on firmer ground. The old chancel comes from a rebuilding of the old body of the church, destroyed by the flood of 1698. St Werburgh's has clung to its old stones, and it has kept some of its old furnishings, notably those of Robert Bakewell's smithwork. One of the most splendid examples is an iron crown used as a font-cover; others are the screen across the entrance to the old chancel, and an iron gateway to a small garden close to the churchyard. The brass pelican, now a lectern in the chapel, was once part of the wrought-iron font-cover.

In the old chancel is a sculpture by Chantrey, a memorial to the wife of Edward Whinyates who saw much fighting in the Peninsular War. Here also is remembered Thomas Parker, who preached for 64 years, seeing the passing of Henry VIII, the short years of Edward VI and the terrible years of Mary Tudor, the glorious reign of Elizabeth I, and its unhappy decline to the Stuart dynasty.

But St Werburgh's pleasantest memory is of one summer's day in 1735, when Samuel Johnson brought his beloved Mrs Porter to the altar of the old chancel. A strange pair they must have looked, she twenty years older than her ungainly husband, dressed fantastically and affected in her manners. Here they were married after driving over from Birmingham, and from Derby Johnson went to be a failure as a schoolmaster at Edial, near Lichfield, and an immortal in London.

St Michael's church, near the cathedral, entirely rebuilt in 1858, after much of the old structure had collapsed during a church service, is the fifth of the churches mentioned in Domesday Book.

St Peter's, the sixth, has a 19th century tower and an exterior that looks all Victorian, but it is the only church with any mediaeval remains in the fabric. The east wall of the nave and part of the arcades are Norman, but the interior is mainly of the 14th century. A 13th century coffin-stone built into the inner south aisle wall has an unusual design of a cross-head in a circle, two stars, and foliage. Among the woodwork are a pillar almsbox by a Flemish craftsman, with a panel showing a woman and her child giving alms outside a castle gate, and, finer still, a big 14th century chest, the masterpiece of some other Fleming, with elaborate tracery and grotesque animals among a wealth of exquisite carving. An Elizabethan carved oak sanctuary chair, stolen from the church, probably in the Civil War, was discovered at an auction sale in Surrey.

In St Peter's churchyard is an old stone building with a greater fame than the church, for in it Derby School was established when, after four centuries, it was removed from its first foundation. Its second foundation was in 1554, and it is of curious interest that after another three centuries Derby School should have returned to its original site, for in 1863 it moved to St Helen's House, a splendid 18th century mansion in King Street, on the spot where Darley Abbey, to which the school belonged, had an establishment. In 1966, however, the school was moved again, to new buildings in the suburb of Littleover. The old school house, in its centuries of teaching, received many men of worth, including John Cotton, the Pilgrim Father, John Flamsteed, the first Astronomer-Royal, several Lords High Chancellor, and Edward Venables Vernon, who became Archbishop of York.

If in the past the town has seemed to neglect its antiquities, it has always held in high esteem its great men and women. William Hutton, the historian, was born in Full Street in 1723 and worked in a silk mill before he was tall enough to reach the machine without standing on tiptoe. He was a bookbinder in a small way; he afterwards became rich through the paper trade in Birmingham, and then retired to spend the rest of his life writing about Derby and other places he knew or had visited. He had the writer's knack and the scholar's industry, but his work contains many inaccuracies that have misled later historians. His fame was a local one. That of Herbert Spencer, who began life in 1820 in one of a row of plain old brick houses in Exeter Street, near the Derwent Bridge, belongs not to Derby alone, for he set his mark in the 19th century on the thought and philosophy of the civilised world.

There are others, such as Joseph Wright, the painter whom all knew in the 18th century as Wright of Derby, and who refused to become an academician, though he was both fashionable and famous. His real worth as an artist has won a new recognition; but in his lifetime he was noted most for his subject pictures and for his skill in painting candlelight and firelight. The subjects lent themselves to reproduction in mezzotint, and two at least are extremely well-known, the *Experiment with an Air-Pump* (now in the Tate Gallery in London) and the *Orrery*, which is in the Museum and Art Gallery. There, sharing the galleries with remains from Little Chester, the Roman camp on the other side of the river, the fine carved Saxon stones and the splendid sarcophagus from St Alkmund's church, and exhibits of local industry (including a large working model of the old Midland Railway), is a magnificent collection of the Derby porcelain which brought new fame to the town; and this brings us to another of the town's worthies, William Duesbury, who came from Longton, in Staffordshire, in 1756.

After taking over the first china works in Derby which had been established about 1750, he bought the Chelsea china factory and the plant at Bow, and reproduced their figures from the old moulds as Chelsea Derby, giving their patterns a second life, and a more successful one. For three generations the works remained in his family, and in the famous Royal Crown Derby Porcelain Company, refounded in 1876, they flourish still. Duesbury's porcelain is his incomparable monument, but the museum keeps alive the fame of other men of Derby. Beside the library which it adjoins have been placed the old silk-mill gates of about 1725, another of the masterpieces of Robert Bakewell.

One name has this town dear to the hearts of all, Florence Nightingale, who belongs to the county. On a stone pedestal near the huge buildings of the Derbyshire Royal Infirmary, her lovely white marble statue looks down on the busy traffic passing by. A shawl is thrown loosely about her shoulders over the nurse's dress she wore in the Crimea; she has a frilled cap on her head, and in her hand a lighted torch such as she carried through the wards of Scutari.

Among the bricks and mortar of a town which always seems to be multiplying them is a green oasis with banks of lawn and formal flowerbeds, and a variety of fine trees. This is the Arboretum, and over its entrance gates is a lifesize figure of Joseph Strutt, who gave it to the town in 1840. There is another statue by the side of a fish pool, where stands a little bearded bronze man with his hands in his pockets, looking thoughtfully down at the flowers growing about his feet. He was Sir Henry Royce, who made the engine of the first aeroplane to cross the Atlantic direct, and the engine of that which made the first flight to Australia. He was a working boy, one of a family of nine and he sold papers in the streets and delivered telegrams at a halfpenny a time. By his own character he won for himself the applause of the world, for all unaided by influence he forced himself upon the attention of the motor industry. He began with neither capital nor influence, with nothing but a faith in his own powers and in the future, and he it was who fashioned the Rolls-Royce car, and, in partnership with Charles Rolls, who died too young, raised its reputation to the height at which it still stands throughout the world. The manufacture of the car, however, has been transferred to Crewe, in Cheshire, to make more room for the manufacture of the now equally famous jet-propelled aero-engine.

Henry Cavendish, the father of Chemistry, was born at Nice in 1731, a grandson of the second Duke of Devonshire. He left Cambridge without a degree. He inherited a fortune of over a million, yet he made his great rambling house at Clapham in South London a laboratory and a hermitage. A shy and nervous man, with a stammering speech, he could not tolerate the presence of women and would leave written instructions as to his meals, which always meant leg of mutton for dinner, two legs if he had guests. He would converse only with scientists whom he could not avoid.

With his laboratory in the drawing-room and a forge next door, with his observatory aloft, he first weighed carbon dioxide, experimented with hydrogen, which he found the lightest of gases, and mixed oxygen and hydrogen in a large glass vessel, exhausted of air. By means of an electric spark he fired this mixture and found that only fluid remained, so startling the world by his revelation that water consists of these two elements.

Cavendish first revealed the fact that carbon dioxide prevents combustion and is incapable of sustaining life. One of his ancestors was among the first to sail round the earth; Cavendish, by a simple home-made apparatus, was the first to weigh it, and made an estimate wonderfully near the truth, finding it to be 6000 million million million tons.

His work was fundamental, and on his foundations chemistry has erected a structure that has transformed human knowledge and activities. Most of his researches were unknown to his contemporaries, for no man ever spoke fewer words to his fellows. He died at his London home in 1810, left over a million of money to a nephew, a remarkable page of new learning to all who wanted it, and the memory of one of the most extraordinary characters of his age.

Herbert Spencer, the great educator and philosopher, born at Derby in 1820, was a schoolmaster's son. Sent to his uncle's school near Bath at 13, he walked home, 115 miles in three days, a first proof of his resolute character. His own schooling formed the basis of his book on *Education*, a veritable masterpiece which made him the chief educational reformer of his age. At 17 he began eight years of service on a railway, where he invented an apparatus for testing the speed of engines; following this, when he was famous, with an attempt at a flying machine, a successful invalid bed, and—a mouse-trap!

In early manhood he wrote a series of papers on the rights of the individual, maintaining that the function of the State should be limited to the maintenance of justice at home and the repelling of aggression abroad, while every man should be free "to do that which he wills, provided he infringes not the equal freedom of any other man". Elaborating many essays, he formulated his great system of *Synthetic Philosophy*, a work of many volumes into which he put 30 years of labour, ruining his health. The founder of evolutionary philosophy, he traced the progress of laws, customs, men, matter, and the universe itself to evolution. It was he who gave currency to the word Evolution in its modern sense; he who, when Darwin's great work appeared, suggested the substitution of Survival of the Fittest for Natural Selection.

He had to spend all he had to secure publication of his work, which long kept him poor; but triumph came eventually, in money and in world-wide fame, but although he lived 83 years he was an invalid and much given to eccentricities. His closing years were spent at Brighton, where he was disheartened by the thought of failure and the sense of having achieved so little with so great a labour.

Dethick. High above the Derwent, with a fine panorama of the lovely valley, is this secluded village with a story of one of England's conspirators. In the farmhouse nestling close to the tiny church are the remains of the manor house where was born Anthony Babington, who was to bring dire tragedy on the splendour of his family.

Thomas Babington had married the heiress of the Dethicks, and was at Agincourt. His son John was killed at Bosworth Field; his brother William was a famous Lord Chief Justice. Anthony was sixth in descent from Thomas; he spent his boyhood in this village, and he must have known the grand old kitchen which is still here with its old turnspit, its oak beams, and its stone arches.

His father died when he was 10 and he was brought up in a strong atmosphere of the Roman Catholic faith. At 16 he was page to the captive Queen of Scots, and it was his pity for her plight which was to bring him to the scaffold. In a few years he was plotting for the death of Elizabeth and the release of Mary, his own share to be the actual deliverance of the queen, who was then imprisoned at Wingfield Manor, nearly four miles away. Well he knew this old church, whose fine tower was built in 1530 by one whose name he bore; it has a band of 15 shields of arms of his family and their alliances, and a great shield of Sir Anthony and his wife Catherine Ferrers.

The church had its beginnings in the 13th century. Among the remains of those days is the lower masonry of the side walls, two tiny lancets, the south doorway, and the piscina. The clerestory is of the 16th century. It would be the bell in Dethick's tower which rang out a welcome to Florence Nightingale when she arrived home from the Crimea, alone and unguessed at, while all England was talking of her. She had stolen her way to London, hid herself there for a night, and, refusing triumphal bands and presentations of addresses, had come quietly home to Lea Hurst a mile or so away, after the two years which had made her the most famous woman in the land.

94

Anthony Babington, head of a house which was then still secretly clinging to Roman Catholicism, inherited great estates at Dethick and beyond the Derbyshire border. During the imprisonment of Mary, Queen of Scots, at Sheffield Castle, he acted as one of her pages, and, fascinated by her charm, formed a passionate attachment for her, although she was 19 years older than he.

Married at 18, he won immediate recognition at the court of Elizabeth I, his wealth, wit, and good looks making him a conspicuous favourite. His Roman Catholic sympathies, however, soon led to his becoming the centre of conspiracies which gradually crystallised into a plot for the furnishing of money and troops by Philip of Spain, the sack of London, the murder of Elizabeth's chief advisers, and the crowning of Mary as Queen of England and Scotland.

All this depended, of course, upon the assassination of Elizabeth, and that fearful mission Babington himself undertook. Plot and counter-plot ran their course, but happily the secret was revealed by the discovery of Babington's letter to Mary detailing the plot. Babington fled in disguise, his hair cut off, his face and body stained with walnut juice. He hid first in the wilds of St John's Wood, near London, and then in the house of a sympathiser at Harrow, but he was arrested with 12 other conspirators and condemned to death.

Anxious to save his life, he betrayed the cipher in which Mary had conducted this terrible correspondence, and the day before his execution he wrote this letter to Elizabeth:

"Most gratious Souvraigne, if either bitter teares, or pensive contrite harte, or any dutiful sighte of the wretched synner might work any pitty in your royal brest, I would wringe out of my drayned eyes as much bloode as in bemoaninge my drery tragedye should lamentably bewayle my faulte, and somewhat (no doughte) move you to compassion.

"But since there is no proportione betwixte the qualitye of my crimes and any human commiseration, Showe, sweet Queene, some mirakle on a wretch that lyeth prostrate in your prison, most grivously bewaylinge his offence, and imploringe such comforte at your anoynted hands as my poor wife's misfortunes doth begge, my child's innocence doth crave, my gyltless familye doth wishe, and my heynous trecherye leste deserve."

It was in vain that he pleaded. The terrible sentence of hanging and quartering was carried out in the manner of those days.

Dove Holes. It is now bordered by huge limestone quarries, but it has still something like the shadow of an ancient past, for a little is left of what once was the great stone circle 260 yards round, one of the three most important prehistoric circles in Derbyshire. Known as the Bull Ring, its stones were broken up and used for building 200 years ago, and what is left for us to see is the ditch, with two entrances which were old before the Romans came, and an isolated mound, close by.

Doveridge. On the border of Staffordshire in a charming setting, it spreads down from the highway towards the winding Dove. A quiet lane leads to the church in a green retreat. It was on the old bridge which takes the road towards Uttoxeter that a schoolboy was told that he would be thrown into the river if he did not curse the Methodists. He did not curse them and he was not thrown in; he showed his tormentors the courage which made him famous as the great Michael Sadler, long remembered for his great work for the poor in the 19th century, and especially as a fearless agitator against child slavery in the factories.

In the peaceful garden of the fine old church is one of Derbyshire's magnificent living treasures, an old yew whose fine upstanding trunk is 22 feet round. Its spreading branches shelter a patch of ground about 260 feet round, making with the help of another yew a green tunnel from the gate. Near it are the shaft and steps of a mediaeval cross, reminding us that Doveridge was a market centre in the 13th century; they are now part of a War Memorial cross.

The lower part of the church tower is Norman work, the upper part, with its beautiful windows, is of the 13th century, with a 15th century spire. The graceful lancets of the chancel are some of the finest 13th century work in Derbyshire. The piscina is 700 years old and the font is also of this time, in spite of its youthful appearance. The nave arcades are of the 14th century. The 15th century oak roofs have fragments as old as the walls. A 17th century chest with a gabled top and three locks is nearly three feet high.

An alabaster stone in the chancel has engraved portraits of a knight and lady fading away after 450 years, Radulphus Okevere and his wife; and another stone has a priest in robes, his head on a pillow held by angels. He was perhaps Robert Kniveton, who founded a chantry in 1392.

A monument with two angels holding back curtains is to Thomas Milward and his wife, who entertained Charles I; and another shows the kneeling figures of their daughter Mary and her husband. He has the dress of a Cavalier, with rosettes to his high boots, and she wears a full-skirted gown. Below kneel three daughters, dressed like their mother and with lace-trimmed collars; and with them is a wideawake baby in a cradle with pretty draperies.

Dronfield. In the valley of the River Drone, it grew into a town and had a market until modern transport gave it easy access to Chesterfield and Sheffield, between which it comes midway, and to both of which it is now almost joined by continuous ranks of housing. Collieries, iron foundries, and steel works have given it a workaday dress, but some fine 18th century houses remain, and with all its stir of spades and shovels, tools for the workshop and sickles for the field, it has not forgotten how to treasure the old church on the hill.

A beautiful building without and within, it has been the glory of Dronfield for over 600 years. In its churchyard is the shaft of the old preaching cross. The fine tower and spire, 138 feet high, is of the 15th century, though the spire was much restored after a storm. The nave arcades, 600 years old, were crowned with a clerestory a century after.

The joy of the church is the lovely 14th century chancel, one of the finest in the county, long and lofty and light, with traceried windows, and a carved band of wavy moulding below the parapet. In the chancel windows is ancient glass through which the light has been falling 600 years. There are coats-of-arms, and three roundels with quaint figures playing musical instruments. A man is sitting with an ancient guitar, a monk has a clavichord, and another man is playing a primitive kind of fiddle. In a border round a medley of fragments are St Cecilia with an organ and other strange little figures.

Splendid woodwork old and new adds to the charm of the church. Worked into the choir stalls are bench-ends and poppyheads 500 years old. There is a Jacobean pulpit handsomely carved, and a fine old chest with seven locks. The handsome carving of the altar table,

97

and the reredos with Christ and the Four Evangelists in canopied niches, are among the finest work of a modern Derbyshire craftsman, Advent Hunstone of Tideswell.

The old font was found in the vicarage garden. Among the beautiful silver is a paten of about 1530. There is a little sanctus bell, and among other survivals is a chained book. On an alabaster tomb adorned with angels lies Sir Richard Barley in armour, his hands in prayer but his dagger by his side; he lived at Dronfield Woodhouse 500 years ago.

Set in a stone against the chancel wall are brasses of John Fanshawe with his wife and four children, and another of a woman and a child. They lived at Fanshawe Gate three or four miles away; a barn and a dovecot remain of their old home, and they are remembered in Dronfield as the founders of the grammar school in the time of Elizabeth I. On the chancel floor are fine brass portraits of two 14th century priests who were brothers, Thomas and Richard Gomfrey, said to be the only example known of a brass engraved in memory of two brothers.

Duffield. It lies in a hollow where the Derwent flows under a fine old bridge after gathering the waters of the Ecclesbourne. It has graceful 18th century houses, an Elizabethan and later Hall, now a girls' school, and a charming Baptist Chapel built in 1830. Its church is in a delightful river setting, with limes and yews in and round the churchyard; and to the north is the site of one of the greatest castles in England.

From the road above the river is a glorious view of the valley, with Castle Hill, where Henry de Ferrers, who came over with William the Conqueror, built his Norman stronghold. The powerful Ferrers family fell out with the monarch, and the castle was razed to the ground in 1266. The foundations of its keep were accidentally laid bare many years ago, and it was found that it must have been bigger than any other Norman keep in England except those of Colchester and the Tower of London. It was nearly 100 feet square, with walls 16 feet thick, had a well 80 feet deep, and a moat of which we can see remains to this day.

The church of many gables has a 14th century tower and spire and a fine peal of 10 bells. Nothing is left of the Saxon church except its dedication to St Alkmund, whose tomb has recently been discovered in Derby, but there are fragments of Norman work in two small shafts and capitals under the 14th century chancel arch, and a corbel table with 12 grotesque heads on an outer wall of the chancel, now enclosed by a chapel. An arched recess in the chancel may mark the burial-place of the founder of the Norman church, though the stone with a cross lying under it is new.

From the 14th century come most of the nave arcades, the south porch, the doorway letting us in, and a fine corbel of a bearded head under the north aisle roof. The arches of the north arcade may have been altered in the 17th century. There are windows of three mediaeval centuries; and in the chancel screen, the pulpit, and the screen-work in the arches of the chapel is good modern woodwork.

On a fine alabaster tomb in the chapel (now the vestry) lie the figures of Sir Roger Mynors and his wife who were buried here more than 400 years ago. He is in armour with his sword and gauntlets at his side; she has a girdled gown with many folds and a mantle with wide sleeves, and lovely pointed headdress showing her hair held by a ribbon. Everything is very rich; both have rings on their fingers, she four on each hand; a big jewel hangs from his collar, and her collar has a double chain with a cross; his feet are on a lion, and two tiny dogs are holding the hem of her robe. There are angels and two priests on the tomb. Sir Roger was a sergeant in the household of Henry VII and his son, and knew Sir Thomas More.

The wall monument in the north transept, with a marvellous company of Anthony Bradshaw, his two wives, and 20 children, is very unusual. He set it up in the year 1600, or the children would have been three more. We may wonder if anywhere else in England three children came too late to have their pictures on their father's monument. The figures of Anthony, his wives, and children, all with their initials, are engraved across the middle of the monument between long inscriptions. Worked into the inscription is a rhyming acrostic on Anthony's name.

A queer fellow was this Anthony Bradshaw, great-uncle of the John Bradshaw who sat in judgment on Charles I. He was a barrister, and Deputy-Steward of the then important Duffield Frith, a stretch of forest land between Duffield and Wirksworth where wolves abounded in the 13th century and Edward I hunted the fallow deer. He wrote an extraordinary poem of 54 stanzas about Duffield and Duffield Frith, and lived in the village for a time. He founded an almshouse here, which was pulled down last century, and left instructions in his will that the old folk who lived there should sit at the back of his pew and keep his monument clean.

Some of the family of Anthony Bradshaw lived at the old hall at Makeney, a stone-built hamlet at the end of a lovely climb from Duffield along the road where coaches used to travel. An old stone near the inn has the words *Derby Coach Road* 1739.

Earl Sterndale. It is surrounded by a wonderful array of hills, which fill the horizon with the wild scenery of the limestone country of the Peak. Keeping watch above are Hitter Hill and Aldery Cliff, and High Wheeldon, a hill given to the nation as a memorial to the men of the Staffordshire and Derbyshire regiments who fell in World War II.

An old inn, the Silent Woman (i.e. one without her head), stands by the green, and the 19th century church, on the site of an ancient chapel, shelters a crudely shaped font, said to be Saxon. Overlooking the Dove to the west are the curiously shaped cones of Parkhouse Hill and Chrome Hill, and above the head of the valley is the long moorland of Axe Edge, rising over 1800 feet above sea-level.

Eckington. It has a charming corner about the church, where the little coal-mining town throws off its workaday garb. The church is its glory, with the work of the later Normans in two splendid nave arcades with massive pillars. The fine tower is of the early 13th century, with a round-arched west doorway and with lancet windows below the parapet of quatrefoil and ballflower ornament. The sturdy spire is of the 14th century. The 13th century arches of the tower and chancel rest on capitals carved with foliage. The fine south aisle, with the south porch, were rebuilt in the 18th century.

The chancel is rich in old oak chairs, for it has seven of them as well as a seat. There is a very unusual peephole at the end of an aisle, designed so that it gave a view of two altars. The reredos is a beautiful painting of the Madonna with the dead Christ, a copy made about 1600 of a work by Annibale Carracci in Bologna, bought by Sir Sitwell Sitwell in Spain. In the east window are shields and medallions of old glass.

One of the queerest things in the church is an extraordinary monument showing the kneeling figures of George Sitwell and his wife in comically theatrical attitudes. After losing heavily by his loyalty to Charles I, he recovered his fortunes by founding the Renishaw ironworks.

Renishaw Hall, the old home of the Sitwells, in a fine setting near Eckington, is a 17th century house built by George Sitwell and much enlarged about 1800 by Sitwell Sitwell. The noted gardens were laid out by Sir George Sitwell, lord of the manor for over 70 years and the father of a famous literary trio, Sir Osbert, Sacheverell, and the late Dame Edith Sitwell.

Edale. It is in the broad and smiling dale which bears its name, through which the River Noe goes gathering countless mountain streams. High moorlands surround the valley, from the glory of the Kinder Scout range, with Grindslow Knoll and Ringing Roger, to Brown Knoll, Rushup Edge, and the long sharp ridge from Mam Tor to Lose Hill which separates the dale from the Castleton Valley.

A secluded little place, it has pretty gritstone houses and lovely gardens, an inn (the Nag's Head), 300 years old, and a delightful wayside dell where a one-arch bridge crosses the Grinds Brook on its way to the Noe. The 19th century church is the third in three centuries.

One of Derbyshire's wonderful walks begins here, crossing the Kinder Scout range by way of Upper Booth, Jacob's Ladder, and Oaken Clough to Hayfield. On the ridge we pass Edale Cross, a mediaeval boundary stone, rudely shaped, near the old packhorse track, from which another track ascends on to the moorland plateau of Kinder Scout.

From the road which climbs Mam Tor is a superb view of this quiet village and exquisite vale, and of the splendour of the southern mass of Kinder Scout bounding its farther side.

Edensor. Its houses, gathered by a green and wayside edged with lawn, are built of every style and shape, with irregular roofs and chimneys, with gable or turret or battlement; all at different angles, all in gardens, all looking up to the handsome church, and all built in the same decade.

Everywhere about it is the loveliness of the English countryside, for it stands on the threshold of Chatsworth. We may come to the village from Beeley's fine old bridge, across the park, with a view of the Palace of the Peak, an approach enchanting when the woods are turning to gold and the bracken to bronze. We may come from Baslow by another stretch of the park; from Bakewell through Pilsley for the joy of views and fir plantations; or by the steep way which climbs via Ballcross, passing an ancient road stone in a corner of a field. Well worth while is this by-road for the glorious panorama of Bakewell encircled by hills, and the fine views over Chatsworth as we drop down into Edensor.

The elaborate tower, with its slender spire, has reared its great height since 1867, when the old church was made new in the 14th century style by Sir Gilbert Scott. A spacious place of fine arches, it has tall canopied sedilia and finely carved corbels on the pillars supporting the roof beams and the chancel arch. The fine pulpit and the font are made from alabaster and marble, but the church has also an old font like a chalice, the eight sides of its shallow bowl carved with traceried arcading. The embattled porch, sheltering a restored Norman doorway, and with a stone roof, is mainly of the 14th century. On one side is a gargoyle with an ugly human face, and on the other an angel holding arms; and in the walls are fragments of ancient coffin stones.

We think at Edensor of the tragedy of Mary, Queen of Scots, for there is a brass in the chancel in memory of her faithful servant John Beton. He helped her to escape and was imprisoned with her at Chatsworth, dying there. The plate, three feet long, with a Latin inscription below which is a tiny figure in armour lying on a tomb, was set here by his two brothers at the wish of the queen, his most kind mistress.

A huge and costly monument in the Cavendish Chapel is in memory of two sons of the famous Bess of Hardwick and her second husband, Sir William Cavendish. At each side is a mythological figure, and at the top a display of arms. Fame with a trumpet is holding Latin inscriptions to Henry Cavendish, and to William, first Earl of Devonshire, a friend of James I who is said to have helped to colonise the Bermudas and has an island named after him. Beneath the open tomb lie two figures, one a skeleton and one in a winding sheet with its head uncovered. In the upper part of the monument are represented Henry's suit of armour with helmet and gauntlets, and the earl's robes and coronet; they are lifesize, and as if the brothers had just stepped out of them at the call of death. In the ostentatious style of the time, this monument was the reredos of the old church.

The glass of the east window of the chapel, and the fine alabaster tablet below it, recall a tragedy of nearly a century ago, for they are in memory of Lord Frederick Cavendish, who was murdered in 1882 in Phoenix Park, Dublin, within 12 hours of his landing in Ireland. This quiet village had its share in the shadow which fell on Chatsworth when they brought him home, for in the peaceful churchyard he was laid to rest, borne from the chapel of the stately house, across the park where thousands came to do him honour. A plain granite cross marks his grave.

A plain inscription pays tribute to Sir Joseph Paxton, who left the world more beautiful than he found it when he died in 1865. For more than a generation the gardens at Chatsworth became even lovelier under his care. He made glorious plantations and designed the colossal conservatory which covered nearly an acre of ground and was one of the wonders of Chatsworth until it was demolished in 1920. It was from this inspiration that he designed the Crystal Palace.

While at Chatsworth, Paxton became a devoted friend of the sixth duke, who helped him with his plans. Known as the Good Duke, it was he who rebuilt the village of Edensor, after 1839, and the north wing of Chatsworth. He is said to have spent £50,000 on his mission to Russia for the coronation of the Emperor Nicholas. His collection of books and pictures were among the finest in England. He was buried in the churchyard in 1858 under a tomb with a cross and a simple inscription.

Here also are buried the seventh and eighth dukes. William Cavendish, the seventh duke, was M.P. for Derbyshire when the Reform Act was passed, but devoted his energies to science and industry. He contributed £200,000 towards the Irish railways, and did much to advance the iron and steel works of the north. He was one of the founders of the Royal Agricultural Society, and his name is preserved in his gift to Cambridge University of the Cavendish Laboratory. The eighth duke loved nothing better than entertaining royalty in this magnificent house. Better known as Lord Hartington, he was the chief supporter of Mr Gladstone until the split on Home Rule, when he formed the Liberal Unionist party.

Edlaston. The lowly church of this scattered village stands on a hilltop by a lovely lane, looking away to the pyramid height of Thorpe Cloud and the long ridge of Bunster, those twin guardians of Dovedale, and to the Weaver Hills of Staffordshire.

Much of the church is of the 14th century, including the chancel and the chancel arch, but most of the windows are a century younger. The bowl of a very old font is still here, though a 19th century one is now used. A corner of the 17th century altar table serves as a shelf in the chancel. The curious bellcote was added on the west end in 1900.

In the churchyard are an ancient yew, with widespreading branches and a trunk 16 feet round, and the old churchyard cross, now crowned by a ball. The pretty hamlet of Wyaston lies about a green hollow near by.

Egginton. It lies in rich meadows, near the Roman road of Ryknild Street (which ran from Wall, near Lichfield, to Derby) and the River Dove, here near the end of its journey and crossed by five bridges. A bridge with a single span has been joined by a new bridge of 1968 to take part of a double carriageway road. These have kept for company the old Monks' Bridge a few yards away, a monument of more leisured days. Over this narrow graceful bridge, built perhaps by the monks of Tutbury Priory, Dr Johnson must have come with his darling Tetty, the widow nearly twice his age, on their way from Birmingham to be married at Derby, he making up his mind as he rode never to let her get the upper hand of him. A stone's throw from the Monks Bridge the river is crossed again, this time by a canal raised on sturdy arches, the building of which was one of the triumphs of James Brindley in the 18th century, and farther downstream is the fifth bridge, carrying the railway.

The church is in a quiet setting at the end of an avenue of limes, with the buttressed brick wall of the rectory on one side of the churchyard. Much of it is from the end of the 13th century, when the Norman church was rebuilt. Of this time are the north arcade, with two tiny 14th century clerestory windows (an early date for

The pre-Conquest cross in Eyam churchyard.

Eyam Hall.

Haddon Hall
(a) From the north-east.

(b) The Long Gallery.

a Midland church), the chancel with a priest's doorway, a stone seat and a piscina, and the fine east window with remains of 14th and 15th century glass, including small figures of the Madonna and St John, with a Crucifixion scene.

Perhaps the joy of this bright place is the south aisle of about 1320, its fine arcade with clustered pillars, and its long wall a mass of recesses and niches and of odd windows of later time. In one recess lies the stone figure of a woman with a heart in her hands, perhaps Elizabeth Stafford, a 14th century heiress. The tower was added to the church in the 15th century.

Elmton. It has lost the glory of its elms, and today Elmton has nothing for us to see but a plain church of the 18th century and a churchyard in which is buried an Elmton man who has curiously written his name into books all over the world, though here he is without a stone to mark the place. Here he was born in 1707; here they laid him in 1772, Jedediah Buxton, son of the village school-master.

There were many odd circumstances in his phenomenal career, but almost equalling his astonishing faculty for figures was the strangeness of the fact that Jedediah, although grandson of the vicar and son of the schoolmaster, never could learn to read or write. He passed his life as a labourer in the fields, dreaming in arithmetic. The theory of the men who studied him was that, having a genius for mathematics, he unconsciously developed it to the entire exclusion of other mental attributes. Working away in the open, he was constantly creating and solving problems with which normal mathematicians found it difficult to grapple.

However limited his knowledge, his power of concentration on his favourite subject was baffling. He chatted briskly while working out such a problem as this: In a body whose three sides measure 23,145,789 yards, 5,642,732 yards, and 54,965 yards, how many cubic eighths-of-an-inch are there? As he walked over a field he could estimate its area to an inch with the accuracy of a surveyor. One of his rapid feats was his calculation of the product of a farthing doubled 139 times. When mathematicians had proved his answer correct, Jedediah calmly multiplied his answer by itself. He could break off a calculation at any point and resume it in a week.

After a short season of triumph in London, where he was disappointed not to see the royal family but was delighted to appear before the Royal Society, Buxton returned home and died here at 65. His widespread reputation was not forgotten in his death, and a learned hand placed a Latin inscription on his coffin. Could poor Jedediah have seen it, it would have been no more puzzling to him than the complexities of that native tongue which he was never able to read or write.

Elton. Green limestone uplands and rocky ravines are round about this village, which has 17th and 18th century houses, a 19th century church, and ancient memories. It was perhaps through delving for lead that the foundations of the ancient chapel were weakened in the 18th century, causing the old steeple to fall in Trafalgar year. Some of the old stones are still in the rectory garden with one that may have been the base stone of the village cross.

The church of 1812 has a font with a story. Of most unusual design, it has on one side a small stoup fashioned out of the same block of stone, seeming to be held in the mouth of a dragon carved on the bowl. But, alas for Elton, this font is only a copy of a rare treasure it had but did not value, now the pride of Youlgreave, a Norman font perhaps unique in England, with a bracket beneath which the head of a dragon peeps out.

It is curious to learn that when the new church was built after the fall of the steeple, the old font was cast out. Twenty years later it found itself in the vicarage grounds at Youlgreave, and there it was taken into the church. The day came when Elton asked for it back again, but nothing would persuade Youlgreave to let it go, and Elton must be content with its copy of the priceless thing it threw away. One of its bells was here before the Reformation; exceptionally fine and ornate, it is inscribed, *Jesus be our Spede*.

Elvaston. It is five miles from Derby, completing a quiet group with the hamlets of Ambaston and Thulston on a level stretch of meadows near the winding Derwent. Away from the road, facing a fine avenue, are the blue and gold gates of Elvaston Castle, from a royal palace in Madrid. These grounds were famous for their avenues and groves of trees, their gardens with lake and rockeries, and a lovely yew garden where one of a maze of yew hedges, fashioned into many arbors, encircles a lawn.

The stately house, remodelled after 1817 to the designs of James Wyatt, was a home of the Stanhopes for over 400 years. The first Stanhope of Elvaston was Sir Michael, who lost his head in 1552 for being faithful to Protector Somerset; the story of some who followed him is told in the church by their home. Before the Stanhopes the Blounts were here for generations, and traces of the home they knew are said to survive in the castle. The first here was Sir Thomas, Treasurer of Calais during the wars of Henry VI; and here is said to have been born his son Walter Blount, who was Lord Treasurer to Edward IV and became the first Lord Mountjoy.

A fine embattled tower, with eight pinnacles above the high tree-tops, crowns the church which came into Domesday Book but has now nothing older than the 13th century lancet in the aisle. The chancel arch, the nave arcade, the porch, and the beautiful font are of the 14th century; many of the windows and most of the fine nave roof (with carved and gilded bosses) are of the 15th century.

The handsome mediaeval chancel screen is carved both east and west; two richly carved stall-ends once attached to it are in the chancel, with poppyheads of an antelope seated and a lion chained. Another lovely 15th century screen encloses the Stanhope pew, where is also some 17th century carving.

In the chancel, on a monument with a wonderful canopy and a shield which is almost a monument in itself, lie the marble figures of Sir John Stanhope and his second wife, he with golden hair and gilded armour, she in a black hood, resting on a tasselled cushion of red, green, and gold. He was knighted when James I came to England. One of his sons was the Philip who became Lord Chester-field in 1628. Another son John sat in Charles I's first Parliament, and his striking monument of white marble shows him wide awake, resting on his arm. He died in 1638, and this costly monument is said to have been damaged by Sir John Gell (his bitter enemy) when the Parliamentarians plundered the castle. We read how Sir John Gell wooed the widow and married her, only "to destroy the glory of her husband and his house".

The great-grandson of this Sir John Stanhope became first Earl of Harrington. The fifth earl lies in the Stanhope pew, a fine marble figure, and in the chancel we see his eldest son Algernon, who died at nine years old, a fine sculpture of a sleeping boy, by Westmacott. On the chancel wall is the brass portrait of the sixth Earl of Harrington, who died before he was 21, showing him in a scholar's dress.

The Derby County Agricultural Show is held on Spring Bank Holiday Monday in the fields to the south of the main road.

Sir Aston Cokayne, the poet of his family, was born at Elvaston early in the 17th century. Made a baronet by Charles I, he suffered heavily by his loyalty, and after an extravagant life, joined with his son in selling Ashbourne Hall and other estates. He died a poor man.

Etwall. Like a bit of the old world among the undulating South Derbyshire countryside, it has a church high by the wayside with a shapely yew, and a delightful group of almshouses with a central archway adorned with painted heraldic panels, and two sundials on the chimney stacks. The old hall of the Ports has gone, making way for two fine new schools, but three generations of the family, three gentlemen of Tudor times, have memorials in the church where they are buried, two having found a place in our national roll of fame.

The first is Henry Port, a merchant of Chester who died in 1512. His brass has gone, but those of his wife in her widow's mantle, and groups of their 17 children, are here. His son Sir John Port has an unusual tomb with a small battered figure of himself in his judge's robes, and his two wives. He was a benefactor to Brasenose College, Oxford.

Under the finely carved canopy of his tomb are the charming brass portraits of the next Sir John, who died in 1557, his two wives and five children, all kneeling in prayer. He gave Etwall its almshouses, which were made new in 1681, and he founded Repton School, whose badge (a pigeon with a cross) is seen on his armour and in the heraldry of his monument. His heiress married Sir Thomas Gerard, a Roman Catholic suspected of plotting to get Mary, Queen o Scots, out of prison. Sir Thomas tried to evade Elizabeth's spies by attending service in the church, but trouble came one day when he compelled his younger brother to accompany him, for he began chanting like a good Roman Catholic as soon as the minister began the reformed service in English, and the scene ended in his being seized and carried out of church.

Much of the old work left in the church is of the 15th and 16th centuries, including the low embattled tower. Part of the chancel walls and its buttresses are of the 13th century, and three round arches remain of the Norman arcade. The massive font is 500 years old, there is a stone lectern of the unique Derbyshire pattern (probably of the 13th century) on the chancel wall, and in the Port Chapel are beautiful carved seats and a prayer desk of the Elizabethan period.

Eyam. In a land of moorland heights, ravines, and pretty dells lies this charming Queen of the Peak, whose old stone houses line the long, wide, old-world street on a terrace of the hills. It looks up to Eyam Edge, rising 400 feet above the village, and reaches down to the grand gorge of Middleton Dale, with its own delightful Cucklet Delf and Eyam Dale, shut in by rocky heights and a fine plantation. Its hills are riddled with caverns and the earth with old lead mines; its moor, crowned by Sir William Hill, 1407 feet above sea-level, is rich in burial mounds and stone circles, among them the Wet Withens.

It has a fine house, an old church, and in the churchyard one of the finest Saxon crosses in the land: it has associations with a group of lettered folk through whom it came to be called the Athens of the Peak. It has its humble cottages, its simple graves, its memories of simple folk, and it is with these that its imperishable story lives.

It was in September 1665 that a box of tailor's cloth and some old clothes came from London to a cottage near the church, and with it bitter tragedy for Eyam, tragedy which turned the peaceful village into a place of death, for it brought the plague that had raged in London many months. The first of its victims was the journeyman who opened the fateful box; he died within four days. By the end of the month five more had died, in October a score and more. For more than a year the pestilence pursued its savage way, abating with the winter months only to burst out with greater violence in the spring. In March, 56 are said to have perished. All the time this village of grief and despair was a place of quiet heroism, the heroism of a little band who stayed to serve, of a panic-stricken people who in the very face of death resigned themselves to follow the path they were asked to tread.

Names that will live while man has memory are those of William Mompesson the rector, his wife Catherine, and Thomas Stanley, who had been ejected from the church for nonconformity but had remained among his people. They set themselves to isolate the village for the sake of the outer world, asking no more of the others than they were willing to do themselves. They arranged for food to be brought from outside and left at certain places on the boundaries they fixed, the money left for payment being carefully washed before it was taken away. One of the appointed places, since known as Mompesson's Well, is covered with a block of stone, on the edge half a mile north of the village.

The horror of it all increased as the months went on, and deaths were so frequent that the passing bell ceased to toll, and the grave-yard ceased to take the dead. Graves were dug in gardens and fields and often those yet spared had to bury their own loved ones. At one house a woman watched her family die within eight days, husband and six children. The Riley Graves of the Hancock family can still be seen, a pathetic circle of six headstones and a tomb. The tomb of John Hancock, the father, is in its original place, the stones having been brought together from about the field.

Time came when the church door was closed, and the rector took the remnant of his flock to Cucklet Delf, a haunt of peace and loveliness among the trees which June had filled with the song of birds and the joy of flowers. The pitiful procession was to grow pitifully less as the days went by, wending its way down grassy slope and slowly up again to where Mompesson found his pulpit on a picturesque rock with natural arches, and carried on his ministry to the stricken people. Every year when Feast Day comes, on the last Sunday in August, a great procession treads the way to the simple Cucklet Church in memory of the sufferers of nearly three centuries ago.

In August, Catherine Mompesson died and was buried in the churchyard, a yew tree now sheltering her tomb. By October the last toll had been paid, and according to the register out of 350 village folk 259 had died. Among those left were the two ministers, William Mompesson and Thomas Stanley; they saw this bitter tragedy through to its appalling end. Mompesson left the village soon afterwards for the living of Eakring in Nottinghamshire, and became a prebendary of York and Southwell. Very different was the reward of Thomas Stanley, who remained at Eyam until he died in 1670, for after all his labours there were those who would have turned him from the village for his nonconformity.

In the church is a brass tablet in memory of Stanley and the two Mompessons, and an old oak chair is carved with *Mom. 1665. Eyam.* In the vestry is a little oak cupboard said to have been originally in one of the Plague Cottages, as those near the church are called.

Much of the old work of the church has been lost in rebuilding and restoration, but from Norman times there are two fonts, one of them with round arcading. From the 13th century come the chancel and the north arcade of the nave, from the 14th century the archway to the tower, and from the 15th the south arcade and the clerestory windows. There is an old oak chest, ancient tiebeams and bosses in the nave roof, an 18th century oak pulpit, and remains of an urn found in a barrow on Eyam Moor. In the chancel is a lancet window in memory of a rector who helped with his own hands to restore the church last century. Here too is a memorial to Ralph Rigby, a curate. Three Yorkshire clergymen who had been to his funeral in 1740 were lost in the snow while returning; one was found next morning and survived, but the other two perished. On the walls are rare 16th century paintings, brought to light in 1962.

The churchyard with its fine trees is rich indeed in story. There is an elaborate sundial of 1775 on the wall of the church showing "the parallel of the sun's declination for the months of the year, the scale of the sun's meridian altitude, points of the compass, and a number of meridians". Many of the epitaphs were written by two poets who knew this place. One was Richard Furness, a village boy born in 1791 and buried here, a preacher and soldier before he was 20 and afterwards schoolmaster of Dore, where he designed a new school-house and was doctor for all. The other was Peter Cunningham, who was curate here for 18 years and wrote poems that no-one reads. While he was curate the rector was Thomas Seward, who thought himself a playwright, poet, and author, and published an edition of Beaumont and Fletcher. He was buried in Lichfield Cathedral, where he was a prebendary.

It was his daughter Anna who made his name familiar. She could repeat a poem of Milton's before she was three and she became known as the Swan of Lichfield. Her poetry was very affected and has been forgotten, but while she lived at Lichfield, where the Sewards were often visited by Dr Johnson, she became the friend of many men of letters of her day. The rectory where she was born in 1747 has recently been rebuilt.

The most precious thing the village has is in the churchyard, a Saxon cross which has come through more than a thousand years in almost all its glory, complete with head and arms, only two feet of the top of the shaft missing. It stands eight feet high and is carved all over with fine design. On the head and arms are angels with crosses and trumpets, while the shaft has knotwork and lovely scrolls with foliage, and figures of a man with bugle horn, and the Madonna and Child.

In the centre of the village is the charming great house, at the roadside facing the stone pillars of the ancient stocks. Grey-stoned and many-gabled, set in terraces and lawns, it was built by the Wrights in 1676, and is said to be a copy of the old Bradshaw Hall of Eyam whose stones were used in it. A Well-Dressing Festival, the last to be held each year in Derbyshire, takes place on the Saturday before the Plague Commemoration Service.

Fairfield. It is almost on Buxton's doorstep, but it keeps a character of its own, for all at once the busy road opens out to a breezy common where men play golf 1100 feet above sea-level, one of the highest courses in England.

Just beyond the common is Water Swallows, its name coming from the curious behaviour of a stream near the wayside, which disappears into the earth with swirling eddies and runs underground for about three miles until it bursts out in Chee Dale.

The church of 1839 has an old font which may have been in the chapel here 700 years ago, when the Dakins were living in the village. One of two 19th century memorials to them has on it the strange motto: *Strike, Dakin, the Devil's in the hemp.*

Fenny Bentley. It is watered by the little Bentley Brook, which found its way into Izaak Walton's *The Compleat Angler*, thanks to its trout and grayling. The old Hall is picturesque with gables and a square tower making it look like half a house and half a castle. The tower is part of the old manor of John Beresford who fought at Agincourt with a soldier son now lying in the church across the way.

This great soldier, who is said to have marshalled his 16 sons for the wars of Henry VI, has one of the most extraordinary monuments in Derbyshire, an alabaster tomb on which he lies with his wife Agnes, both in shrouds tied up above the head, at the ankles, and below the feet, so that no part of them can be seen. Round the edge of the tomb are helmets, shields, breast-plates, swords, banners, and drums, the things these Beresfords loved, while on one side and at one end are engraved the tiny shrouded figures of 21 children, five of them girls. In a window of the chapel, with a great heraldic display, are Thomas and Agnes with their son James, who became Canon of Lichfield.

Another window showing the death of St Edmund is in memory of Captain Hans Busk, the gift of a daughter who married a Beresford. Born in the year of Waterloo, Hans Busk was the founder of England's volunteer army, author of many books about rifles and shooting, and one of the earliest advocates of lifeboats. The east window shines with good 19th century glass.

The fine church has nothing older than the 14th century, except the red bowl of the font and a doorway perhaps Norman. From the 19th century comes the hammerbeam roof of the nave and chancel, with 26 angels looking down; some are singing, some playing instruments, others praying. There is a splendid chest with ironwork perhaps 700 years old, and a bench with 14th century carving; but the precious possession of the church is its 16th century screens. The chancel screen, the older of the two, still keeps its rood-loft, though the fine vaulting and exquisite cornice have been made new. In one of the spandrels is a fox with a goose in its mouth. The other screen, now between the aisle and north chapel, once enclosed a chantry founded by James Beresford.

Findern. Though Derby is creeping nearer, it still remains a quiet old place, gathered round a shady green on a little hilltop. It has a charming tale, belonging to the Crusades and the Findernes, who were here 200 years. Sir Geoffrey fought in the Holy Land, and when he came home he brought a narcissus to plant in his garden. The flower took root and flourished. It saw the great days of the

Findernes and said goodbye to the last of the line when Jane Finderne married Judge Harpur and went to Swarkestone. When the last traces of the old home had gone the narcissus went on blooming, growing wild as the garden became a field, until it seemed, as the villagers believed, that it would never die. It found its way into the gardens of the cottages and vicarage, and it saw the rebuilding of the Norman church before a careless hand uprooted it from the soil.

No stone is left of the old home of the Findernes, and for long there were no monuments to be seen in the church. An old inhabitant, asked what remained of the Findernes, said, "Nothing, except the little flower in the vicarage garden". Walls and tombs had gone, but the little flower brought to England by a Crusader was growing and blooming still. Now there is only its memory, but in the church an alabaster floorstone has come to light bearing traces of shields in memory of Isabella Finderne of 500 years ago.

All that is left of the Norman church, rebuilt in 1863, is a tympanum crudely carved with a cross, a pattern of squares, and little figures like Dutch dolls. One of the church's great treasures is an exquisitely engraved chalice of beaten silver; it is of 1564 and among the oldest in Derbyshire. The church-register is said to record the burial of John and Sarah Woollet, who lived together for more than 60 years and were buried in one grave on January 14, 1747, he being 91 and his wife 92.

It was at Findern that Jedediah Strutt, the inventor of the ribbed-stocking frame, served a seven-years' apprenticeship with a wheelwright, and no doubt learned much about hoisery from the family with whom he lodged.

Foremark. It is all charming here, high above the Trent, and lovely are the ways bringing us to it from Repton or from Ingleby. Fine gates lead to the handsome stone Hall with a huge portico and corner bows with domed roofs, built by David Hiorns in 1755 for Sir Robert Burdett. Now a preparatory school for Repton, it stands at the head of a lake in grounds with groves of trees and noble yew hedges.

One who loved this quiet place and made it his home was Sir Francis Burdett, a 19th century opponent of injustice and a vigorous champion of liberty. He had denounced flogging in the army and

Mugginton
Nicholas Kniveton
and wife, 1475

Ashbourne
Francis Cockayne
and wife, 1505

Dronfield
Thomas and Richard Gomfrey, 14 c.

Chesterfield
Sir Godfrey Foljambe
and wife, 1529

Kedleston
Richard Curzon and
wife, 1496

Etwall
Sir John Port (founder of Repton School) with his family, 1557

BRASS PORTRAITS OF OLD DERBYSHIRE FOLK

advocated its abolition for fifty years when Queen Victoria was still advocating its continuance as the only means of keeping order in the navy. He was imprisoned more than once for his advanced views, and suffered through his protest against the Peterloo massacre. His courageous efforts brought about some of the early prison reforms; and as far back as Trafalgar he was urging reforms which were not accepted for another generation. He died in 1844, a man widely loved, generous to the poor and a supporter of every good cause.

The church with the low tower was built in the Gothic style in 1662, when the old chapel and the chapel of Ingleby downstream fell into decay, the stone and wood from Ingleby being used to rebuild it. There are three sundials on three buttresses, and above the chancel window are the Burdett arms and figures of Faith and Hope.

Most of the old woodwork has been saved. The flat roof has massive beams, the nave walls are lined with oak panelling, and the box-pews are so high that we do not wonder the parson climbs up into a three-decker pulpit, a fine Jacobean piece. An extraordinary oak screen between the chancel and the nave is crowned with a pediment of contemporary glass showing angels and a dove. The 13th century font has a 17th century wooden cover; the 18th century altar rails were made by Robert Bakewell, the great Derby ironsmith, who also made the beautiful gates between the churchyard and the park of the Hall.

Foston. A patch of beauty on a now-busy highway, it has a few picturesque houses, a Hall in a park, and a brook winding to Scropton, where the hamlet people go to church.

But it has given England a distinguished antiquary. Its present house took the place of the old Hall burned down last century, the home of the Agards, who had lived here from the 14th century until the time of Charles II. Arthur Agard, who was born here in 1540, spent most of his time in London, a patient searcher among old documents in the chapter house at Westminister. He made a wonderful collection of writings, some of them still used by students. A friend of Camden, Stow, and Cotton, he loved nothing better than ancient manuscripts on law and heraldry. He died in 1615 and was buried in the cloisters of Westminster Abbey, close to the marvellous old chapter house in which he had spent the happiest hours of his life, doing things that would have been tedious to most men. He was one of the first members of the Society of Antiquaries.

Froggatt. It lies on a gentle slope above the Derwent, mantled in trees and with gay gardens that are a joy to see, a village so girt with beauty that only those who have time should seek it.

There is a charming view-point from the 17th century bridge which spans the river with two arches odd in size and odd in shape. It is a scene of a wide stream making a marvellous curve, of the softness of lovely meadows and the grace of fine wooded slopes, of the rugged strength of Froggatt Edge stretching like a rampart behind the village.

The glory of the village is this gritstone 'edge' under which it nestles, magnificent in length and in its precipitous height, with great boulders jutting from its sides and all of it softened by the green of heath and fern and tree.

A winding road climbs to a scene of great beauty at the top. With moorland all about us and across the valley, we look deep down below to where the Derwent stretches like an endless snake of trees, winding to Grindleford Bridge and Padley Woods, on towards Hathersage, and beyond to the glorious background of Bamford Edge and Win Hill.

The land rises across the river to the heights of Eyam. Between them and the river are the deep woods sheltering Stoke Hall, the 17th century home of Sir William Cavendish, the famous Royalist who smoked a pipe at Marston Moor and spent nearly a million pounds in the cause of Charles I, losing his estates in the end.

Glossop. It is Derbyshire's textile town, busy with cotton mills and rayon printing works, and also producing paper, ropes, and canned foods, but finding romance in its glorious situation as the northern gateway of the High Peak.

It stands at the beginning of a magnificent 12-mile stretch of road unrivalled in this lovely county, beside the wild grandeur of Kinder Scout, a world of mountain and gorge, moorland and trackless waste and many a waterfall, and the beauty of green valleys as the Ladybower Reservoir draws near. Four miles from Glossop, after climbing nearly 1700 feet above sea-level at the Snake Pass, the road is joined for a spell by the course of the Doctor's Gate, which leaves it again near the inn which is the first sign of life.

The Doctor's Gate is part of the old Roman road from Brough to Melandra Castle, known to the Romans as Ardotalia, where, on a slope between the meeting of the Etherow and a brook, can be seen the walls of the fortress, excavated in recent years. In Dinting Vale an impressive railway viaduct 120 feet high, with 16 arches each 125 feet wide, strides across road and valley, and north of the town the Etherow is dammed up into five miles of lakes to supply Manchester and its neighbouring towns with water. South of the town, on the old Monks' Road, is the Abbot's Chair, perhaps the base stone of an ancient cross; and a mile from the Chair are Robin Hood's Pickling Rods, twin monoliths set in a massive stone.

The sombre "new town" around the marketplace was mostly laid out after 1830; the charm is in its older haunts to the north-east, where 17th century gabled houses climb the road by the church and the tall market-cross stands in the square.

The church of Old Glossop has little old work left, the nave having been made new in 1915 and the chancel and a lady chapel added in 1923. The tower and spire were built last century by the Duke of Norfolk, whose arms are on the spandrels of its doorway. There is an elaborate reredos, coloured and gilded, with a rose window above it, a fine oak pulpit and three old oak chairs, and the choir stalls and the reredos in the lady chapel are of fine modern craftsmanship. The unusual font of pure white marble has a bowl in the shape of a shell held up by two children. William Bagshawe, the Apostle of the Peak, was vicar here till his ejection in 1662.

On a hill to the west of the church is a Roman Catholic chapel, built in 1836, with a lovely view of dipping moorlands. Between the church and the chapel is Glossop Hall, a fine house of 1850, once the Duke of Norfolk's and now a school, in a public park of rare delight, with a wealth of trees, stream and waterfalls and lake, and playgrounds for all.

Great Hucklow. This limestone village of charming old grey houses is in a secluded position below the slopes of Camp Hill, the summit plateau of which is the launching-ground of the Derbyshire and Lancashire Gliding Club. Their gliders can be seen taking off from the hill on fine Sundays during the summer and swooping gracefully over the Bradwell Dale towards the heights beyond. The Northern Gliding Championships are held here each year, usually in July or August, and the World Championships have also taken place here, one of the only two places in England.

Great Hucklow is well known for the fascinating little theatre of the Village Players, a company formed in 1927 by L. du Garde Peach, the playwright and producer, and still directed by him. The performances of the Players draw enthusiastic audiences from over a very wide area of Yorkshire and the North Midlands.

Great Longstone. It lies under Longstone Edge, a gritstone ridge over three miles long rising to nearly 1300 feet at Bleaklow, where human skeletons have been found in a barrow. A splendid row of 14 great elms by the roadside adds to its charm, and on the small green is the old cross on its steps. Facing the manor house and the Crispin Inn (with its sign of the cobbler's saint) is the attractive 18th century red-brick Hall, reached by an avenue of fine elms and lawn, keeping still a ball-crowned gable of the older home of the Wrights who lived here most of the time from the 14th century onward.

The church, in company with two fine old yews, comes from the mediaeval centuries. The south doorway and the north aisle windows are of the 13th century; the west tower, the priest's doorway, and the nave arcades are a century younger. The church's glory is in its splendid 15th century roofs with fine moulded beams, embattled cornices, and bosses of flowers and foliage and arms, one showing a man holding the cover of a tub from which a weird figure has just come out. An old oak screen with a deep cornice shuts off the end of an aisle which was once the family pew of the Eyres. On the wall is an engraved copper plate of 1624 with the portraits of Rowland Eyre and his wife, kneeling as if in a chapel with a window at each side; he in a long robe with lace ruffs at the wrists, she with a ruff and a flowing veil. Both have a rosary.

The eight panels of the fine old font were splendidly carved early this century by a Tideswell sculptor, and its fine new cover has eight figures of kneeling angels. A cross built into an outside wall may once have adorned a gable. There is a tribute here to a hero of

Great Longstone, Dr Edward Buxton, who early last century, as an old man of 73, sacrificed himself to tend the villagers during an outbreak of typhus. Though the fever visited every house but one, no-one died.

Grindleford. Time brings changes even here, in the new houses of commuters from Sheffield, beyond the moors, but nothing can rob it of its lovely setting in the dale of the Derwent. It lies under Froggatt Edge, where the river comes down through a glory of woods and meadows to its three-arch bridge, only lately joined by the Burbage Brook, which left a moorland home for the joy of a sylvan glen.

The village keeps its charm of other days on the hillside where the road descends steeply from Sir William Hill, on Eyam Moor, to the creepered inn; where grey cottages gather round a green with an old sundial. It lies at the point of a triangle of roads enriched with scenes it would be hard to surpass, 10 miles of river and rock, of lovely woods, of hill and moor. We climb from Grindleford Bridge through Padley Woods to the heather moors, past Longshaw Lodge to the Fox House Inn. The lodge is an old shooting box on whose pastures (now the property of the National Trust) famous sheep-dog trials are held in September; the inn, standing where the roads divide is a spot believed by some lovers of Charlotte Brontë to be the Whitcross where Jane Eyre was set down from the coach during her flight.

And then the road rides by the moors from east to west. We see Burbage Brook near the beginning of its journey, passing under the road where the Toad Rock rears its realistic shape. On the moor beyond the rock we see Carl Wark, where nature and man combined to make a remarkable fortress, mysterious yet in its name and age, perhaps of the Saxon period, perhaps earlier. Farther north rises Higgar Tor, 1350 above sea-level, its great mass of rocks heaped in fantastic fashion and weathered to curious shapes.

At Millstone Edge an entrancing panorama comes upon us with such startling suddenness that it is known as the Surprise View. From this top of a moorland world which is wonderful whatever its mood, kind when the heather is all aglow and magnificent under snow, we look far down to the Derwent in its wooded vale, joined by the Highlow Brook at the end of its journey between two moors with ancient graves; we look beyond Hathersage nestling round its charming church to Bamford Edge, and on to Crook Hill rising between the Woodlands Valley and the reaches of the Upper Derwent; we look from Win Hill, Lose Hill, and Mam Tor to a dim horizon of Kinder Scout and other Peakland heights beyond the broad and lovely Hope Valley. From Hathersage back to Grindleford the road runs in the Derwent Valley, through deep plantations under the slopes rising to Eyam Moor.

Haddon Hall. Set on its gentle hill with the Wye flowing at its feet, it is not a vast mansion like Chatsworth, but a lovely English home that has taken nothing but beauty from the centuries it has seen. It stands as a mirror of the history of the Vernon family, who came here in the 12th century, and of the Manners family, Dukes of Rutland, who succeeded in the 16th century and whose roots were planted by our Norman conquerors. Mostly built about 1370, it is one of the finest mediaeval houses and one of the best pieces of domestic architecture now existing, and is magnificently preserved. A gateway in the great tower built by Sir George Vernon, "King of the Peak", gives entrance to the lower courtyard, a gem of architecture with stone steps, turret and tower, and traceried windows. Here is the oldest part of Haddon, the chapel, still keeping its Norman font and one round 13th century column of its arcade. It has 15th century wall paintings, including a St Christopher with the Christ Child, 15th century stained glass, and a 14th century altarpiece carved from Derbyshire alabaster.

We cross the courtyard to the banqueting hall, which rises to the full height of the building. It has a minstrel gallery fronted by a splendid screen, and at the opposite end is the raised dais, its high table lit by a traceried window. The kitchens, on the other side of the screen, are a rare and complete survival from Tudor and earlier times. We pass the dining room, one of the alterations made by the Tudor Vernons. One end is filled by a window of eight lights brilliant with heraldic glass, the other end having an exquisite oriel window. Over the fireplace are the royal arms and the motto, *Drede God and honor the kyng*; and on two of the panels are the heads of Henry VII and Queen Elizabeth I. The painted 16th century ceiling is a rare survival in an English house. From this room we climb stone stairs to the state apartments and find ourselves in the Great Chamber, the Tudor drawing-room, which has a fireplace with a surprising splendour of metal work.

The Long Gallery, 110 feet from end to end, was altered and extended in the early 17th century by Sir John Manners, son of the Earl of Rutland. It is reached by six semicircular steps of solid oak cut from the root of one tree, and it is said (though truly it seems incredible), that the whole floor of this room came from the timbers of this oak. The wainscoting here is probably unequalled anywhere. Big and little arches are divided by pilasters with flowering capitals, and running along the top is a frieze and a battlemented cornice. The design, with its flutings, its geometric patterns, its shields, its wealth of carving, all exceedingly intricate, is an early example of classical style of decoration.

A doorway in the adjoining ante-room is known as Dorothy Vernon's Door, and through it, according to tradition, the only daughter and heiress of Sir George eloped to meet Sir John Manners and fly with him to Belvoir Castle, in Leicestershire, thus linking the Vernon estates with those of the Earl (and now the Duke) of Rutland. The beautiful terraced gardens at Haddon, mostly laid out in the 17th century, afford a charming view of the River Wye winding in the meadows below and the limestone uplands beyond. Across the river is an old packhorse bridge over which Dorothy is said to have escaped.

Hardwick Hall. It has been called the "supreme triumph of Elizabethan architecture" and it cannot fail to impress us by its six lofty towers, its tremendous front of nearly 200 feet, and its mass of closely packed windows seeming to occupy almost the whole of its great wall space, so that there has grown up an old Derbyshire rhyme, "Hardwick Hall—more glass than wall". It was one of the great houses of the Cavendishes, Dukes of Devonshire, but after the death of the 10th duke in 1950 the death duties on the estate were so enormous that the house was taken over in lieu by the state and it was subsequently made over to the National Trust.

In the balustrading above the house can be seen, repeated many times, the initials, "ES". They stand for Elizabeth, Countess of

Shrewsbury, better known as "Bess of Hardwick", a commanding woman even in the days of Elizabeth I. After quarrelling with the fourth and richest of her four rich husbands, the Earl of Shrewsbury, she returned to Hardwick and began to rebuild the old manor house where she had been born. But the death of the earl in 1590 left her the richest woman in England, after the queen, and she immediately began the building of the new hall, leaving the old to fall into the ruin which still stands.

Bess called in Robert Smythson, the great Elizabethan architect, who had been responsible for the noble Renaissance mansions of Longleat, in Wiltshire, and Wollaton Hall, near Nottingham. The building was completed in 1597, less than seven years after work had started. Bess was then 75 years old, but she lived on at Hardwick Hall until she died at the age of 87, when she was buried in All Saints, Derby (now the cathedral).

The magnificent interior of the house amazes us by its balanced proportions, the richness of its decoration, and its unequalled tapestries and needlework, a national treasure in themselves. From room to room we pass at Hardwick in an ascending scale of grandeur. The Entrance Hall is imposing, the Presence Chamber is magnificent, the Long Gallery is overwhelming. In the Presence Chamber a great plaster frieze of forest glades, branching trees, browsing deer, and other realistic English animals, and curiously unreal elephants, goes round the room, the work of an English craftsman, Abraham Smith. Under the frieze hang 16th century Brussels tapestries coloured with old dyes and shimmering with gold and silver. The Long Gallery, 166 feet from end to end, with deep window recesses, is a royal spectacle, the architectural masterpiece of the house. It has a painted frieze, and a vast range of tapestries illustrating the story of Gideon. It has paintings famous all over the world, portraits of Elizabeth I and Mary Stuart and numerous Cavendishes, including the first Duke of Devonshire, the builder of Chatsworth, and among them is one of Bess herself when she was growing old, her beauty gone, though still she looks out as one having great authority.

Hartington. Fine limestone hills and dales surround this up-land village of old stone houses, already a market centre in the early 13th century. Here an ancient church and a fine old Hall look across to each other from opposite slopes, and an inn reminds us that this is a place our most famous angler loved.

Here a lovely reach of the Dove divides two counties and, within a mile of the village, flows through Beresford Dale, an exquisite haunt of precipitous rocks, luxuriant trees, and green banks mirrored in a crystal stream. Here is Pike Pool in still and green seclusion, with a great lichen-covered rock rising like a slender spire from its depths. Among the trees, and now quite inaccessible, is the one-roomed Fishing House built by Charles Cotton in 1674, where he and Izaak Walton talked of everything to do with rod and line. Here, too, is the cave where Cotton is said to have hidden from his creditors.

The picturesque and gabled Hartington Hall (now a youth hostel) was built in 1611 by one of the Batemans and restored 300 years later by another. Robert Bateman was born at Hartington in 1561 and became a merchant in London, one son being knighted by Charles II and another becoming Lord Mayor of London.

The church in the shape of a cross is chiefly of the early 14th century, including the fine west tower, the nave arcades, the chancel with its priest's doorway and east window, and the two-storeyed porch with a niche for a saint. The sundial on the porch says, *So marches the God of day*.

Fragments of ancient stones are built into the walls, and some engraved with crosses are in the porch. Oldest of them all is a small Saxon stone in the wall of the north transept; carved with interlaced knotwork, it is the oldest thing Hartington has. The church has mediaeval glass fragments, four piscinae, and a 15th century font with shields and tracery. In a south transept recess is a long tapering coffin-stone showing in openings, at each end, the sculptured head and shoulders of a 13th century woman holding a heart, and her feet. Found under the floor of the nave, it is thought she may be Margaret de Ferrers, Countess of Derby.

Hartshorne. It gave England a great preacher, and has in its church an unfortunate historian. The first was George Stanhope, born in the village after Cromwell's day, a few years before his father became rector. He grew up to be a famous preacher, a bold critic, and a daring writer of Queen Anne's reign.

The historian was Stebbing Shaw, Hartshorne's most pathetic

rector, who followed his father in 1799, and was buried here in 1802. With Sir Egerton Brydges he travelled much in Staffordshire, Leicestershire, and Derbyshire, and together they edited the *Topographer*. In 1788 he published a diary of his travels in Scotland but no one read it. His only popular book was about Cornwall, but he was always trying to write something that everybody would read, and his failures made him bitter. It was during his three years here that he wrote what was to have been a monumental history of Staffordshire, though only the first volume was published. A disappointed man, sometimes insane with grief, he walked about the rectory garden with his eyes to the ground; and often he would be found playing his fiddle to try to while away his melancholy.

His church was rebuilt in 1835, but it keeps a 15th century tower with a row of carved stones in an outer wall, one with arms, and two with figures of dogs. The lancet windows have tracery made of cast iron, and the west gallery has cast-iron columns. The font is probably of the 14th century. A splendid old chest has nine iron clamps; two bells are older than the Reformation, and a silver paten, of about 1480, is one of the oldest pieces of plate in the county.

On a fine altar tomb lie the alabaster figures of Sir Humphry Dethick of 1599 and his wife, both with ruffs; Sir Humphry in armour has a pointed beard, his wife has a pretty French cap and lies on a cushion with an embroidered border. On the front of the tomb are three sons, one an infant, and three daughters. It was one of the Dethicks who went to Cleves to find a fourth wife for Henry VIII, and his son Sir William laid a pall of rich velvet on the coffin of Mary, Queen of Scots.

Hassop. It shelters under Longstone Edge, charming with its cluster of pretty houses, its great house, and a fine Roman Catholic church. For centuries the home of the Eyres, it has seen the waxing and waning of the splendour of this family, once with 20 manors in the country and 20,000 acres in Derbyshire. They built the Hall, set in a noble park with a fine lake, in the late 17th century. A mighty chestnut and a giant beech are among the splendid trees guarding the gates to the drive enclosed by an ivied wall and a high yew hedge.

The Eyres garrisoned their house for Charles I, fighting the Parliamentarians at its gates. One of them won distinction at the siege of Newark, and later had to pay £21,000 to redeem his estates. One married Lady Mary Radcliffe, whose father and his brother (the Earl of Derwentwater) were also friends of the Stuarts, both being captured at Preston in 1715, when the earl was beheaded. Charles Radcliffe escaped from Newgate, only to be taken off the Dogger Bank in 1745, when he too was beheaded. It was through Mary Radcliffe that the Eyres were for 40 years Earls of Newburgh, and one of them built the Roman Catholic church, in a classical style like a little temple, just after Waterloo. On the Italian baroque altarpiece is a fine painting of the Crucifixion by Lodovico Carracci.

Hathersage. It comes into our literature; it is said to have the grave of Little John; and it has a lovely treasure-house. For long it knew the Eyres, and some of their old homes are near. Highlow Hall and Offerton Hall stand high across the valley, and beyond the church and towards the moors are Moorseats and North Lees Hall. A 16th century house in a lovely setting is North Lees Hall, mantled in trees. From here the Eyres fled when James II ran away, and near by are ruins of their tiny chapel.

Charlotte Brontë knew Hathersage and brought it everlasting fame in *Jane Eyre*, giving her heroine a name which breathed association with this place and using the glorious country round about for her moorland scenery. North Lees Hall is in the story, Moorseats is the Moor House where the Rivers sisters lived. The house has been much altered, but the little window through which Jane peeped is here, now inside the hall. The cross-roads three miles off are said to be the Whitcross where Jane left the coach to find her way to Morton, which is Hathersage. She stayed at the vicarage, high up on a hill, helping Ellen Nussey to get the house ready for her brother and his bride. In the vicarage are now kept Charlotte's writing desk (inlaid with pearl), one of her shawls, and slippers worn by her and her sister Anne.

Close to the vicarage is the handsome church, coming mainly from the 14th and 15th centuries. Lighted by splendid windows, its battlemented walls have pinnacles and gargoyles, among which are quaint faces, a tiger's head, and a muzzled bear. The fine 15th century tower has a lofty spire as old as itself, and an arch with beautiful capitals. The nave arcades with fine capitals, the priest's doorway, the graceful canopied sedilia, and a lovely piscina are also of the 14th century. Of the 12th century church all that is left is the base of a pillar in the north aisle. In the porch is a broken coffin-stone 600 years old. Incorporated in the modern vestry are windows, stones, and slates from Derwent church, now beneath the waters of the Ladybower Reservoir.

The arms of the Eyres are over the porch, and their fine array of brass portraits is indoors, all in armour. The 15th century font has their arms, too, and a beautiful little sanctus bell asks for a prayer for Robert and Joan, whose brass portraits have been for over 500 years on an altar tomb under an elaborate canopy in the chancel. Robert has his sword and dagger, his wife has a fur-trimmed gown, and their 14 children are all in a row.

On the wall above this tomb kneel their eldest surviving son Robert with his wife, four boys kneeling behind; two little kneeling figures on the other side of the chancel may be missing daughters. The brass portraits of Joan's son Ralph and his wife are against the chancel wall, and brass figures of a knight and his lady of two generations later kneel at desks on which there are books; they are Sir Arthur Eyre and his wife.

The churchyard is lovely with trees and has splendid views; it has also four feet of the old cross, and a grave that everyone comes to see. It is by an old yew, and we read that here lies buried Little John, the friend and lieutenant of Robin Hood.

Little John is said to have disguised himself as a servant in the house of the Sheriff of Nottingham and to have carried off the silver plate. According to legend, he came back here with a broken heart after laying Robin Hood to rest at Kirklees. It was he who gave the dying Robin his bow and arrow, and sent him from the world with the praise of his last feeble shot ringing in his ears. The wise will be content with the story, content to hear how his little cap and his bent bow used to hang in this church, and how there was found in his grave a thigh-bone 32 inches long, of a man of tremendous stature.

Hatton. This expanding village must have had a great share in Tutbury's pageantry, for such near neighbours are they that as we stand on the five-arch 19th century bridge spanning the Dove with one foot in Tutbury and one in Hatton, we look up to the ruins of the castle crowning the wooded hillside. Hatton saw the rising of the noble castle walls in Norman days and their dismantling in the Civil War; saddest of all its memories was the passing this way of Mary, Queen of Scots, to be a prisoner there.

It has known the days when a treasure chest was thrown into the Dove while Thomas, Earl of Lancaster, was fleeing from the castle with the king's men after him; and it has known the excitement of finding some of the treasure a century or more ago, when 100,000 silver coins were picked up in the gravel of the river-bed near this bridge. Some of them are now in the British Museum.

Hayfield. It is on the threshold of the mighty range of Kinder Scout, the great tableland wild and savage in rock and ravine, menacing with trackless wastes of moss and heath and bog, charming with mountain streams and delightful waterfalls, and kindly when the sun lights up the moorland hues of purple, gold, and green. It is a region of solitude with a lofty grandeur culminating in a height of 2088 feet above sea-level.

We can cross this mountain mass from Hayfield by walking up the valley of the Kinder River and then over Nab Brow and up William Clough to Ashop Head, with fine views of the cliffs of Kinder Downfall. It was round these haunts that Mrs Humphry Ward laid the early scenes of her *David Grieve*. A few miles across the moorland bring us to the Snake Inn on the wild road over the Snake Pass from Glossop.

Standing over 600 feet above the sea, on the banks of the vigorous little River Sett, Hayfield is busy making paper and printing calico. Like the rest of the village, the church suffered from floods before it was rebuilt in 1818, for a lusty stream flows beneath it. The new church was built on the old foundations, and the level has been raised, the pillars of the old arcades being shortened to serve as props for the new floor. The chancel was added in 1894.

In the church is a fine marble bust of Joseph Hague, sculptured by John Bacon. Born at Hayfield, he began life as a pedlar, carrying his wares till he was able to afford a donkey; in 1717 he went to London and there made a fortune, which he gave away. It is said that when his own 12 children died, all before they were 21, he adopted another family. He ended his days at Park Hall, a house of 1811 to the north, below the moors, and he was buried in Glossop church, where this bust was originally set up. At the rebuilding of the chancel there the bust was placed for safety in the lock-up, where all was well with it until one night it had a drunken man for company, and he, enraged with the silence of his white companion, set about it savagely. It was then rescued from its indignity and set up here in memory of a village boy.

Hazelwood. It lies on an airy upland between the valleys of the Derwent and the Ecclesbourne, glorying in its fine views; it has a pleasant group with the gabled vicarage and the gabled schools, gathered round the churchyard, from where we see Alport Height and the tower on Crich Stand.

The church, built in 1840 was restored after a fire in 1902. Some of its lancets have memorial glass, one commemorating one of the Strutts who helped to make Belper famous, another to the Alleynes, one of whom made for the church its finely carved lectern. Above the altar are three fine new windows by Carl Edwards.

To the east of Hazelwood stretches the long sandstone ridge of The Chevin, sometimes called the "last of the Pennines". From it there are wide views, both up and down the beautiful valley of the Derwent.

Heanor. This hilltop market-town, busy with hosiery, coal, engineering, and pottery, has more to remember than to see. It knew William Howitt who, with his wife Mary, was writing books for nearly 60 years when there were not so many books to read. William and his brother Richard were born in a house called the Dene, now demolished. Close by the site of their home is the old chapel the family knew, built for the Quakers in 1839. The house, the chapel, and an array of seven stones in its graveyard with the names of Howitt and Tantum (the family name of William's mother) are the only memories in Heanor of its most distinguished son, who is buried with his wife near Rome.

Heanor has known Samuel Watson, who was buried in its church in 1715. A marvellous craftsman, he was responsible for the exquisite carving at Chatsworth, where his work is of such striking beauty that when Horace Walpole called he imagined it to be by the great Grinling Gibbons. His epitaph in the church speaks of his *wondrous works in Chatsworth Hall*, and declares that his skilful art represented nature *to the very life*.

It is possible that Samuel Watson may have been present in his youth at the funeral of a brave rector who is buried somewhere in the churchyard, John Heiron of Breadsall. He was one of the Non-conformists turned out of their pulpits at the Restoration, a man known in a hundred churches and chapels all over the country, believing in God and fearing nobody. He seems to have escaped from death many times when face to face with it, for he was tossed by a cow, he fell from a window, he was caught in a whirlpool, and fell into a river. But in the end he died a quiet death, and was laid here in 1682.

In the church is a fragment of stone with an inscription of Roman carving, recalling that 1700 years ago a Roman buried a vase at Heanor with 800 Roman coins in it. Here they lay undiscovered until the railway came.

Only the massive 15th century tower is left of the old church re-built in 1868. There is a small crucifix made from an old oak beam of the belfry, but all else is modern. The oak pulpit has good tracery and a cornice of vine and grape; the oak font-cover was given by the parents of one child who was baptised along with 250 others in 1908; and a window whose interest is in its story has a group of martyrs in memory of a brave sufferer, Jane Burns.

Sons of a wealthy Quaker surveyor at Heanor, William Howitt, born in 1792, and his brother Richard, seven years his junior, inherited a love of learning and a gift for languages. After school-days they practised together as chemists in Nottingham but at 29 William married Mary Botham, a Quaker of martyr stock, whose name became inseparable from his own in a long literary career. Leaving the shop for the study, they wrote jointly a number of books such as the *Rural Life of England* and volumes resulting from their wide travels to places of fame and interest, old halls, battlefields, and homes and haunts of our poets.

Mary, like her husband, was a poet and novelist, and was widely esteemed for her books for children. Quiet as was their lives, there was a spice of adventure in their blood, and they settled for some years in Germany, doing excellent translation work there, with works on German life and manners, and the first complete examination in English of the chief Scandinavian and Icelandic writers.

After their return to England, William, accompanied by his two sons, joined the gold rush to Australia, worked in the goldfields, and returned three years later, at 63, to publish work which stirred Young England to follow where he had led, and travel about the world. One whom he so inspired was his own son, Alfred, who made a memorable Australian journey to find and carry to Melbourne the bodies of the two heroic explorers, Burke and Wills.

It was a Heanor boy, Henry Garnett, born in the middle of the 16th century, who grew up to be a central figure in the Gunpowder Plot. The son of a Protestant schoolmaster, he left Winchester for London and the Law, but, turning Roman Catholic as a young man, went to Italy. He proved such a brilliant scholar there that it was with great reluctance that the Papal authorities permitted his return on a mission in which his friends pictured him as a lamb going to slaughter. He was to take part in the plots against the Throne, stirring up rebellion first against Elizabeth I and then James. It was the Gunpowder Plot which brought to light documents by which he was incriminated.

Garnett fled to Hindlip Hall, in Worcestershire, where he lay with a companion hidden for four days in a secret chamber, nourished by broth and other warm drinks conveyed by a reed through a hole in a chimney. He was driven out at last by foul air, and more than twenty times he appeared before his judges, but threats of torture and tricks of eavesdroppers failed to betray him into more than one admission. He acknowledged himself "highly guilty, and to have offended God" in not revealing it. He pleaded that he was struck with horror at the proposal, and saw that, as he could not disclose the secret, he used every endeavour to prevail on the conspirators to abandon their undertaking. Sentence of death was passed on him, and he was drawn on a hurdle from the Tower of London to St Paul's Churchyard and executed.

Heath. The village has left the hollow for the fine view from the hill; it can see Hardwick Hall and Bolsover Castle, both standing proudly on their long, finely wooded ridge of limestone. It has charming brown stone cottages, and in a churchyard bordered with

131

limes is the church of 1853, with embattled tower and spire and high roofs, looking down over the fields to all that remains of the old church left for the new.

All but the porch was pulled down, but on to that a little chapel was built from the old material which served for a while at funerals. It is lonely and forsaken now, and the great new motorway roars past.

Higham. It lines the road by which the Romans tramped to Chesterfield from Derby, its houses (stone-walled and some of them set in gardens), a charming frame for a wayside cross.

Higham was a market centre from the 13th century, and the fine flight of seven steps (now supporting a modern cross) reminds us that butter and eggs were brought here for sale. The cross looks afar to a lovely countryside, or nearer to the busy road at the end of the village, pitying, we may think, the people who hurry on, not heeding that this pleasant village is near.

We have beautiful views whichever way we come to it, and especially fine is the panorama from the road from Stretton, looking over the Amber Valley to the Ashover hills and Crich Stand.

Hilton. Standing on a busy highway, with the traffic roaring through, it has little to show. The unhappy Mary, Queen of Scots, would come this way on her journey to Tutbury Castle, one of the many prisons she was to know before she reached Fotheringhay. It is said that she called at the timber-framed Old Hall by the roadside, which was Hilton's glory in other days, built perhaps five centuries ago and known as Wakelyn, from the old family whose home it was.

Hognaston. The village is built along a pleasant road climbing from a sparkling brook to the Wirksworth–Ashbourne road, which rides nearly 1000 feet high along the top of Hognaston Winn. Its old church has fine views of sweeping hills and valley, the trimmed limes making a frame for the sturdy tower. The tower walls, five feet thick, come from the 13th century, the belfry with its pinnacles and gargoyles is of the 15th and the tower opens into the nave with a fine pointed arch.

The glory of the church, sheltered by the porch, is a handsome doorway of the Normans. The sides have beak-head moulding, the arch has chevrons, while the fine old tympanum is engraved with crude carvings of quaint figures. One is a man wearing a tunic and bearing a staff; he stands between a holy lamb and a group of wild beasts as if to convey the idea of a pastor protecting his flock from attacks. In this doorway still swings an ancient oak door. The round bowl of the font is Norman, with sunken arches; the chancel arch and the east window are of the 14th century.

Holbrook. It stands on a hilltop with a Hall of 1681 (now a convalescent home), other old houses great and small, and a charming outlook on a pastoral countryside. In a field near the hall a Roman pottery kiln, where the well-known "Derbyshire ware" was made, was discovered and excavated in 1962.

The church, in a pleasant churchyard enriched with flowers, looks out to Horsley's ancient steeple in a wealth of trees on the facing hill. It was rebuilt in 1841, incorporating part of the private chapel built for the Hall which stands above it, and was enlarged early in the present century. It has much contemporary woodwork, and a memorial to Samuel Bradshaw who built the original chapel and died in 1768. A round west window has glass in memory of William Leeke, who was vicar here and who is buried in the churchyard, his gravestone telling us that he carried the colours of his regiment at Waterloo.

Holloway. Sheltering under the crest of a wooded ridge, it seems to be at the top of the world as we climb up to it from Whatstandwell. It looks out magnificently over valley and hill, rocks and trees, which seem to have no end. It has a pleasing church built in 1903, with a tower standing above the chancel, nave walls lined with oak, a fine oak pulpit, and an alabaster font.

One summer's day in 1856 a lady left a convent on the banks of the Thames, took a train to the nearest station to Holloway, and walked from there to her home. She was unattended and hardly expected when she opened the door of Lea Hurst to reveal herself to her astonished household. She was Florence Nightingale home again.

She was the most talked-of woman in Europe. She had astonished the government by her courage and frightened every old woman in the army by her daring, for she had torn the red tape of the army to shreds. She had made memorable the insanity of the Crimean War with the opening of another chapter of humanity; she had soothed the last hours of soldiers wounded by war and murdered by neglect. In all our history there was no woman like her, and when it was all over and she came home, all England waited to acclaim her. The navy offered her a warship and would have brought her home in state, but she would not have it and came home privately. When it was known that she would go to her Derbyshire home there was talk of triumphal arches, addresses from mayors and corporations, all the panoply and pageantry of regimental bands.

But Florence Nightingale would have it not. She arrived unknown in London and early the next morning knocked at the door of the home of the Bermondsey nuns and spent a few hours with them. Then she went to the station and caught a train at an unusual hour. She arrived unseen in this stone house with many gables in the charming garden above the Derwent which her father had built in 1825. Florence, who was born in Florence, came here when she was five. Here she loved to be, to visit the old folk in their cottages, to help with village entertainments; she could be well content, she said, to do this all her life.

Her balcony was a great joy to her, commanding a view of the garden with its stone terraces massed with flowers, and of a meadow beyond, losing itself among the trees running down to the river. Often the sound of the Derwent was in her ears, and she had recalled it one night in hospital at Scutari. There was a great storm, and suddenly Florence Nightingale said: "How I like to hear that ceaseless roar; it puts me in mind of the Derwent. How often I have listened to it from the nursery window!" If ever she lived to see England again, she wrote from the Crimea, the western breezes of her hilltop home would be her first longing. It was to Lea Hurst that she came home again, to this house that we may see, now fittingly being used as an old people's home.

Holmesfield. Standing at a height of over 800 feet, on a ridge of the Pennines which separates the headwaters of the River Sheaf from the headwaters of the Rother, it looks far over Derbyshire to Hardwick Hall, the ruins of Bolsover Castle, and the crooked spire of Chesterfield, while to the north are the hills round Sheffield.

Where the road along the ridge begins to drop from Holmesfield into the Cordwell valley is a low weather-beaten house of about 1600 with many gables, some panelled rooms, mysterious recesses, fine carvings, and beautifully moulded ceilings. This is Cartledge Hall, home of the Wolstenholmes. One of their sons, Sir John, was a most energetic merchant adventurer, a founder of the Virginia Company. He helped to fit out the ill-fated expedition of Henry Hudson, and his name is preserved by Baffin in his map of the inhospitable region of Wolstenholme Island.

In this ancient hall lived, wrote, and died in 1917 Robert Murray Gilchrist, the Derbyshire novelist, who was born in Sheffield in 1868. From boyhood he was a writer, and he wrote a dozen or more novels illustrating either modern types of character or 18th century romance and fashion. Almost invariably his work had a Derbyshire setting. Whether his stories were long or short, his literary workmanship was fastidious, and he had the power of making his characters intensely real in the simplest way. He never wrote a best-seller, but many thoughtful judges have held that his stories have qualities that will always call for notice in any wide survey of fiction.

Gilchrist had a natural gift for friendship, and not a few writers of his day visited him at the old hall on the hilltop, and with him traversed the dales and moors of the Pennines' Derbyshire fringe. He was a huge man, full of humour, who could rattle off anything on a piano and surprise the stranger with the sweetness of a tenor voice coming from his massive frame. He died suddenly in his prime and had a great funeral, including a contingent of Belgian refugees to whom he had been kind, and who had found their way to this remote upland village. He was buried in Holmesfield churchyard, on the edge of the hill country he peopled with his fancy. There is a memorial to him in the church of 1826, built on the site of an ancient chapel.

Holmesfield was held by the Deincourts from the Conquest until the 15th century. The old Hall near the church, though now a farmhouse, is still adorned with a great shield of some of its owners. A mile below, in the Cordwell valley, is the hamlet of Millthorpe, where Edward Carpenter, the Socialist poet, lived the simple life and evolved his philosophic theories.

Hope. We find it in the rich green Vale which bears its name, changing with modern days but with an ancient story. Hereabouts the Peakshole Water meets the River Noe as it flows from the Vale of Edale between Win Hill and Lose Hill, two fine landmarks towering above the village for another 1000 feet.

Only a mile away is Brough, which the Romans called Navio, and where many relics have been found; some are in Buxton's museum, with an ancient milestone. There is little to see at Brough today, for the excavations have been filled in, but they revealed an enclosure with walls six feet thick, measuring 340 feet long by 280 feet wide. There was a gateway on every side, and a western tower. Traces of the Praetorium were found, and a sunken chamber dating the fort to the 2nd century. For 600 years Brough has had a mill by the bridge, given in early days to the Strelleys for the service of attending the king on horseback whenever he should come into Derbyshire.

Hope had a Saxon church which may have stood where the church now stands amid fine sycamores. It is thought the round bowl of the font may have been in it; certainly it is very early. In the churchyard is a fine fragment of a cross which was perhaps here before there was a church at all. Seven feet of the shaft remain, carved with knotwork and foliage, and with two figures holding a cross. It is over 1000 years old, and was found in pieces in the walls of the old school.

From the 14th century, when the old church was made new, come the nave arcades of lofty bays, three priest's seats and a piscina, the south doorway, the tower with its short spire, and the lofty tower arch like a lancet window, which gives a charming effect to the interior. The clerestory and the fine windows of the aisles are of the 15th century; two of the windows have glass after the Annunciation of Leonardo in the Uffizi Gallery at Florence.

The chancel has Kempe glass in the windows, the east showing the Crucifixion in eight panels. Lining the side walls is fine old panelling, some of it the remains of the 16th century family pews in which sat two great families, the Balguys and the Eyres. They lived at Aston Hall, now a farmhouse, and at Hope Hall. On the chancel wall is a tiny brass with a quaint engraving of old Henry Balguy, who died in 1685; it shows him in breeches, doublet, and pointed hat, pen in one hand and a book in the other, and it has this epitaph:

Hardwick Hall
(a) The west front.

(b) The Presence Chamber.

Kedleston Hall
(a) The south front.

(b) The Marble Hall.

Wained from the world, upon it yet I peepe,
Disdaine it, weepe for sinne, and sweetly sleepe.

There are fragments of old heraldic glass in the windows, ancient tiebeams with quaint corbel heads in the nave roof, a curious old hymn board with a picture of David playing the harp, four big 18th century pictures of Moses and Aaron, Time and Death, a fine carved oak pulpit from 1652, and two 17th century chairs. One of these, in the sanctuary, is said to have been the schoolmaster's chair, and has on it the words, *A Mercury cannot be made out of bent wood.* Two coffinstones at the west end of the church are perhaps of the 13th century, and are engraved with crosses and bugles, one having also an arrow and a sword. The 15th century porch has a turret with steps which once reached to the roof of the aisles.

Hope has a Well-Dressing Festival (like Tissington) on St Peter's Day or the Saturday before, and an agricultural show and sheep-dog trials on the Summer Bank Holiday Monday.

Hopton. In this delightful green hamlet, with its handful of cottages, is a great house which has long been the home of the Gells. Here was born Sir John Gell, the Parliamentary General of the Civil War, an extraordinary man who, with a rough and rather brutal spirit, led the forces of the fairest army raised in England. His doublet, colours, and other relics are still preserved at Hopton Hall, an Elizabethan house much altered in the 18th century.

Very different was Sir William Gell, a famous classical scholar and traveller, born here in 1777. Gentle and kind-hearted, he spent most of his life in Italy, where he wrote books on Rome and Pompeii. His greatest joy was to entertain distinguished people in his lovely home at Naples, where he was often found with his books, drawings, and maps, his guitar, and two or three dogs. There he died in 1836, and he was buried on a hill above the famous bay. Sir Philip Gell, another baronet, founded the almshouses in the village in 1719.

The name of the Gells will long be remembered in Derbyshire, for the Via Gellia, a lovely road through a romantic woodland valley, was named after one of them who made it. One of Hopton's joys is a lovely lane which climbs through a glorious hillside plantation, the way we take to find the Via Gellia two miles away to the north.

There were Gells who stayed in and about their ancestral Hopton

K   137 to strike shrewd blows for the Commonwealth against the Stuarts, but in happier days the family produced in Sir William Gell an even more conspicuous figure in the life of peace. A Royal Academy student, he went to Greece, exploring and sketching what he believed to be the site and environs of the old Troy, and tracing, as he believed, the footsteps of Ulysses in his little island kingdom.

He settled down in Italy, with homes in Naples and Rome, where he was a centre of an artistic and learned society. Byron, Moore, and Scott were among his friends. Surrounded by noble books, writing, drawing, and publishing, he was a prince of hosts and one of the best known men in Europe. He comes into one of the most pathetic chapters in Lockhart's *Life of Scott*. Gell and Scott had met in England and immediately became friends. They did not come together again until 1832, when, although neither knew it, both were dying.

At Naples, Gell arranged Scott's plans, being warned by him that those who had tried to get classical antiquities into his head had always "found his skull too thick". The two friends went to Pompeii. Scott could not walk, so Gell surrendered his chair to him, and himself obtained another which was tied together with cords and handkerchiefs. So they rode side by side, the old poet surveying the scene in romantic rapture.

In Rome the old friends laboured at sightseeing, with Gell as guide so solicitous as to remember to tie a glove round the end of Scott's walking-stick lest he should slip on the floor of the Vatican. Scott begged Gell to return home and visit him, and Gell replied that if his health and means permitted he might do so. Four months later Scott was in his grave, and Gell came no more home to England, for he died three years later at Naples.

Horsley. On a hilltop about a mile south of the village, stood a castle which knew the mightiest people in the land. Known as Horeston Castle, it had Montforts, Shirleys, and Dukes of Lancaster and Norfolk among its owners, but very little of it now remains, hidden among the trees. It is the glory of another building which brings us here, an ancient church in a beautiful setting, with carpets of narcissi and daffodils in spring, roses in summer, and always kindly trees. It is seen from afar, and reached by a tree-lined road.

The church is charming to look at, with a strongly buttressed tower and spire, a pretty porch with a mediaeval crucifix, and a lovely array of windows, with the fine 15th century clerestory under a handsome parapet of battlements and pinnacles. The church of the Conqueror's day was made new 600 years ago and from that time comes the north arcade and the tower and spire, with two tiers of lights, rising to 130 feet. To the 15th century belong the chancel with its grand sedilia, the large font with roses and foliage, and perhaps a remarkable gargoyle projecting about two feet from the wall.

Seen in profile, the head of this gargoyle is like some forbidding catlike creature, while a full view of the face shows debased human features. It is remarkable for the carving underneath, which can only be seen standing right below it, showing the figure clothed in vestments with draped sleeves, an open book in one hand. Another great gargoyle has a grotesque head projecting even farther from the wall, on the other side of the porch.

The south arcade was rebuilt in 1860, much of the old stone being used again. The reredos is an oak carving of the Last Supper; the chancel screen with tracery and a cornice of vine and grapes is a War Memorial. Kept in a glass case is a fragment of the 15th century chancel screen.

Hulland. At the end of a fine ridge of high land, it has a magnificent outlook over the hills and dales. From the top of the sturdy embattled tower of the church we can sometimes see the Wrekin in Shropshire, 40 miles away. The church, built in 1851, has an enormous font, its eight sides carved with the symbols of the Four Evangelists. Its bowl is over ten feet round and stands over four feet high. A new chancel was added to the church in 1961.

On a pretty stretch of the Ashbourne–Belper road, shaded by lovely trees, stand the old Hall and the new, the old one now a farmhouse, said to have been built with stones from a moated house in the valley which was destroyed in the Civil War.

Idridgehay. In the lovely valley of the Ecclesbourne, this small village is part of a golden land in spring, when hills and vale are thick with flowers. Charming ways bring us to it, but especially pleasing is the long mile from Alton Manor, a fine 19th century house in Elizabethan style, built of stone from its own estate. The small church was built in 1855 with a distinctive tower and spire. South Sitch near by is a well-preserved house, partly timber-framed.

Ilkeston. It has fine wide views from the hillside above the valley of the Erewash which here bounds the county, and its church-crowned hilltop is a landmark from afar. A market and textile-manufacturing town, in a colliery district, it has nothing finer than its church, whose story is one of many changes since its building late in the 12th century.

The church has grown with the town, and is today a spacious place with fine windows and arcades like a graceful avenue. Of the three eastern bays of each arcade, dividing the old part of the nave from the aisles, those on the north are of about 1300; those on the south are of special interest, for, coming from the close of the 12th century when the Norman style was changing to English, they show the two styles in the chevron moulding on the slightly pointed arches. Their capitals are square, resting on the original round pillars, which have been lengthened by about five feet.

The church is truly notable for its window tracery, especially in the six windows in the older part of the church, three in the north and three in the south walls of the aisles. They were rebuilt after the old design in 1855, when an architectural report said that "no church in England possesses any to equal them, and they can never be surpassed in the lightness and elegance of their tracery". The great east window, with a wheel in its tracery, is of the same time.

From about 1280 come the sedilia and the double piscina, of beautiful workmanship. The piscina is divided by a round pillar into two arches. The chancel arch rests on corbels carved with lilies and passion flowers, wheat, and vine. Across the chancel is an unusual 14th century stone screen, its five arches springing from marble pillars.

Since the middle of last century the arcade of three lofty bays between the chancel and the spacious chapel of St Peter has become again the glory of the church; it is all that is left of a 14th century chapel and was long walled up. The capitals of its clustered pillars are carved with foliage cunningly contrived to represent gnome-like faces (more than 40 of them) which escape the casual eye. In a bay of the chancel arcade is the stone tomb of a knight in chain mail, his

140

legs crossed, his feet on a lion, and on his shield the arms of the Cantelupes. He may be Sir Nicholas who died about 1355, or his father, Sir William.

Many adventures the tower has had. A lofty tower and spire came to grief in a storm in 1714; only the tower was rebuilt, and this gave place to another in 1855 on the old foundations. This was moved westward when the nave was doubled in length in 1907. One thing it has kept through all the changes, its 13th century archway. Other old relics are a tiny piscina in one aisle and a founder's recess in the other. An altar table in the chapel is of 1622, and a 15th century chest has two medallions, carved with a rose and a tiny head. Ilkeston has one of the few churches in which the organ is interesting, for it has built up within it one from a London church on which the great Mendelssohn is known to have played.

Ingleby. It comes at the end of a lovely drive, whether we approach from Repton or Ticknall or Swarkestone; the loveliest way is perhaps the lane from Swarkestone in company with the winding River Trent.

It is only a handful of dwellings sheltered by steep wooded cliffs, quietly situated by the river. Even its church has gone, being in such sorry plight in the 17th century that its stone and wood were given away towards the building of Foremark church a mile or so away. Strangely enough, it has another church it is hardly likely to lose. We come to it higher upstream at a bend of the river, where the bank is broken by deep clefts and sharp rocks out of which have been fashioned several rooms with windows and a doorway. It is called Anchor Church, for it is said to have been the cell of a mediaeval hermit or anchorite.

Kedleston. It is an oasis of quiet in a glorious park, with groves and plantations and a stream of many waterfalls all making a lovely setting for the Hall. On the road from Quarndon and Derby we have a splendid view of the great house, with its fine background of trees and the beautiful Adam bridge with its cascades. When the house was built the whole of the village, except for the church, was moved some distance away to allow the land to be brought into the park. The turnpike road was given a bend, and the Cutler Brook found itself filling a lake among the trees.

One of the stately homes of England is Kedleston Hall, built in 1761–70 by James Paine and Robert Adam for the first Lord Scarsdale in the classical style, after the fashion of the time, with massive Greek columns and fine statuary, and beautiful rooms abounding in treasures. Its north front, designed by Paine, is 360 feet long, a central block and two wings connected by corridors. A double flight of steps leads to a rather austere portico with six Corinthian pillars 30 feet high, supporting a pediment with large sculptured figures on the top. The south front, by Robert Adam, is much more elegant; it has graceful curved staircases and the heavy pediment is here replaced by lively classical figures.

The great Marble Hall has a vaulted ceiling supported by 20 huge Corinthian columns and pilasters, each 25 feet high, made of alabaster from the Curzon estates. The floor is of Hopton Wood stone from Derbyshire and the graceful ceiling was plastered by Joseph Rose, who worked extensively with Robert Adam. The whole of the interior, in fact, was designed by Adam and the state rooms are a wonderful example of the style of decoration associated with the Scottish architect. Perhaps the handsomest room is the round Saloon or Rotunda, 62 feet high to the top of the dome. In the rooms are many vases of "blue john" from Castleton. Yet Boswell tells us that Dr Johnson described the house as being more suitable for a town hall, and that he was more delighted in finding his *Dictionary* here than in all its treasures.

The story of Kedleston is that of the Curzons, an illustrious family whose home it has been for nine centuries, of father and son without a break until the 19th century, when a nephew came into this noble heritage. The first of them was Richard de Curzon, whose father came over with the Conqueror: two of his grandsons divided their estates, Richard settling at Croxall, Thomas at Kedleston.

All along the line we find distinction in their train. Robert Curzon was a 12th century cardinal, hated by the clergy because he exposed their vices, by France because his diplomacy was always on the side of England, and by the rich because he championed the poor. He gathered great companies of Crusaders, and was present at a Council in 1215 when part of France was handed over to Simon de Montfort. The Curzons were among the most loyal of Charles I's supporters; they became baronets with John Curzon in 1641, the fifth baronet being made the first Lord Scarsdale in 1761. It was he who built the Hall.

The most distinguished of them was George Nathaniel Curzon, known to all in the generation of the Great War. Born here, he became Viceroy of India and Foreign Secretary, and was leader of the House of Lords until he died as Marquess Curzon of Kedleston in 1925. He gave this church the beautiful chapel in which he is buried, building it in memory of his first wife, Mary Leiter. Her serene figure lies on an exquisite tomb of white marble, her husband beside her, and two angels bending over them with a veiled crown.

The chapel, in the 15th century style, was designed by G. F. Bodley. Its decorative features and furnishings were the work of Lord Curzon himself, who also designed the iron grilles, and the monument is by Sir Bertram Mackennal. The oak roof has fine carving and bosses; the floor is of green marble from the Central Asia Lord Curzon knew so well. In the west wall are two Italian marble panels, reproduced from famous sculptures in St Maria Maggiore in Rome. The altar covers are of old Genoa velvet. Two candlesticks and a lectern are of Spanish silver, and a Portuguese silver-gilt crucifix is nearly 300 years old. There are two silver lamps, and a great pendant made by a German craftsman in the 18th century.

All that is left of the 12th century church is the south doorway with chevrons and beak-heads and a tympanum showing traces of a man on horseback blowing a horn. Most of the church comes from the late 13th century, including the pointed arches supporting the central tower. The upper stage of the tower, with its embattled parapet and four pinnacles, is of the 15th century.

A great piece of sculptured stone about seven feet long, now making a canopy over a recess in the chancel, may have belonged to a founder's tomb; it comes from the 14th century, and has a crocketed finial and pinnacles. In about 1700 the high oak pews with finely carved panels of open work were placed in the chancel. The oak ceiling of the tower and the oak roof of the nave were raised in 1885, the rest of the church and was restored when the memorial chapel was built. There is a Prayer Book of 1687, the gift in 1715 of Lady Sarah Curzon, who gave also a lovely silver chalice 300 years old.

In the church are many memorials of Curzons, from the 13th

143

century to our own time. A 13th century coffin-stone, carved with a cross, was found over 50 years ago covering a skull, perhaps that of Thomas de Curzon. A most unusual memorial lies under the chancel floor, where two wooden lids lift up to show the heads of a 13th century knight and his lady sculptured within quatrefoils, the knight in a hood of mail and the lady in a coif and wimple. Although they appear to be separate, they are part of a great stone four feet wide and ten inches thick, sunk more than a foot below the floor.

Under a canopy in the chancel lies the figure of Sir John Curzon. who attended parliament for Derbyshire when Richard II was king. He is in plate armour, his head on a helmet and his feet on a lion. Another Sir John Curzon, who died about 1450, lies with his wife on an alabaster tomb with two groups of their seven boys and ten girls. The knight is in armour, his head on a helmet and his feet on a dog; his wife has a square headdress with lappets and veil, a mantle tied with a tasselled cord, and a triple chain round her neck. The 15th century brass portraits of their son Richard and his wife are in a stone on the chancel floor, with a group of eight daughters; their four sons are gone.

A 17th century monument shows two angels unveiling the figures of Sir John Curzon and his wife; below them are four sons and three daughters all in curtained niches, the girls with ringlets like their mother, and the boys with long hair. In the south transept is a bust of Sir John Curzon, who sat in Queen Anne's Parliament and lived to see the Stuarts go and the Georges come. In the north transept is a great marble monument with two 18th century figures in flowing robes, Sir Nathaniel Curzon and his wife Sarah; another monument with a group of four figures is to their son Nathaniel, father of the first Lord Scarsdale.

Killamarsh. On the borders of Yorkshire, it is busy with coal and steel, but it has two fine things in its church, crowned by a 15th century tower, and keeping a few windows as old.

One is the doorway inside the porch, adorned with chevron moulding by the Normans; the other is a small window of 15th century glass showing a crowned Madonna with a sceptre, and the Holy Child, whose hands are grasping a lock of her hair. Killamarsh has lost much, but she treasures this precious bit of loveliness.

King's Newton. A market centre in the Middle Ages, it is now a village of rare delight, on one side the winding valley of the Trent with Weston's spire in the trees, on the other, Breedon's church high on the hill.

Its road, with wayside lawns, is packed with charming pictures. On a great square flight of steps is a cross of 1936 marking (perhaps uniquely) the accession of Edward VIII, and taking the place of the old cross whose richly carved head is now in Melbourne church. Near it is the 18th century church house with round steps. The gabled Chantry House looks across to a charming row of brick and timber cottages. A little inn and the delightful house called Four Gables (both built of brick and timber) look over the way to the great house behind a charming garden wall lined with trimmed limes. Rebuilt in 1910, it followed the style of the Elizabethan Hall, long the home of the Hardinge family, which was burned down.

Two men who loved the outdoor world are remembered here. One was William Speechly, who early in the 19th century was gardener to the Duke of Portland. He was a noted agriculturist and wrote a useful country book. The other man was John Joseph Briggs, whose father spent 88 years on a farm close by. John, a patient naturalist and topographer, was content to farm the same fields, happy to watch the life of the country round about. A careful observer of every sort of life, he was the faithful chronicler of the seasons for thirty years and a student of antiquities of Derbyshire. When he died in 1876 he left behind him a valuable collection of notes and records which are still waiting to be given to the world.

With his deep love of the country, Briggs acquired from his school-master an instructed taste for natural history in all its rural aspects; but his bent for recording in diary and journal was innate in him as in Gilbert White of Selborne. Day by day, year after year, Briggs set down in his manuscript volumes all that could interest the sympathetic observer of nature throughout the area over which his activities carried him. He published endless notes and sketches in news-papers and periodicals, of places of interest in the Midland Counties unnoted in their triumphal progresses by the grand monarchs of antiquarian literature. Several volumes of Derbyshire history and antiquities, mainly parochial in character, were issued during his lifetime, but the bulk of his work, fruit of half a century of collecting

145

and writing, including the biographies of nearly 700 worthies of his native county, was left in manuscript.

King Sterndale. We come to it down the high road from Buxton, through Ashwood Dale and Wye Dale, then climb by a steep and winding way, with a magnificent view, to burst suddenly upon the village. All at once the road opens on to a spacious green with the broken cross in the middle and farmsteads gathered round. The neat 19th century church, along the lane farther south, is built of the local stone.

A path opposite the church leads into the rugged gorge of Deep Dale, wild and romantic, where precipitous limestone rocks rise on each side of the rock-strewn path, running down to Wye Dale by Topley Pike. In a great cavern here many Roman relics have been found. Here, too, there lay down and died, in some far-back prehistoric age, a great brown bear who in course of time was found embedded in a cave of Deep Dale.

Kirk Hallam. It looks across to the church-crowned hill of Ilkeston. Its own little church has a low tower and walls 500 years old, its oldest relics being two fine fragments of Norman beakhead moulding (once part of a chancel arch and now built into the porch), and the bowl of a Norman font. There are three old sedilia, and a piscina niche which is rare for having a tiny niche at each side.

In the church are memorials to the Newdigates who have had land here for many generations and had for their ancestor a Saxon chief. A brass tablet has a rhyming epitaph to old Patrick Rice, one of the queer fellows who pop up in our village histories. He wrote his epitaph two years before his death in 1766, and at the same time had his coffin made, keeping it behind his bed and using it regularly until his death as a home for his Sunday clothes.

Kirk Ireton. Its old church with a sturdy tower and a leaning porch and crazy stone walls inside is 700 feet above sea-level. It looks over the village and the Ecclesbourne valley to miles of lovely country. The churchyard is entered through an 18th century pillared gateway.

The Normans began the church tower, which was finished in the 14th century. They built the doorway through which we enter, and

146

a pointed arch was built inside it when the porch was added six centuries ago. They raised the nave arcades with round pillars and boldly carved capitals, but their font came to a tragic end last century when, after being used for a time as a water butt by the chancel, a plumber made a fire under it to melt some lead and split it to pieces. In the fine 14th century chancel we find the great joy of the church, a charming doorway under six feet high, with a slender pillar on each side, and flowers in the moulding of the pointed arch. It is an architectural gem.

It was in the hamlet of Blackwall, nearly a mile south-west, that Anthony Blackwall, the distinguished classical scholar, was born in 1664. He was headmaster of Derby School when only 24, and while he was headmaster of Market Bosworth, Samuel Johnson was perhaps his assistant. One of Derbyshire's great schoolmasters, he had many brilliant pupils, one of whom gave him a living in Surrey. He was over 50 when he went to London for ordination, and as a young chaplain began questioning him on the Greek Testament the examination was cut short by the Bishop of London entering and saying to the examiner: "Mr Blackwall knows more of the Greek Testament than you or I".

Kirk Langley. We find two Langleys, divided by a brook, around the road to Ashbourne from Derby: Kirk Langley, the old village with the church, and Meynell Langley recalling the family who have known it for 800 years. Their Tudor home gave place to what is now Langley Hall, a handsome brick house with lovely views, built last century by A. W. N. Pugin.

The great 19th century stone house where the Meynells live today is seen from the Ashbourne road, its lovely park with drive and fishpond made in the first years of last century; for Meynell Langley's ancient deer park of over 500 acres was destroyed in the Civil War, when it belonged to the Royalist Duke of Newcastle, the timber being cut for charcoal.

Very pleasant is Kirk Langley with its old brick houses, a beautiful church, and a fine 17th century rectory which has a lovely garden. standing where there has been a rectory since the time of Henry VIII. Nearby is an old tithe barn with a 19th century archway.

The way to the church is through a lychgate and under a fine yew like a bower. Made new over 600 years ago, it is spacious and full of light. There are three beautiful stone seats with trefoiled heads and clustered shafts in the chancel, three piscinae, mediaeval tiles in the Twyford chapel, and an old font which has come into its own after being for a time in a farmyard and then used as a poor-box. The bowl has a lead lining which overlaps the rim and forms a border with a finely embossed design. There is colourful 19th century glass in the east window, and a fine modern chancel screen. Screens of the late 19th century enclose two chapels, one with a fine cornice and traceried panels having some of the 15th century screen worked into it.

The chief treasure of the church is a screen under the tower, where the light is all too dim to do justice to what is said to be the oldest timber screen in Derbyshire. It is what is left of the 14th century chancel screen, unusual in design, with a band of trefoils above an arcade of trefoiled openings, while below is a band of quatrefoils with flowers.

The church has many memorials to the Meynells of Meynell Langley. On an altar tomb in the south aisle are the engraved figures of Henry and Dorothea Pole, he in 16th century armour with his head on a helmet, she in a French cap and a fur-lined cloak. A stone on the north wall has the portrait of Alice Beresford of 1511 in pointed headdress and a close-fitting gown with a long girdle. One of Kirk Langley's much-loved rectors was Henry James Feilden, who died in 1885 after being here 64 years. He used to put on a black gown and a pair of black gloves before he entered the pulpit.

Kniveton. Tucked away in a land of winding lanes and little hills and streams are its grey stone houses, looking up to a small church which has seen Norman days. It stands in a churchyard with a trickling stream and a gate shaded by a great sycamore, an aisleless building with a low tower and a short spire. The Norman remains are in the arch of the porch and the doorway within, which has a hood adorned with a stone head in the middle and crude carvings at the ends. A round stone with a cross, let into the wall of the nave, is thought to be Norman too.

The font is of the 13th century, the bowl carved with an effective

148

border round the top, and resting on clustered pillars. The chancel arch is of the 14th century. Fragments of mediaeval glass in the chancel glow with the arms of the old family of Kniveton; it was Lady Frances who gave the altar its lovely flagon and chalice in 1572. Sir Andrew Kniveton became so impoverished through his loyalty to Charles I that he had to sell most of the family estates.

Ladybower Reservoir. Now the centre of Derbyshire's own Lake District, it has changed the landscape and character of the eastern side of the High Peak. Here the valleys meet below the grandeur of rugged heights, long gritstone edges, and rolling moors, Win Hill and Crook Hill, Derwent Edge and Bamford Edge, following the compass round.

Down their valleys come the Derwent and the Ashop, one from the moorlands of the Yorkshire border, the other from the vast solitudes of Kinder Scout, the rivers now mingling in the reservoir. This was constructed between 1935 and 1945 to supply the needs of Sheffield, Nottingham, Derby, and Leicester. Its waters have drowned the old villages of Ashopton and Derwent, whose church and charming old hall are now only a memory.

The 17th century packhorse bridge at Derwent was taken down stone by stone and has been re-erected higher up at Slippery Stones, above the Derwent and Howden Reservoirs, two earlier man-made lakes, built in 1912–16 and now enclosed by beautiful pine plantations.

The Ladybower is at the end of one of the finest stretches of road in Derbyshire, the modern highway from Glossop which climbs to 1680 feet on the Snake Pass and then winds down into the charming Woodlands Valley. Could any road stir us more than this, glorying in the lonely windswept moorlands of Kinder Scout on the one hand and Bleaklow on the other? On the north of the valley opens Alport Dale, penetrating deep into the peaty recesses of Bleaklow, and overlooked by the impressive crags of Alport Castles. At the solitary Castles Farm, in the dale, an unusual Methodist "Love Feast" takes place, as it has done for centuries, on the first Sunday in July.

Who can forget the splendid panorama from the peak of Win Hill, rising above the reservoir, with the green dales of the Ashop and the Noe, the conical Lose Hill rising to over 1560 feet, the deep Hope Valley with the villages of Hope and Castleton, the isolated Shatton Edge and Abney Moor to the south, and beyond the Derwent Valley the long rampart of Stanage Edge, bounding the county from Yorkshire?

Little Eaton. This village of old stone cottages is sheltered by a fine line of hills, with a little brook running by the busy road to Derby. We get a fine aerial view of its housetops as we drop down from Breadsall Priory, with the churchyard climbing as high as the church tower and making a fine look-out over the village playing-fields and the Derwent Valley. There is little in the church for the pilgrim, but an odd thing is that before it was rebuilt in 1791 it had been a blacksmith's shop. It was greatly restored in the Norman style of architecture in 1837.

In the churchyard are a War Memorial lychgate and a cross with the name of Theodore Percival Cameron Wilson, the brilliant son of the vicar here when the Great War started. He loathed war as the hideous thing it is, and he loved this countryside and the vicarage garden of which he wrote on leaving his home:

"Never again a thrush in the lilac at six o'clock, a bee droning up the sunlit silences, a poplar pointing against the stars, the village voices and cries, the faint scent of wet lavender in the night."

He went in the first fortnight of the war, enlisting in the Guards. One spring day in the last year of the war, hearing that one of his men had been left wounded on the barbed wire, he crawled out in the face of machine-gun fire and brought him in on his back. The next day, in a moment when he was joking and laughing, a bullet struck him and he fell. The enemy was 200 yards behind. No trace of his burial has been found.

Among his papers they came upon letters which showed what those who knew him thought of his chances in life; and indeed he had qualified himself for a place among the poets. He had the great delight of seeing himself printed by J. A. Spender in the old green pages of the *Westminster Gazette*, the best evening paper ever offered to an intellectual Englishman. He wrote for *Punch*, and he wrote a novel which his publisher thought one of the best-reviewed books of the year.

Little Longstone. Sheltering under Longstone Edge, this quiet hamlet is a joy to find, with remains of the old stocks and charming houses on its mile-long road. One of the houses is the twin-gabled manor behind fine hedges of holly and yew, built perhaps in the 17th century by one of the Longsdons who have lived at Little Longstone all the time, but not always at the manor house.

At the end of the road, at Monsal Head (or Headstone Head), is a surprise in store for all who come, for with startling suddenness there opens out one of the finest natural sights in Derbyshire, a glory of rock and wood and water. It is a view of the Wye deep down in the valley, flowing at the foot of fine hills as it comes from Millers Dale, and making a glorious curve round the foot of Putwell Hill on its journey through the lovely Monsal Dale. It is an enchanting river scene, where the Wye forgets its impetuous ways and flows in broad and gentle fashion, now through bright green meadow, now mirroring the lofty hills.

It is true that we see the railway bridge on its five high arches, but nature can well hold her own. It was this bridge that vexed the spirit of John Ruskin, bringing from him these bitter words about the valley:

"You might have seen the gods there morning and evening, walking in fair procession on the lawns, and to and fro among the pinnacles of its crags, but the valley is gone and the gods with it, and now every fool in Buxton can be in Bakewell in half an hour, and every fool in Bakewell at Buxton."

But this is no longer true, as the stations at Monsal Dale and Millers Dale have been closed, together with the branch line to Buxton.

Littleover. It is now a favourite residential district, a dormitory for Derby, but its church of many gables and its fine vicarage share a glorious distant prospect over the Trent Valley.

The church has a Norman doorway and a huge Norman font, its oldest possessions. There are 14th century windows in the chancel and the north arcade is of this time, but the north aisle was rebuilt in 1856 and the south aisle in 1908, and in 1961 the nave and aisles were extended to double their length.

On the chancel wall is a coloured monument to Sir Richard

Harpur and his wife. They are kneeling at a desk, Sir Richard in a long gown with hanging sleeves, his wife in a hood and ruff, three sons and three daughters below with an infant in swaddling clothes. It is a typical 17th century group. The Old Hall here, built by Sir Richard's father, a judge of Elizabeth I's day who lived at Swarkestone, has been rebuilt and extended as a research centre for Rolls-Royce.

Litton. Nearly 1000 feet above sea-level in a land of stone-walled fields, it has old limestone dwellings on a road graced by little greens. On one of these are the square steps of an ancient cross with a modern pillar, and at one end of the village is a small church with just a nave and chancel. The village has little else, but its name has travelled far, for it was the home of the ancestors of the Earl of Lytton.

A farmhouse stands on the site of their old home, which was in Charles I's day the birthplace of William Bagshawe, the Apostle of the Peak, the great Nonconformist who is buried at Chapel-en-le-Frith.

The rocky ravine of Litton Dale leads down from the village to Tideswell Dale, which ends at Millers Dale, a lovely stretch of the Wye embosomed in sheer cliffs and hanging woods. Here is Litton Mill, gladdened today with flowered cottages and gardens, but with memories of the bad old days of more than a century ago when terrible cruelty to the pauper apprentices sent many of them to an early grave in Tideswell churchyard. Cressbrook Mill, farther down the river, belonged to William Newton, the Minstrel of the Peak, and conditions there under this carpenter-poet were much better.

Long Eaton. At the lower end of the rich mineral valley of the Erewash, a quiet old-fashioned village almost within living memory, it has outstripped its neighbours and become an active town, busy with many industries from dainty lace to heavy railway waggons.

Once it belonged to Sawley; today it has made Sawley part of itself. Churches, chapels, and fine schools have come into being in this place which has set its playing-fields in gardens and its library in lawns. On the Derby road is Trent College, a public school founded in 1866, while a mile or so away the Trent flows on through peaceful meadows.

At the heart of the town, just off the marketplace, is a link with the

Melbourne Hall.

Melbourne Church.

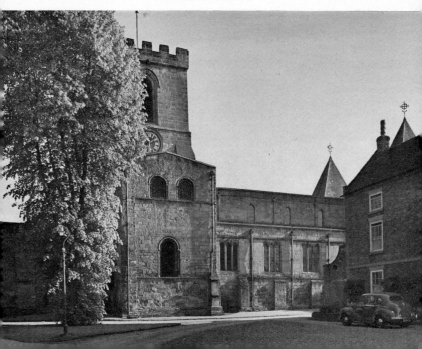

(*above left*)
The monument in Morley Church to Jonathan Sacheverell and his wife.

(*above*)
The pre-Conquest tympanum in the west wall of Ault Hucknall Church.

The vestry doorway at South Normanton Church.

past in a church the Normans and the Saxons knew. In the early days a chapel of Sawley, it was refashioned 600 years ago, when the tower and its spire were built. Now the old nave and chancel have become the aisle and chapel of a larger building designed by G. E. Street in 1868; and so wisely were the additions made that the ancient stones have lost little of their simplicity and strength. There is a splendid Norman doorway in the porch, with beak-head mouldings and an unusual chain pattern. A fine round arch between the old nave and chancel, and a small deeply splayed south window with long-and-short work, are said to be as the Saxons left them. The old chancel has a 14th century window with flowing tracery, and in the old nave is one a century younger.

One of Long Eaton's playgrounds is Trent Lock, where three counties meet. Here the Soar comes into the Trent, which has only lately gathered the Derwent to itself below Wilne, and the waters leap the weir under Red Hill, a headland looking into Derbyshire and Leicestershire from Nottinghamshire. A gay scene it is in summer with its pleasure boats, and the white wings of the yachts racing by.

Longford. We come to it across the spacious park, seeing the graceful façade of the Hall, which is partly Tudor, but was much altered about 1700 and damaged by fire in 1942, and coming to the splendid 15th century tower of a beautiful church set in magnificent limes, with a great yew and a great beech.

All that is left of the Norman church are three bays of the north arcade with round arches and pillars, three pillars of the south arcade, and the bowl of the font which fell from grace as a cattle trough but was restored in 1897 and returned to the church. The pointed arch of the north arcade and those of the south are of the early 14th century, and it was at this time that the Norman capitals of the south arcade were given their present mouldings. There are three old oak poppyheads and graceful sedilia arches, and the nave roof has five old bosses and six heads on each side. A great treasure of the church is the oak pulpit, on which a modern craftsman has set in canopied niches little figures carved with exquisite detail: St Aidan is with a book, St Chad with a model of Lichfield Cathedral, and Bede writing.

It is an attractive group of monuments which draws the traveller here. Under a recess in the chancel is a priest sculptured in his robes, perhaps John de Cressy, rector 600 years ago. There are alabaster monuments of three generations of the Longfords, as well as one to the last of the family, every one a knight and every one a Nicholas. The oldest is Sir Nicholas Longford who died in 1357, lying in armour and helmet, his feet on a dog. His son, Sir Nicholas, who died in 1403, is wearing armour and helmet and has a fine belt of square medallions with a beautiful clasp. His sword is gone, but his dagger remains; his feet are on a lion, and his head is on a remarkable crest like plumes of feathers. His son is in armour with his feet on a lion; he has a richly ornamented helmet, and on his smiling lips is an odd little moustache. The last of the Longfords, dying a few years before Shakespeare, lies with his third wife, he in armour and she in a high-waisted gown of many folds.

With the passing of the Longfords the estates went to the Cokes who were here about 300 years. There are memorials to Sir Edward of 1727 and his son Edward of 1733. Under an elaborate canopy is a fine white marble bust of Thomas William Coke, who died here in 1842 but is buried in Tittleshall church in Norfolk. The bust is by Chantrey's pupil John Francis. Known as the handsome Englishman, Coke was Father of the House of Commons and famous as an agriculturist. He was made first Earl of Leicester at the beginning of the Victorian era, and married a Keppel, whose marble monument is near his in the chancel.

Lullington. It lies in the extreme south of Derbyshire, near the Staffordshire border. A fine lime shades its tiny green in summer; a glorious daffodil carpet spreads in the grounds of its great house in spring. Its 19th century church is at the corner of a tree-shaded road. Yews and hollies make the churchyard beautiful, and the pleasant gardens of the vicarage open out beyond the church tower.

The 14th century tower is all that is left of the mediaeval church. The spire, rebuilt in 1766, is most unusual, for its eight sides rise from the edge of the tower in an almost upright line for several feet, forming a kind of lantern. Among the treasures of the church are an ancient unused font with crude carving, said to be more than 600 years old; a reading desk of wood finely carved by an Italian craftsman; and two unusual windows in the chancel. One of these, of 1882, shows Christ in white and gold and a woman in a blue dress, a child in her arms; the other is the east window, painted in Brussels by Jean Baptiste Capronnier in 1862 and showing scenes from Bible stories.

Mackworth. An arresting picture is the church as we see it from the highroad in a green dip of the countryside, beautiful in its trim churchyard. A huge elm that once topped the tower crashed down in 1959, damaging part of the fabric of the church.

The church comes mainly from a rebuilding of the 14th century. About 50 years older than the rest is the beautiful chancel, with buttresses crowned with crocketed pinnacles, and a priest's doorway with ballflowers. The tower has a spire with dormer windows, and the cross-bow loopholes, rare in a church, suggest that the tower was for defence. The little room over the porch has two peepholes for vanished altars, once at the ends of the aisles.

The modern interior of the chancel is a blaze of colour, with an almost overwhelming display of alabaster. It has a great alabaster reredos inlaid with coloured marbles, a richly carved canopy of 1886 over a door, two angels with candles like guardians of the sanctuary, altar rails of white alabaster and blue stone, and a lectern magnificently carved in 1903 from an alabaster block, its column encircled by an entwining vine, with leaves and clustering fruit forming the table.

The chancel has three stone seats and a piscina of the 14th century, all with trefoiled arches, and in the north aisle are two 15th century canopied niches for saints and a canopied recess, restored in 1851. A fine chest of 1640 has handsome clamps and hinges. Some old carved panels in the back of a seat in the porch are perhaps 15th century bench-ends.

Under a recess is an alabaster stone with the sculptured head and finger-tips of a priest sunk in a quatrefoil; he is thought to be Thomas Touchet, a rector older than Agincourt. On an alabaster tomb lies Edward Mundy, grandson of a 16th century Lord Mayor of London. He wears a long gown with hanging sleeves and ruffs, and in front of his tomb are tiny figures of six sons and two daughters. The window above this tomb shows the arms of the Mundys for 600 years.

To the west of the church, and reached by a switchback lane, is a great stone gatehouse of about 1500, all that is left of a proud castle which was long the home of the Mackworths and is said to have been destroyed in the Civil War. The old home of the Mundys, the 18th century Markeaton Hall has been demolished, but the fine park belongs to the people of Derby. On a hill above the park are the distinctive buildings of the Derby and District Colleges of Art and Technology, designed by the Building Design Partnership. First opened in 1959 and extended in 1966, they are the finest example of modern architecture in the county.

Mapleton. In the quiet meadows of the Dove, it has houses of mellowed brick and a tiny church with a curious octagonal dome. An 18th century structure, it has only a few remains of the older church in some fragments of glass, and perhaps the five great beams supporting the roof. The oak chair is of the 18th century.

Five great beeches overhang the road to the one-arch bridge across the Dove, where we may stand with one foot in Derbyshire and one in Staffordshire, seeing two miles away the peak of Thorpe Cloud and the great mass of Bunster, the two splendid guardians of Dovedale. Beyond the river are a fine church at the doorstep of Okeover Hall and the deer park which we may cross to Mayfield, where Tom Moore wrote his *Lalla Rookh*. One of a great Derbyshire family, Thomas Cokayne, born at Mapleton in 1587, was the author of an English and Greek dictionary for New Testament students.

Marston Montgomery. Its lanes in springtime are glorious with damson blossom, and a charming picture of the village is made by the church, looking all roof from the road, the lychgate, the old pump shelter, and a beautiful old black-and-white house with a massive stone chimney.

They were building the church about 900 years ago. The Montgomerys had owned these lands 400 years when the last of them died some 400 years ago, but the stones in this tiny chancel arch and a small window in the west wall were here before then. They are among the oldest masonry in Derbyshire, for the arch is of the early Norman period. It saw the later Normans come and build the doorway for the people and the doorway for the priest, and it saw them bring the round font. It has stood unchanged while a stripling in the churchyard has become a venerable yew. The church has two 13th century windows in the chancel and a 14th century nave arcade, but the north aisle is of the 19th century, as is the distinctive belfry over the west gable.

Marston-on-Dove. We do not wonder that the Dove seems loth to leave its charming seclusion, encircling its meadows with winding streams. Set in a churchyard like a lawn, looking across to the big house which has something left of the manor house of long ago, is the old church with a tower and spire nearly 600 years old, proud of one of the oldest singers in Derbyshire, for one of its bells, with a prayer in beautiful Lombardic capitals, has been ringing as long as the tower has stood.

The chancel, with six lancets and the priest's doorway, comes from the 13th century (though the east window is modern), and the nave arcades are perhaps a century younger. The south aisle, with unusual tracery in its windows, is of the 14th century, and in the 15th century windows of the other aisle is a little old glass. But the oldest possessions here are the top of a tiny Norman window built into an outside wall, and the massive Norman font looking like part of a round pillar. Something of its simplicity and strength has been put, by a local craftsman, in the modern oak choir stalls, the pulpit, the prayer desk, the rails, and the solid screen across the east end of the chancel.

The most remarkable thing in the church is the list of vicars, with a continuous run of four for nearly two centuries. George Gretton was here for 65 years, from 1685 to 1750; John Edwards was here for 54 years up to the eve of Trafalgar; Frederick Anson was here 36 years, and his successor was here another 36. The first two of these vicars preached for 119 years in this place. George Gretton saw the Stuarts go and the Georges come; John Edwards saw Napoleon come and his successor saw him go. It is an astonishing record.

Matlock. Stretching along the depths of a narrow limestone ravine and spilling over at the north end into a broader vale, its glory has often been sung. One called it the most dazzlingly beautiful spot in Britain, another a romantic fragment of Switzerland set in the heart of England. Lord Byron and John Ruskin praised it.

But this place of ancient story which the Romans worked for lead has grown to a string of Matlocks stretching for more than two miles, and houses now fill the valley and climb the slopes. They reach almost from Cromford to where the valley broadens out in Darley Dale: Matlock Bath, Matlock Dale, Matlock Bridge, Matlock Town, and Matlock Bank.

The story of Matlock Bath comes from 1698 when the first bath was built over a warm spring, with a few small rooms for visitors. Today it is an over-popular week-end resort, abounding in hotels and villas reached by startling ascents, with riverside gardens and Lovers' Walks, illuminated during the "Venetian Nights" in late-summer; yet there are delightful paths through woods and over the hills, for it is here and along the dale that the most beautiful scenery is found. Masson's stupendous bulk, rising 1100 feet above sea-level, shuts in one side of the dale, its wooded Heights of Abraham crowned by a look-out tower commanding a charming view. On the other side of the river the magnificent crag of High Tor rears its naked head straight from the valley floor, a sheer height of more than 350 feet from head to foot. Something to remember is the magnificent panorama from the broad summit of Masson where we see the lovely valley up and down edged by woods and moors, and great hills which only end in the dim outline of Kinder Scout. In the side of the hill are the Rutland Cavern and the Great Masson Cavern, consisting partly of abandoned lead mines said to have been first explored by the Romans.

The thermal springs, with their constant temperature of 68° Fahrenheit (20° Centigrade), for which Matlock Bath was once noted, now feed a fishpond beside the Pavilion and the swimming pools at the New Bath Hotel. The old Petrifying Well survives, beside a new promenade which runs alongside the river. The wayside church of 1841, beside the Cromford road, has an elegant crocketed spire, but was enlarged in 1873.

Matlock Bridge, where five ways meet, is busy with shops and pleasant with riverside walks and gardens. The fine 16th century four-arch bridge was widened on one side in 1903. Matlock Bank, on the steep hill-slope above the bridge, came into being with John Smedley, a hosiery manufacturer who, having recovered from a breakdown through a visit to a spa, sought to practise the water cure on others. He made his first experiments on his workpeople at Lea Mills, and the beginning of the great Smedley Hydro was a small house on a site he bought in 1852. Out of the fortune he made with air and water John Smedley built Riber Castle, where he might catch the breezes from 850 feet above sea-level, and he died here in 1874. The vast hydropathic establishment was converted in 1958 into the offices for the county council, who were transferred from Derby.

All Saints' Church, high on the hillside, was built in 1884 and stands in a garden of lawn and flowers and trees, with a fine view to Masson. It is lighted by lancets, three in the east wall of the chancel having stained glass designed by William Morris and Burne-Jones with figures of saints and the four Evangelists.

Matlock Town, high above the river, is the oldest of the Matlocks and the original village. Old houses line the steep and narrow road through it. On a knoll close by is a church with an old story, though much rebuilt; above the church by a green is a 17th century house which has been an inn. A lychgate opens to the fine churchyard, from whose upper end we look up the Derwent Valley. The embattled tower with four handsome pinnacles is of the 15th century, almost the only old work left in the fabric now. The chancel was rebuilt in 1859 and the nave in 1871. Some older relics are outside the church, including carved and moulded stones, and a Norman coffin-stone with a cross and sword. The strangely carved font, also Norman, is now back in the church after being long in the rectory garden. One of the eight bells is older than the Reformation.

The most engaging possession of the church is hanging just inside the door, a set of six paper garlands. They have a pathetic appeal, for they were carried in the funeral processions of betrothed maidens who died too soon to marry. Such garlands are to be found also at Ashford-in-the-Water and Trusley.

The alabaster stone of a tomb in the south aisle has engraved portraits of Anthony Woolley and his wife, with four boys and two girls below them. Anthony has a fur-lined gown, his wife's is tied with bows down the front, and she wears a close-fitting cap of Tudor days. There is another Woolley stone on the west wall near the tomb, telling of the burial here of Adam Woolley and his Grace. They were man and wife for 76 years, Adam dying in 1657 in his hundredth year and Grace in 1669 at 110.

This is surely a record. Adam was born in the year Elizabeth I was crowned and died a year before Cromwell's work was done. His wife lived to talk of the Fire of London, and together they remembered the coming of the Armada, the passing of Shakespeare, and the execution of Charles I. This memorial was put here in 1824 by their grandson four times removed, who has an inscription in the church. He was Adam Woolley, who died in 1827, and he collected much material for a History of Derbyshire, bequeathing it to the British Museum, where it lies. The home of the Woolleys was the Old Hall at Riber, which belonged to the family for seven generations.

Melbourne. We come upon its old haunts with delightful suddenness, a green corner of England which gave its name to Queen Victoria's first Prime Minister and through him to one of the chief cities of the Commonwealth. All about us here are limes, elms, and sycamores. There are two little greens, one with a shapely tree. Here is the gabled stone vicarage a century old, and the fine tithe barn 700 years old in its lower part of stone, with a doorway 500 years young and some fine old beams.

Melbourne Hall had its Tudor walls refashioned nearly 250 years ago, when Francis Smith of Warwick added graceful new rooms, and his son, William, completed the work in 1744 with an elegant new front. The lovely gardens, which have been growing more beautiful since the 18th century, are a place of endless fascination with terraces and lawns, noble limes, cedars, and pines, fountains and lead statues, and a summerhouse like a bird-cage of hammered iron by Robert Bakewell, the great Derby ironsmith. There are fine yew hedges and a yew tunnel 100 yards long like an aisle of weird shapes as we walk along it. A stone urn with cupids, garlands, and wreaths is a memorial to Thomas Coke, the maker of these gardens, who was born at the Hall and is buried in the chancel of the church. He was Chamberlain to Queen Anne, who gave him the lovely monument near the urn, made by John van Nost, its carvings representing the seasons. On the stone pedestal is a lead vase supported by four monkeys and crowned by a bowl of fruit and flowers; there are four heads round the edge of the vase, which has 24 figures of children at play.

It was while staying at the Hall in 1650 that Richard Baxter wrote some of his *The Saint's Everlasting Rest*. In the 18th century the house passed to the Lambs, who took the name of Melbourne for their peerage; it was the Prime Minister, Lord Melbourne, who gave his name to the Australian city. Later it passed to the Kerrs, one of whom, Lord Walter Kerr, an admiral who died at the Hall in 1927, had among his many honours the Silver Medal of the Royal Humane Society for jumping overboard and rescuing a man who had fallen into the Tagus.

Melbourne Pool, across the road from the Hall, is delightful with its island trees. The pool is said to fill a quarry which gave the stone for Melbourne Castle, the almost vanished stronghold to which the Duke of Bourbon was brought a captive from Agincourt. Here he remained for 19 years until released for a ransom of £18,000 and when set free at last, he left Melbourne for London on his way to France, but died before he could set sail. Sir Ralph Shirley, one of the commanders at Agincourt, was a Governor of the Castle, and in the church of Staunton Harold, three miles from here, are the tattered banners he captured on that glorious day, with flags taken by his relatives at Crécy and Shrewsbury. By the time of Charles I, the castle had fallen into ruin, and now its only remains are a fragment of a massive wall bounding a farmyard by the square near the church.

The wonderful church of Melbourne, one of the finest and most complete Norman churches in England, stands open to the road, built in the shape of a cross with a central tower, and two small and unfinished western towers with a fine doorway between them open-ing into a portico with a vaulted roof. This unique kind of entrance in a Norman village church opens at each side into a smaller portico with vaulted roof, these opening in turn to the aisles.

It is a majestic place inside, with a great forest of round arches built by the Normans for bays and windows. The glory here is the Norman nave with five bays each side, their fine horse-shoe arches adorned with chevrons and resting on massive pillars 15 feet high and over 12 feet round. Above the arches are the triforium arcades, opening on to the clerestory windows, the two sides of different dates. The north side is Norman, each bay having three arches divided by slender pillars and opening to a single Norman window in the outer wall. The south side has one Norman bay; the rest are of the 13th century.

Three tiers of Norman arcading adorn the walls of the central tower, the lowest open and the rest blind. The capitals of two of the massive pillars supporting the tower are intricately carved with grotesques, heads, birds, and animals among the foliage. The belfry stage was raised in the 17th century.

The chancel, divided from the nave by a mediaeval screen made new, is dim in contrast with the full light of the nave. Both chancel and transepts had apsidal east ends until the 15th century. Three chancel windows are a tribute to Colonel Gooch, who lived for a time at the Hall, and went out to Waterloo, where with two soldiers he closed and held the door of a farmhouse against a strong column of the French army. In the chancel is a tribute to John Middleton, vicar for 47 years, who was followed by Joseph Deans for 57 years of last century. The fine font is Norman or of the 13th century, and in the south transept is a projecting Norman piscina. On a bracket in the other transept is the head of a mediaeval village cross from near-by King's Newton.

In the south transept, now used as a vestry, is a 13th century coffin-stone, and in a 15th century recess lies a battered 13th century knight, with a jewelled bandeau round his head. Here too, against a wall, is an odd little company of stone portraits of the famous Hardinge family (originally spelt Hardie) of King's Newton, three alabaster stones with four queer figures. One shows Henrie Hardie and his wife Elizabeth of Shakespeare's day, Henrie in armour, with hair which looks as if he had had a fright; his wife with a great ruff all round her face, and hair like a fountain playing. On the other stones are extraordinary figures of Sir Robert Hardinge and his wife, who died towards the end of the 17th century. He has a gown with many buttons and a mop of hair flowing to his shoulders; she has a gown with pointed bodice, a necklace, and her hair in ringlets.

In the busier part of the large village is a group of 14 cottages and a chapel adjoining them, built and endowed by Thomas Cook whose name is known to every tourist. It is odd that he should have been born in a cottage, still here, and that in the great house was born a man who carried the name of Melbourne across the world.

The answer to the problem of how our ancestors travelled in

roadless mediaeval days is that as a rule "they didn't". When Thomas Cook was born a poor boy here in 1808, people were still parochial and inert, and seldom left their villages; they were still mediaeval in habit. Cook, alternately gardener, wood-turner, and local missionary, travelled on foot nearly the whole of the 2700 miles of his first evangelical tour. Forty years later he compassed the earth in 222 days. His real mission as a pioneer of popular travel began in 1841 when he induced the Midland Railway to take 570 passengers, a temperance party, from Leicester to Loughborough and back for a shilling each.

Setting up in Leicester as a tourist agent, the first of his calling, Cook, aided by his son John, quickly developed his business. The son proved the chief organiser; at 17 he conveyed 165,000 people to London for the Great Exhibition, engaging a brass band to play in the streets and persuading into his trains persons who flocked out to listen. Never since the Crusades had the world seen such hosts of travellers as Cook and Son personally conducted throughout the Old World and the New. They planned the tours, booked trains, ships, and hotels, established their own banking system, and prepared every detail.

It was the Cooks who carried provisions to starving Paris after the armistice that ended the Franco-Prussian war; they who took General Gordon and his forces up to Korosko; they who transported the relief expedition. This was an enterprise of great magnitude for a private firm, involving the carriage from rail-head to Wady Halfa of 18,000 troops, 130,000 tons of stores, 70,000 tons of coal, and 800 whaling boats. The work was executed punctually and without a hitch.

Thomas Cook died in 1892, but the work continued unchecked, with headquarters in London and branches throughout the civilised world, making travellers of multitudes in many lands who had been inveterate stay-at-homes. The Cooks translated into terms of modern method and mechanism the fable of the magic carpet, and helped the world to bridge the gulfs separating nation from nation.

Middleton-by-Wirksworth. It is an old lead-mining village and now has large limestone quarries in the neighbourhood. It stands on the road that climbs steeply from Wirksworth, then descends just as steeply to the Via Gellia, with a marvellous view as it winds down to the dale. Deep below the cornice wall, the sea of green unfolds as we draw near into the loveliness of the dale, which is shut in by wooded cliffs. Luxuriant with all the trees that grow, with violet and primrose, forget-me-not and lily of the valley, it has nothing lovelier than the view we have of it on the road from Middleton.

Middleton-by-Youlgreave. Enshrined in trees above the lovely Bradford Dale is this charming corner of Derbyshire with something left to remind us of a sad story of the Fulwoods to whom it once belonged.

In a field of Castle Farm are remains of their 17th century home, now but a few stones and fragments of a wall about a mound known as Fulwood's Castle. The farmhouse was built out of the ruins. Here lived Christopher Fulwood, a Derbyshire justice loved for his mercy in the time of Charles I. From here he went to muster more than 1000 men of Tideswell for the service of his king, and it was here that he was surprised by a party of Parliamentarians when fleeing for shelter to a rock across the brook, where he was found and shot. Fulwood's Rock is at the head of Bradford Dale within a few hundred yards of his home, a huge boulder with enough room for a man to hide between it and the cliff of which it was a part.

Middleton is in one of the prehistoric regions of the county, and half-way between the village and Youlgreave is Lomberdale Hall, the home of William and Thomas Bateman, father and son, who gathered together a fine collection of antiquities. The result of their findings during years of excavations in the many barrows of the districts can be seen in Weston Park Museum at Sheffield. Thomas Bateman, dying young last century, is buried in a field by the roadside, two yews shading his tomb.

Two miles away on Middleton Common is the great stone circle of Arbor Low, impressive in its isolation on the brow of a hill, and looking out over a wide stretch of the green limestone uplands from 1230 feet above sea-level. This sacred site of the New Stone Age or the early Bronze Age has over 40 stones mostly lying round the edge of a plateau. Thought to have been once upright, they now all (except one) lie flat on the ground. Between the plateau and the high earthwork, which is 250 feet in diameter, and has an entrance at each end, is a wide ditch. In a large burial mound near one entrance were found two urns, the shoulder blade and antlers of a deer, and many rat bones.

About 300 yards away from the circle and once connected with it by a rampart of earth, is a great burial mound known as Gib Hill; and in another mound at Benty Grange, a mile away, has been found a leather cup with a silver edge, enamels, and a helmet.

Milford. The hamlet which grew into a flourishing village with the coming of the Strutts shelters under steep wooded cliffs by the Derwent. It was Jedediah Strutt who built the cotton mills about 1780 (one has recently been demolished) and the house where he spent the last years of his life.

The Strutts made the bridge over the river; they gave the village its school and the site for the church of 1848. The east window of this is to George Herbert Strutt who was born here and who built the grammar school at Belper.

Millers Dale. This tiny village shares the name of the dale in which it lies, one of the loveliest in Derbyshire, a reach of the River Wye under whose magnificent limestone cliffs are the glory of wild flowers in spring and surpassing scenes in winter snow.

There are old houses and the textile mills from which the dale took its former name of Millhouse Dale, and opposite the weir is a small church of 1880, built by Samuel Andrew, vicar of the mother church at Tideswell, where we see his finely engraved brass.

The rocky gorge of Monk's Dale climbs from the middle of the village. On the hillside are foundations of a chapel of the monks, and a fine fragment of a 14th century stone screen found here is now in Tideswell church.

Just upstream is the luxuriant Chee Dale with its magnificent Tor rising 300 feet, rent with fissures and crowned with a fringe of trees. With the Wye rushing round its foot in a grand horseshoe curve, it is one of the finest scenes on a river of great beauty.

Monyash. One of the gateways to Lathkill Dale, this quiet place on the limestone uplands, with memories of busy days as a market-town and a lead-mining centre of the Peak, has old stone houses and a 17th century inn gathered round a small green with the shaft of the old cross.

By way of the gaunt ravine of Ricklow Dale, with its old marble quarries, we come to the delightful Lathkill Dale, a deep secluded valley of wooded slopes, steep cliff, and grassy paths, whose crystal stream was said by Izaak Walton's angling friend Charles Cotton to be the purest he had ever seen and to have the best trout in England.

Not far from the head of the Dale is an old farmhouse known as One Ash Grange, said to be on the site of a place of confinement for unruly monks. John Gratton, the famous Quaker who lived in Monyash for many years, used to visit the house in the time of the Bowmans, who were among the last of the Quakers here. A rock at the head of the Dale, near where the Lathkill comes to life, has been known as Parson's Tor since Robert Lomas fell over it to his death in 1776. He was vicar of Monyash, and is said to have planted the fine limes in the churchyard, where there is also a shapely yew.

The stone-roofed church has seen many changes since being built about 1200. The nave arcades are of the 14th century; the chancel, the spire, and much more have been made new in the present century. Three fine stone seats and a piscina and the chancel arch are as old as the church, and some of the tower is of the 13th century. It has something rare, a buttress pierced by a lancet window. The bowl of the mediaeval font rests on columns with capitals seeming to be parts of a lion and a tiger.

A great treasure of the church is a fine old chest 10 feet long, with bands of wrought iron every few inches. Worm-eaten and white with age, it was used for the altar plate and the priest's robes perhaps more than 700 years ago. There is a memorial to Thomas Cheney of 1723, a descendant of John Cheney who was struck down by Richard III at Bosworth Field and left for dead. His helmet being broken, he covered his head with the scalp of a bullock which lay near, and from this incident came their crest of a bull's scalp. He lived to see the Tudor Dynasty and to be given a peerage and the Garter by Henry VII.

Morley. We should come to it when time goes slowly, for it is rich and old, with a story going back to Norman days and a treasure house of lovely things. The church, beautiful without and within, has grown from one of early Norman times, for it is said that when the church was enlarged in the mid 12th and early 13th centuries these fine arcades were pierced through already existing walls. The tower, with a turret and a lofty spire, comes from a great rebuilding extending from 1380 to 1453, when the walls over the arches were raised for the clerestory, the aisles were rebuilt and lengthened into chapels and the chancel was made new.

The churchyard is lovely with old trees and with flowers in summer. The charming approach to it is by a sunken lane and the drive leading to the 18th century rectory (now a diocesan retreat house), crossing a slope which was once the village green.

The interior is of unusual charm, filled with soft light turned into sunshine by the clerestory windows. It is a place of lovely arches, low and round in the arcades, lofty and narrow in the tower, wide and pointed in the chancel. It has a wonderful portrait gallery in brass and monuments in stone of folk of long ago; and the walls of the north aisle are like a marvellous picture book with glass both old and new. There are four old piscinae, a fine old oak chest, and a charming window in the chancel, 600 years old and unglazed.

The story of these remarkable brasses, surely the finest and most complete in any Midland church, begins with Ralph Statham or Stathum, who married Goditha, heiress of the Morley lands. With their son Richard they made the church what it became in the 14th century, and two brass plates tell of their benefactions. Much of the 15th century alteration was the work of their grandson John Statham, in whose memory there are two brass plates asking for prayers, and a set of brasses in the north chapel which are the earliest portraits here. We see John in armour, kneeling on his helmet, his hair cut close above his ears, and his wife kneeling in a loose gown and a veil. Above them is St Christopher, patron saint of the family, who appears several times on the brasses. On an altar tomb are elaborate brass portraits of John's son Thomas of 1470, with his two wives dressed alike in fur-trimmed gowns. Thomas is in armour with a sword, his head on a tilting helmet.

Under a canopied archway, which may be from Dale Abbey, is a stone with brass portraits of Henry Statham and his three wives. Henry wears elaborate armour, and two of the wives have long gowns, the other a long mantle held by a cord, a veil over her head-dress. Below are tiny figures of five children, only one of whom grew up; she was Joan, who became sole heiress and married John Sacheverell, slain at Bosworth Field. Their portraits are in a chapel, John kneeling in armour and Joan in a close-fitting gown, and with them are eight children.

The last of this array of family portraits are those of Sir Henry Sacheverell (son of John and Joan) who died in 1558, and his wife becomingly dressed in a gown with puffed sleeves. The beautiful alabaster figure of Sir Henry's daughter Katherine lies on a tomb in the north chapel. She died in 1563, grandmother of Anthony Babington who was executed for conspiring against Elizabeth.

Jacinth Sacherevell and his wife lie side by side on an altar tomb, their figures evidently true to life. On one side of the tomb are three kneeling children and a fourth is in a cradle. Jacinth was a staunch Roman Catholic and suffered much for his faith. His brother Jonathan is said to have been the first of the family to leave the old faith, and the inscription on his painted monument, showing Jonathan and his wife holding hands, a baby in a tiny cradle and another small child on a cushion, tells us that he died a true Protestant in 1662.

Here also is the altar of Henry Sacheverell of Barton, to whom Jacinth left the property instead of to Jonathan; and the tomb of Henry's son, William, who died in 1691. Speaker Onslow described him as the "ablest Parliament man" of the reign of Charles II. He was belaboured with abuse by the brutal Judge Jeffreys for protesting against cancelling the charters of Nottingham, and he was a bold critic of Charles I and a gallant defender of the British Constitution, on which he left his mark.

One of the glories of the church is the lovely 15th century stained glass in three north aisle windows, once in the cloister of Dale Abbey. In one window we read in eight little scenes the story of St Robert of Knaresborough who shot deer which had been eating his corn. Three of the scenes are in modern glass, but the rest are old. The legend of the Invention of the Holy Cross is told in 10 scenes in the next window, seven of 1847 and the rest from Dale Abbey. The three scenes in the old glass are Christ on the Cross, the beheading of Chosroes after he had removed the cross on capturing

Monsal Dale.

Pinxton Church.

The entrance to Repton School, formerly the gateway to Repton Abbey.

Jerusalem, and the baptism of Chosroes' son. The other two windows in the north wall have 19th century glass in the style of that from Dale, showing the Parables and other scenes. The glass of the east window of this aisle includes an original figure of St Ursula ascending to Heaven escorted by angels, with 11 of the virgins gathered in her mantle.

There is fine old stained glass in the south aisle of St Elizabeth in a blue cloak and white robe and Peter in a red cloak, the kneeling figures of three girls and five boys suggesting that the glass is in memory of their father, John Sacheverell of Bosworth Field. Especially fine is a window with Roger, a Bishop of London who died in 1241, wearing red-and-white robes and jewelled gloves; the four Evangelists writing at desks, with their emblems; St William in the white-and-green vestments he wore 800 years ago, and a monk representing St John of Bridlington.

Morton. The coal mines have not spoiled it, for it has still its old haunts at the top of the hill, with lovely trees, old cottages, the 18th century rectory, and a church with a 15th century tower crowned by battlements and eight pinnacles. The rest of the church, except for the 13th century north arcade, was rebuilt in 1850. Inside can be found an ancient and massive font (possibly Saxon), a chancel screen partly of about 1400, and a Jacobean pulpit. The churchyard has a trim array of low 17th and 18th century gravestones, unusual for their simple inscriptions of initials and the year. The War Memorial lychgate stands in the shadow of a great sycamore and a fine beech.

Mugginton. It has a fine prospect over a green countryside of hills and dales, with a brook below winding to Kedleston Park. Its glory is an ancient church whose life began 1000 years ago. One of two old yews in the churchyard is claimed as one of Derbyshire's oldest inhabitants.

But older than the tree is a tiny window in the west wall of the church, probably Saxon. The tower has Norman work, including a belfry window and the corbel table, though the upper stage is of the 15th century. The Norman west doorway is blocked by a buttress. A small doorway at the east end of the south aisle is of the late 13th century. The south doorway and the nave arcade are

600 years old. The font, most of the windows and the arcade of two bays between the chancel and chapel, its capitals carved with flowers and shields and heads, are of the 15th century.

The upper part of an old oak screen between the aisle and chapel has fine 15th century tracery. Eleven plain oak benches remain out of a number made in 1600 for William Jenkinson, who "gave to this church XXXs that made these forms". A stone bracket on a pillar is carved with a curious face and a very ugly head with open mouth looks down from the roof of the south chapel. An inscription to Hugh Radcliffe of 1678 is like a 17th century advertisement, telling us that he made hats for Charles I and all the royal family.

The treasure of the church is an altar tomb in the south chapel to one of the Knivetons, landowners in Derbyshire for 400 years, who gave all they had for the Stuarts. On the top of the tomb are splendid brass portraits of Sir Nicholas Kniveton and his first wife, with tiny figures of five children in a row. On the wife's long hair is a charming chaplet of roses. Sir Nicholas is in armour with a long sword, and a collar with the rare pendant of a portcullis. His feet are on a greyhound and his head rests on a helmet which has a great heraldic interest, for on it is a crest engraved with a fox. It is one of the rare conceptions of heraldry of which there are only a few examples in England. The familar story is that a tiger (here it is a fox), pursuing the hunters who had carried off its cub, was delayed by their throwing down a mirror in which it imagined its lost cub.

On an outside wall of the church is the crest of the Sanders family which gave Cromwell a colonel for his Ironsides. He was the fine old Sir Thomas Sanders who was buried under the chancel in 1695, having lived to see the rise and fall of the Commonwealth, the return of the Stuarts, and the coming of William and Mary.

In a lovely situation on the crest of billowy hills, reached by narrow lanes, is a small stone chapel joining a brick farmhouse; it was built by a farmer, Francis Brown, in 1723 and has the curious local name of Halter Devil Chapel.

Netherseal. In the extreme south of the county, looking into Leicestershire across the River Mease, and near the borders of two other counties, is this village where elms and limes and chestnuts grow, where cottages look on to a tiny green and where a row of almshouses of 1699 and the gabled rectory look up to the church, mostly rebuilt in 1877. The embattled 15th century tower stands among the noble limes, its lofty arch opening to the nave, and the church retains also its 13th century nave arcade. In an arched recess in the chancel is a tomb with an engraved stone of Roger Douton in priest's robes; he was rector here and died in 1500.

Netherseal has lost a Jacobean house which stood near the church, but it has kept the charming 18th century Old Hall built on the foundations of a Norman castle. We must like it for the peep of its garden and lake, and the sight of its 17th century dovecot over the way, with a fine ladder which turns round like a wheel so that every one of the nesting-boxes can be reached. There is an old mill still grinding corn close by.

Newbold. Chesterfield was once one of its hamlets; now it is almost swallowed up by the larger place. In a field behind an inn is a Roman Catholic chapel about 36 feet long and half as wide. It rang with praise and prayer in Norman England, but it was a barn after it ceased to be a church in the 17th century. Through all its adventures it has kept the little priest's doorway the Normans built, with stone carving over it worn away by centuries of wind and rain. There is Norman masonry in its walls, and the windows and the south doorway are of the 15th century.

New Mills. This town given over almost entirely to industry has old-established textile printing and engraving works, as well as other textile mills, metal and engineering works, and manufactures of confectionery. On the borders of Cheshire, it lies deep in the lower valley of the Goyt and in the tributary valley of the Sett, which descends from Hayfield and the neighbourhood of Kinder Scout. Its industrialists look towards Manchester rather than to the rest of Derbyshire, but its townsfolk look out to the moorland hills around them, to Mellor Moor and Lantern Pike, to Chinley Churn and Black Hill, and the heights above the beautiful Lyme Park, in Cheshire.

Newton Solney. Standing opposite the point where the Dove comes into the Trent, it has houses big and small, from the almshouses in the village street to the great stone house of Newton Park, by a lovely bit of sunken road, and the early 19th century Bladon Castle, on a hill 150 feet above the river. From this high end of the village we look into Staffordshire and away towards the distant hills of the Peak.

A charming grass-bordered road with an avenue of trimmed limes leads to a fine house and the church by the river. In the shadow of the church is buried Thomas Gayfere, his stone telling us that his lasting monument is in Westminster Hall and Henry VII's Chapel, which he helped to restore early last century. In the church are buried three knights whose monuments were old when Henry's Chapel was new, three of the Solneys who were here in the 13th and 14th centuries.

The church which shelters them began to rise in Norman days, and has remains of that time in its north doorway, some stones with chevrons on the outside walls of the chancel and the tower, and perhaps the priest's doorway. Most of the rest is 600 years old: the tower and spire, the nave arcades, and most of the chancel. The clerestory is a century younger, and two windows are of the 13th century, one an unusual double lancet with a head carved on the middle shaft, inside and out. A carved oak flower on a beam under the tower is 500 years old, and four oak benches are of the 17th century. The floor of the tower is paved with old tiles, and in it are two ancient stones with crosses. The corner of one of them has in it another stone with a cross, only 18 inches long; they laid a little child under it eight centuries ago.

The oldest of the Solney monuments is the battered stone figure of a 13th century knight in armour, with his hands resting on a sword. Another stone knight lies on a tapering stone, perhaps Norman de Solney of about 1275; he has a sword and wears a surcoat with some parts of his armour of banded mail visible. There are not many examples of this banded mail in England.

Exceptional for its wonderful detail is the monument of the third of these de Solney knights. Sculptured in alabaster, he lies on a tomb adorned with shields, wearing armour, and at the knees and instep, under the arms and below the surcoat, can be seen the undersuit of mail. His hip-belt is handsomely decorated, his head is on a cushion borne by angels, his feet are on a lion. He is thought to be John Solney, the last male of his line, who perhaps built the north chapel and died towards the end of the 14th century. This is said to be the only example in England where the hood-like camail is shown tied down to the shoulders.

Under the tower, and in marked contrast, is the huge marble figure (by Thomas Carter) of Sir Henry Every of Egginton, wearing a toga and sandals, in the manner of those who loved to look like Romans, a fashion which was popular in the 18th century.

Norbury. Round this meeting-place of Derbyshire and Staffordshire, her "Stonyshire" and "Loamshire", George Eliot laid some of the scenes of *Adam Bede*. At Roston, a mile south of Norbury, is the birthplace of her father Robert Evans and his brother, Adam and Seth Bede of the novel.

Norbury is a delightful village in green country by the River Dove, with a deep-cut shady lane climbing to the church in company with a fine yew, on one hand the charming manor house of the Fitzherberts, mostly rebuilt in the early 18th century, its grounds spread round the churchyard. Here, built after an unusual plan, with a low embattled tower between two chapels on the south of the nave, is one of Derbyshire's most charming churches. It has an outstandingly lovely chancel and a wealth of old glass equalled by few village churches in the country.

This superb chancel was built by Henry Kniveton, rector from 1349 to 1395, and is only three feet shorter than the nave. Its walls are all windows between the fine gabled buttresses and the wavy parapet, the windows having inside and out a double flower at the middle point of their lovely and unusual tracery. The inner walls below the side windows are filled with shallow arches, and the east wall is lined with ancient stall-work, some of which remains in the ends of the choir stalls with old tracery and poppyheads. Very effective is the dark oak screen against the light background of the chancel.

It is in the chancel that we find the glory of the mediaeval glass, much of it of the 14th century, with fine interlacing patterns and scrollwork, medallions, and shields, relieved with colours of red and blue. The east window glass is chiefly of the 15th century, with a representation of the Trinity, the Twelve Disciples, and four saints. The two windows in the south-east chapel (recently restored) commemorate the marriages of Nicholas Fitzherbert, who died in 1473 (his tomb is in the chancel). The south window shows him kneeling with one of his wives and four children.

Splendid are the roofs, almost flat, with beautiful bosses. The chancel was roofed in the 15th century by Henry Prince, a rector seen in his priest's robes on a stone in the chancel. There are three sedilia and three piscina niches, a 15th century font on a pillar of clustered shafts, and a mutilated cross-stone 700 years old on the chancel floor. But rarer far are two fine fragments of 10th century Saxon crosses with interlacing and knotwork, while one has a figure with a staff.

In monuments of stone and brass we read of these Fitzherberts whose glory waxed and waned at Norbury from the 12th to the 17th century. The oldest is the stone figure of Sir Henry in chain armour, with a sword and shield. He rebuilt the manor house at the beginning of the 14th century, and some of the upper windows of his time are in the old manor house still.

Very fine is the alabaster tomb in the chancel on which lies Sir Nicholas, who built the chapel where the old glass still commemorates his two marriages. He is in plate armour with a fine sword and a collar of suns and roses; his feet are on a lion with a tiny angel on its back supporting the tip of the knight's foot. At one end of the tomb are his wives, and in carved niches are their 17 children—some civilians, six women in dress of their day, one a nun with veil and rosary, another a monk with a book, one a lawyer with a scroll, one in armour, and another in a collar of roses. A very worn stone has the engraved portrait of his wife Alice

The son and heir of the proud Sir Nicholas lies also in the chancel on another splendid alabaster tomb. He is Sir Ralph, and has plate armour and a collar of suns and roses. His lady has a mantle over her gown, and wears a necklace with a pendant of the Madonna. Her hair is arranged in a beautiful netted headdress, and at her feet are two dogs. At Ralph's feet is a little bedesman with a rosary on a lion's back, holding up the tip of the knight's right foot. In canopied niches on the sides of the tomb are fine figures of seven sons, and eight daughters in dainty low-necked dresses. Another monument to Sir Ralph's wife, Elizabeth, is an engraved alabaster stone on the chancel floor showing her entirely enveloped in a shroud. Their eldest son John, who built the tower and south-west chapel from his grandfather's design, has an alabaster tomb with a brass plate in the upper stone.

Here lies another of the sons of Ralph and his Elizabeth, Sir Anthony, who inherited the estates after his brother John. He was a great scholar and a famous judge, remembered for his fearless opposition to Wolsey when he seized the monastery lands, and he was a judge of the tribunal which tried Sir Thomas More. The splendid brass portraits of Sir Anthony and his wife are set in a stone on the chancel floor. The judge, whose head is missing, has a scroll in his hand; there is a group of five girls, but the sons are gone. An epitaph in Latin is said to be the judge's own words. Some of this set of brasses have been used twice, the other side of the brass of the five daughters having the fine little figure of a monk under a canopy.

Sir Anthony, who died in 1538, was born in the old manor house and it is said that the oak wainscoting in an upper room was put in by him. Some ancient glass in the house shows the marriages of the family, and there are six 15th century roundels of the occupations of the months from January to June. Sir Anthony was the first man to try to codify all the laws of England, and the first to raise his voice against the danger to agriculture owing to the insecurity of the tenant. He wrote two books on rural life, of great practical value. Sir Anthony's eldest son, Sir Thomas, died in the Tower of London after many years of persecution and imprisonment for his faith.

North Wingfield. Belonging to a busy countryside of coal and iron, it has beauty at its doorstep and can turn its back on the smoking chimneys and see England's green and pleasant land, for it looks towards the wooded park of Hardwick Hall.

The interesting church has a prominent tower over 100 feet high and 500 years old, one of its bells older still. Below the embattled parapet is a cornice with shields and on the west window are heads of a bishop and one with a coronet, and a lofty arch opens to the nave.

Full of light is the interior, a blending of stone and woodwork old and new. The old roofs have much original 14th century work in their beams, their trefoil tracery, their fine kingposts and bosses.

There is a fine old chest and an old table, and a modern oak chancel screen with a loft reached by the mediaeval stairway.

The oldest thing North Wingfield has is perhaps a font which is now not used. A noble relic of the past, it was found lying in the churchyard, a round block of stone well over three feet high, the massive stem hollowed out in deep flutings. It is believed to be either Saxon or early Norman. The oldest masonry is a Norman archway opening into the chapel, with a lovely window above it which is probably from the end of the 12th century, the arch being slightly pointed and so marking the change from Norman to Early English. It may have been a doorway, built here for preservation.

The church has a fascinating group of mediaeval stones and sculptures. In the porch is a small tapering coffin-stone under which was probably laid a Norman child. Set in the wall of the south aisle is a sculpture of St Lawrence bound to a grid, a man at each end turning him round and another standing behind. On two other stones, set in the chapel wall, are kneeling and standing figures, one perhaps representing the Annunciation. In a chancel recess lies a knight in chain armour, and in a recess outside the chancel wall is a companion knight; it is thought that they are both Deincourts of the 13th century.

The nave arcades are of the 14th and 15th centuries, and a 14th century arch opens from the chancel to the chapel. The 600-year-old east window has a glowing 19th century scene of the Ascension, and fragments of old glass. The west window of the tower has an ancient figure of a monk with a book and a rosary. The churchyard has a very old sundial, and close by is an inn which was once the chantry house, and has much 15th century work still left.

It is well over a century since Thomas Greatorex played his last organ voluntary, but his name is still with us. Born near North Wingfield in 1758, he came of a family of musicians. His father was a self-taught musician, and his sister was an organist in Leicester when she was only 13. Thomas, very grave and studious, and fond of mathematics and astronomy, soon turned his attention to church music and was organist of Carlisle Cathedral when he was 12.

In his leisure hours he studied science, and at 18 he travelled in Italy and Germany. Before he was 30 he was earning as much as 80 guineas a week by giving singing lessons. Chief professor of the organ in the Royal Academy of Music, he was long regarded as one of the greatest authorities of his day, and no great performance of Handel or Haydn was thought to be complete if he were not at the organ or conducting the chorus. In the 39 years he was conductor of Ancient Concerts he is said never to have missed one performance. Keenly interested in painting and architecture, he always kept his youthful interest in science, and his invention of a new way of measuring the height of mountains won him the fellowship of the Royal Society.

For 12 years organist of Westminster Abbey, he was famous for his wonderful mastery of the instrument. He seemed to have fifty fingers, and when his hands strayed over the keys the abbey was filled with great surges of sound that rolled out magnificently like awful peals of thunder. He is buried in the cloisters at Westminster, not far from the choir where his music stirred all who heard it.

Ockbrook. Some of it has fine peeps over the Trent and Derwent Valleys into Nottinghamshire and Leicestershire, some of it is in the hollow with the church. A Moravian settlement, one of the only three in England, was founded here in 1750, and its girls' school still flourishes, using the chapel and other 18th century buildings.

With a magnificent beech for company, the church is both old and new. The small tower is of the 13th century and the spire is a century younger; the chancel and the nave are of the 19th century. Its treasures are a Norman font, 16th century window pictures of the Evangelists, and woodwork of about 1500 in the choir stalls and the chancel screen. The lofty screen reaches to the roof, and has an upright border of vines at each end.

These fine possessions of 15th and 16th century craft, once in Wigston Hospital in Leicestershire, were brought here last century by one of the Pares, whose memorials are in the chancel. They lived at the 18th century Hopwell Hall a mile or two away, now a school but formerly the home of the Lakes, descendants of the valorous Sir Edward Lake of Edgehill. He was wounded 16 times there, and when his left hand was shot away he gripped the reins between his teeth and kept on fighting till he was taken prisoner. Then he managed to escape, and the proudest moment of his life

177

was on the anniversary of the battle, when he was received and thanked for his valour by Charles I. He was buried in Lincoln Cathedral in 1674.

Old Brampton. Coal and iron round about the Rother Valley have left Old Brampton its green hilltop, looking out to fields and wooded valley and the moors not far away. It is charming with fine trees, trim-walled roads, old houses, and a church of rust-coloured stone.

High above the road, the church is a delightful picture. The Norman chapel was made new in the 13th century, and we see the actual meeting of the styles when Norman was passing into Early English, for the south doorway has a round arch and a pointed one.

The sturdy 13th century tower was altered a century later, when it was capped with the short broached spire. The stone-roofed vaulted porch is also of the 14th century, as is most of the rest of the church, except for the many 15th century windows. Over the arcades are enormously wide arches built into the walls. What was their original use? In a little gallery of worn figures on the outside walls is Paul with a book and sword, Peter with a key and a book (with little birds on the pinnacles of his canopy), a draped woman and a Madonna, and a quaint corbel over the priest's doorway, with foliage coming from its mouth.

A great treasure is a sepulchral monument against the west wall, found in the churchyard. It is one of those curious old sculptures in which are seen parts of a human body below the surface of the stone, as if the lid of a coffin had been cut away. In a quatrefoil opening at the top are the head and shoulders of a woman holding a heart in her hands, while in a narrow opening below, her feet peep out from the folds of her robe. It is thought she was the heiress Matilda le Caus, who died nearly 750 years ago.

The great wooden cross of Lord Gorell, who was killed in Flanders in 1917, has been brought from his grave.

Osmaston. We come through its lovely trees and quiet lanes to thatched model cottages by a pool with a rockery. Though the 19th century Osmaston Manor has gone, the beautiful terraces and parkland and a glorious grove of limes remain.

The church, with yews among the fine trees of its churchyard,

178

was rebuilt in 1845 by H. I. Stevens of Derby. Five brothers sing out from the tower, a peal of five bells of which one says, "I and my four brothers were hung in this church in 1845." A stranger has now joined them. The windows have beautiful tracery in the 14th century style; fine arcades lead to the wide aisles, and lofty arches to the tower and the chancel. The mediaeval font, the only relic of the old chapel, stands over four feet high, its bowl like part of a round pillar.

Over Haddon. A hardy little village in upland country with endless stone-walled fields, it glories in its place above the Lathkill Dale. It sees the river, only three miles old, shining among the rocks and trees of this enchanting valley, leaping weirs and filling trout pools on its way to the mediaeval Conksbury Bridge, charming with its high wall and low arches. It has old stone houses and a late 19th century church, looking over the dale to Youlgreave's fine old tower.

The village story is of Martha Taylor, a story rare enough to have found its way into many books. Born here in the 17th century, an invalid from a child, she lived for a whole year with only a few drops now and then of sugar and water, syrup of prunes, and the juice of a raisin. She was then 18 and she lived on after that another 17 years.

Parwich. In the shadow of a great hill, watered by a stream, the neat stone houses, the pump in its shelter, and the church of this pretty village are grouped round the green. On the slope of the hill is the 18th century Hall, with its pleasant gardens.

The fine church of 1873, with a tower crowned by a lofty spire, is an exchange for a Norman structure. The nave arcades are Norman in style, with round pillars and arches and square capitals carved with foliage. Genuine remains of Norman work are built into the tower.

The fine arch of the tower was the old chancel arch; the west doorway was in the old north wall. Both are adorned with chevrons; the tower arch has a border of stars and the doorway has beak-heads and grotesques. Over the doorway is a fine tympanum with animals long buried under plaster; among them are a stag, a holy lamb looking like a horse, a wolf with a branching tail, a bird and a boar, and two serpents intertwined. The font is the old Norman one, though it has been carved with the date, 1662; it is shaped like an egg-cup, the upper part of the bowl divided into 16 faces, below which it tapers down to a round base.

Peak Forest. Only its name reminds us that it was the hunting ground of kings; today it is an isolated stone-built village of the limestone uplands. It has one of the few churches, a 19th century one among fine sycamores, devoted to the memory of Charles I, with memorials to the Cavendish family who helped to build it.

In two of its windows are memorials of two tragic pages in our history, for one recalls Lord Frederick Cavendish who was murdered in Phoenix Park in Dublin in the dark days of Ireland before Home Rule, and another shows Charles I in armour, with an axe, a block, and a crown beside him.

The rare dedication of the church to King Charles the Martyr belonged also to the 17th century chapel, built perhaps by a countess whose son died fighting for the king. It was owing to the special privilege of this chapel that the village became a kind of Gretna Green and for a time its runaway marriages averaged one a week. The act of 1753 checked the runaways, but the parsons went on marrying them for another 50 years. A mile and a half to the north is Eldon Hill, 1540 feet high, with ancient graves at the top and the remarkable Eldon Hole in the side. One of the Wonders of the Peak, it was known as the Bottomless Pit till 1770, when the bottom was first reached. It is a great tapering chasm about 180 feet deep, opening to a huge cavern which drops much lower still. Thomas Hobbes tells how he rolled stones into the Hole which dropped "to the depths of Hell".

Pentrich. A mile from the site of a Roman fortlet and near the Roman road that ran from Derby to Chesterfield, this hilltop village is charming with its brown-stone gabled houses, looking up to the sturdy church at the top of a picturesque flight of 48 steps.

The Normans built the lower part of the church tower (recently restored), with walls four feet thick; their arcades still lead to the aisles, and the bowl of the font, on a 17th century pedestal, back in the church after being found last century in the cellar of a house at Ripley, is also possibly Norman.

From the 15th century come the top of the tower, the battlements of the rest of the building, and most of the windows. A striking stained-glass War Memorial window from the workshops of Christopher Whall (1916) shows the warrior saints of England and France and a figure of St Michael. Two valiant men of earlier wars are remembered on the walls; Edmund Horne, a sea captain, who fought against the Spaniards and the French and came back to Butterley, his native place, dying in 1764; and Major Jessop of Butterley Hall. He fought with Wellington and was wounded at Waterloo, but he lived for half a century to tell the tale of how they beat Napoleon.

In 1817 a little company of half-starved labourers, stockingers, and weavers met at the White Horse Inn, where Pentrich post office now stands, and made wild plans for a march to London. Collecting recruits on the way, they set out to overthrow the government. Led by Jeremiah Brandreth, who is said to have been the victim of a spy in the pay of the government, the rebels attempted to provoke a riot. It was soon quelled, but it was made use of by the reactionary government to show what would be the result of further attempts at reform. Near 50 of the men were tried by four judges at Derby, the trial lasting 10 days.

In this trial the wild scheme of the deluded rioters, who had plundered a few farmhouses and shot a servant at Wingfield Park, was made to look like a serious revolution, and the men were accused of high treason and of levying war against the king. A few of them were pardoned, some were transported, but Brandreth and two others were sentenced to a terrible death; they were hung, drawn, and quartered at Derby.

Pilsley. Only a mile from Chatsworth, it has a charm of its own in houses of warm-tinted stone and in wonderful views.

Down below, where the valley of the Derwent is rich in green meadows and in a wealth of trees, nestles the pretty village of Baslow; while beyond, as far as we can see up the valley, great heights rise to sweeping moors; on one hand Longstone Edge and Eyam Moor, on the other the Edges of Baslow, Curbar, and Froggatt, carrying the eye along to Hathersage Moor, all especially beautiful when the heather is in bloom.

Pinxton. Coal has changed this border village, but it gave its name to a now rare china. The fame of Pinxton china was largely due to the beautiful paintings of flowers by William Billingsley, who came here from the porcelain works at Derby. Billingsley was a practical potter, too, and his recipe enabled the factory, founded in 1796 by John Coke, to flourish for a few years. Then he left, and the quality of Pinxton ware deteriorated so much that in 1813 the factory was closed, leaving to Pinxton the name of some lovely and some commonplace works of art.

Tradition tells us that Pinxton belonged for a time to the Cliffords, and that here was born to them a daughter who became Fair Rosamund, the mistress of Henry II. Their house was perhaps near the church, for when the ground was opened in 1686, during the search for coal, traces of walls and lead pipes were found. In the 15th century part of the lands belonged to Sir William Babington, the Lord Chief Justice.

The church, standing high, is a plain building mostly rebuilt in the middle of the 18th century and enlarged in 1939. It has a strange plan, with the newer work standing at right-angles to the 13th century tower and what remains of the nave. The old font is still in use, and on the wall of the new aisle is a remarkable diptych attributed to Guido Reni. It was presented by the Pope to a General Manley who had been in command of his guard, and was given to the church in 1902 by General Coke.

There are memorials of the Cokes of Brookhill Hall, a fine 17th-18th century house in a wealth of trees a mile away.

Pleasley. A market centre since the 13th century, it has grey-brown stone cottages with colourful red-tiled roofs, but its colliery has partly turned it into a workaday village. The little River Meden separates it from Nottinghamshire, winding through the deep Pleasley Vale to the cotton mills downstream. Its old houses and church are on the hillside, and at the crossroads are the steps of a mediaeval cross.

The church is a long and aisleless building with 13th century walls and some lancets among the windows, all deeply splayed. The east window and two similar ones in the nave are of the early 14th century. The embattled tower is a century younger, the iron clamps on the pinnacles reminding us of an earthquake which shook them after Waterloo.

There is a fragment of an old coffin-stone in the floor of the porch; an unused font has a crudely carved figure of a priest perhaps 800 years old; but older than all else here is the richly carved Norman chancel arch. The old oak pulpit, cast out from All Saints' Church in Derby, was recovered from a shop last century and brought here, and its carving made new.

Quarndon. A slow drip of water in a shady lane, and a farm-house with a great brick building on the lovely road to Kedleston, tell of the fame that might have come to Quarndon, for one was a spring of precious water, and the other an inn built by Lord Scarsdale who hoped this spring would make the place a busy spa. It did not happen, for an earthquake is said to have disturbed the vigour of the spring. But Quarndon still has its charming situation among the little rolling hills, though now only just beyond the grasp of Derby, and seen from the farmhouse is a pretty picture of a village climbing to its church.

This church of the hilltop, with a fine view of Derby's towers and spires, was newly built in 1874 and has good woodwork in the pulpit and the stalls, finely carved altar rails, and a font of Derbyshire spar.

Radbourne. High up in its finely timbered park is the fine 18th century brick house of the Poles, who have held these lands for centuries. Their old home was by the Radbourne Brook at the foot of the slope, close by the church where some of their ancestors lie.

The oldest of their monuments is a tomb in the north aisle with the alabaster figures of Peter de la Pole (who died in 1432) and his wife Elizabeth. The knight has long straight hair, his family arms on the hilt of his sword, and his feet on a dog. His lady's cloak is tied by a tasselled cord, and held at the hem by a dog; she has a chain round her neck three times. She was the heiress who brought the knight these lands. On a table-tomb are the engraved portraits of Peter's son Ralph, a judge shown in a long gown with hanging sleeves, a square cap on his head and his feet on a greyhound; Johanna, his wife, has a long mantle and an embroidered headdress. A low tomb adorned with angels has the engraved portraits of per-

183

haps the judge's grandson and his wife, both under canopies; and a great marble monument reaching to the roof of the aisle has an inscription on each side of a sarcophagus to a father and son of the 17th century, both with their wives.

It is a charming church in which they are buried, enshrined in lovely trees with the rectory garden close by. In the churchyard is a wonderful bower of three old yews, whose branches sweep the ground for about 70 yards round.

Most of the church comes from about 1300, including the nave arcade, the chancel, and some windows. The embattled tower is of the 15th century, and the porch of the 18th. There is a piscina in the chancel and one in the nave. The oldest carvings in the church are the double sedilia in the chancel and a curious little carving like the top of a staff; they come from Norman days.

The 14th and 15th century woodwork in the church is said to have belonged to Dale Abbey and to have been brought here by Francis Pole of Radbourne, who bought up the fittings of the abbey on its dissolution. In front of the Pole pew are 13 panels of linenfold vine and grapes, perhaps part of the base of a 15th century chancel screen; one of the poppyheads of some handsomely carved benchends has three faces and a skull with a fallen jaw. The glory of the woodwork is an exceptionally fine font-cover which certainly came from Dale; with eight sides and two projecting rims, it is a mass of rich carving with heads and emblems of the Evangelists, the panel underneath showing the Cross and a Crown of Thorns. The font bowl is very old. In the tiebeams of the chancel roof are Elizabethan bosses. The oak reredos, stalls, and chancel screen are of the 19th century.

Repton. We may wonder if there are more than one or two places in the Midlands where the thrill of something very old touches us as here at Repton, which lies by the quiet Trent meadows. Its history takes in Saxon and Norman and Tudor, for here they have come in a great procession, and their story is enshrined in precious stones. They would worship in the crypt built by the Saxons 13 centuries ago, when Repton was the capital of the kingdom of Mercia, the centre from which the conversion of Mercia began. The crypt comes down to us as part of the first church of the con-

Sudbury Hall.

The Market House at Winster.

Garlanding at Castleton

Well dressing at Tideswell

JUBILEE OF DERBY DIOCESE

BEHOLD I SEND
YOU FORTH

verted Saxons in the Midlands, keeping company with great pillars the Normans set up in their priory guest-house, now part of the school which has been building up a great renown since the days of the Tudors.

We feel that time lingers gracefully here, bridging the old and the new as if it did not wish to leave. Within a stone's throw of the fine mediaeval cross is Repton's splendid village group—the church with a spire like a needle in the sky, sheltering the rare old crypt; the fine school buildings old and new, with grey walls and red walls, gables and red roofs, green carpets and lovely trees about them; and the delightful cottages. Along the road to Bretby is a charming black-and-white house with a room overhanging the porch.

It was in the 7th century that a monastery was founded here, built by Saxons, men who were beginning the thousand years of building which has given us our noble village shrines. They gave it a crypt which grew in fame until it became the Westminster Abbey of Mercia, kings and bishops being buried here. For a quarter of a century the body of the martyred Prince Wystan lay in the crypt after he had been treacherously slain by his cousin, but he was removed to Evesham on the approach of the Danes in 874.

The stairways to the crypt were made about 850, when the remains of St Wystan became a goal of pilgrimage; but the Danes destroyed the monastery which had stood for more than 200 years. When other Saxons built a church on the site of the old abbey, they built on old foundations the chancel walls we see today. The crypt has been called the most perfect specimen of Saxon architecture on a small scale that we can see; certainly it is one of the rarest corners of England. Only 17 feet square, it has a vaulted roof with small round arches resting on four spirally wreathed pillars, and eight half pillars on the walls. Modern windows have been put in to show it up for us; there are still traces of an old altar, and an opening in the western wall is believed to have been a peephole in bygone days through which the shrine could be seen from above. The crypt was desecrated at the Dissolution and forgotten until the end of the 18th century, when a man fell into it while digging a grave. Near an entrance to it from the outside, made for the use of the priory, is a holy-water stoup.

Our great English builders of 700 years ago reshaped the Saxon church, but the chancel walls are mostly as in the 10th century, with characteristic pilaster strips. Two Saxon pillars with square capitals (which were part of the 13th century nave arcades until last century) are in the two-storied porch. Above the porch door, which has been swinging here for centuries, is St Wystan in a niche, his hands on his sword. Crowning the 14th century walls of the church is the charming tower and slender spire with three tiers of lights, rising 212 feet above the churchyard with its lychgate and shapely yews. The tower has a band of quatrefoils below the battlements, a fine west window, and a painted clock face half as big as that on the Houses of Parliament.

On the ancient possessions inside the church a splendid roof looks down, 500 years old, but refashioned, with a fine collection of faces among 40 carved bosses. Remains of richly carved old oak pews, with varied designs, adorn a modern screen across the transept. Most of the windows are 600 years old, including the east window of the Saxon chancel. In a small lancet we see Alfrida, Abbess of Repton, and an angel holding a shield with a picture of the abbey in 697. It was Alfrida who received into the monastery Guthlac, the son of a Mercian nobleman who, after several years at Repton, decided to live as a hermit. He went to Crowland, or Croyland, in Lincolnshire, where he lived in a hut until his death in 714, after which the Abbey was built over his shrine.

A knight in 14th century armour with a belt of carved medallions lies on an alabaster tomb. He has short hair, his feet are on a dog, and his head rests on a helmet. He was probably Sir Robert Frances, lord of Foremark near by. A 17th century wall monument has the figures of George Waklin of Bretby and his wife, kneeling. A fine alabaster stone is engraved with the figures of Gilbert Thacker and his wife, stern-looking Tudor folk; at his feet is a quaint lion with its tongue out, at hers are two boys. Their story is linked with that of the priory founded here in 1172 by Matilda, Countess of Chester, for monks who came from Calke.

The priory buildings, east of the parish church, were granted at the Dissolution to Thomas Thacker, Steward to Lord Cromwell, and he made his home among the ruins until he died. As stern as he looks in his portrait was his son Gilbert, for it was he who demolished in a single day the fine priory church. He had become alarmed at events in the terrible reign of Mary Tudor, and "destroyed the nest lest the birds should build therein again".

While still living in the ruins the Thackers sold part of them to the executors of Sir John Port whose fine tomb we see in Etwall church, and here in 1557 he founded the school which has grown great today. Friction between the boys and the Thackers led to the building of another house known as Repton Hall, once the home of the headmaster. Worked into it is what was an isolated tower, one of the earlier and best examples of mediaeval brickwork with turrets and battlements, built by Prior John Overton after 1437. We see it well from the bridge over the old channel of the Trent.

The priory Guest House, with an old sundial over the doorway, is opposite the east end of St Wystan's church, and, though much altered, has still fine beams and massive Norman pillars. The upper part of it is now the library, where roundels of modern glass tell the story of St Guthlac. The whole of the basement of the Guest House was the cellarium, and is the only part remaining of the 12th century monastery. Here there were originally six Norman pillars, two of which still remain in a small room, and two in the part of it used now as the school museum, with ancient tiles in the walls found in the old tile kiln years ago. The great tithe barn of stone and timber stands by the roadside where the wide 14th century priory gateway makes a delightful entrance to the buildings.

On the site of the old priory church a spacious hall was designed by Sir Arthur Blomfield in 1886 in memory of Dr Steuart Pears, under whose rule this grammar school became in 20 years one of the great public schools of the country. The hall has a fine hammerbeam roof, oak-panelled walls, and great windows filling it with light. The east window has 15 panels of heraldry set between figures of saints and patrons, Guthlac and Sir John Port among them. The school chapel, begun in 1857 and several times enlarged, is away from the rest of the building, on the other side of the main road. Here, too, are the fine new Science Buildings, completed in 1957, on the 400th anniversary of the school's foundation.

Riber. Many know its name, if only for the Castle which crowns this great hill, a landmark 850 feet above the sea; but it is worth knowing for itself, for the charm of its old stone houses and its magnificent prospect, from Matlock at its feet to the hills beyond the Derwent.

Close at hand, the pretentious towers of Riber Castle lose whatever importance they have from afar. It is a great gaunt place, built in 1862 by John Smedley with the fortune he made out of his successful hydro at Matlock. Its ruined walls now enclose a popular fauna reserve, with many species of British animals and birds. In the hamlet behind are the delightful 17th century Manor House and the gracious Elizabethan Hall, with the charm of gabled roof and mullioned windows, with a stone gateway in a balustraded wall, its round steps jutting on to the wayside. It was long the home of the Woolleys.

Riddings. It has little enough to see and it is nothing on the map of beautiful England, but twice men have found treasure hidden here. The first time was in the middle of the 18th century, when they found 800 precious Roman coins; the second time was in the middle of the 19th century, when they found a thing a hundred thousand times more precious, from which has sprung one of the greatest industries in the world, bringing with it the motor-car and the aeroplane, and all the activities depending on the internal combustion engine. It is one of the greatest romances of commerce.

In 1847 James Oakes, a colliery proprietor and ironmaster in a small way at Riddings, discovered a mysterious flow of liquid on his property and called in his brother-in-law, Lyon Playfair, a scholar and man of affairs who happened to be one of the most brilliant practical scientists of his day. He tested the flow and found it to be petroleum, then an unknown product commercially, although as naphtha, "salt of the earth", it had been known from Old Testament days. It was found that a spring was producing 300 gallons a day, but James Oakes was too much occupied with his coal and iron to give time to it.

At Glasgow University, Playfair had a friend, James Young, who was employed to repair instruments at the laboratory in which he afterwards became an assistant. Playfair remembered him when the petroleum came to light and wrote suggesting that Young should take over the product of the spring and manufacture useful oils from it. Young had too much faith in his old friend to entertain any doubt of the feasibility of the proposal, and began in a small way a business which was to grow to world-wide proportions. One day soon after, he went with dismay to his friend, showing him the oil in a turbid condition and fearing that some change had occurred which would ruin the enterprise.

It was obvious to the scientist that the condition was due to the presence of paraffin, and Playfair induced Young to extract sufficient of the paraffin to make two candles. They were the first paraffin-wax candles ever produced. With one candle in his right hand and the other in his left, Playfair illumined a lecture he gave at the Royal Institution. From this small beginning dates the enormous petroleum industry and the rich trade in paraffin and its wide range of products. Young, ever after known as Paraffin Young, made a fortune, but when the knowledge of his work spread about a world-wide search for petroleum was instituted.

Ripley. Now a market and industrial town in a colliery district, it gave London one of its most famous roofs and India one of its most famous men.

It began to flourish with the well-known Butterley ironworks where the roof of St Pancras Station was made; they were founded in 1792 by a group of men that included Benjamin Outram, the engineer who introduced iron railways into collieries. He lived at Butterley Hall, the great house in which was born his famous son Sir James, whose great career in the East earned for him the title of the Bayard of India, and a place in Westminster Abbey. The church we see was not here when he was born; it was built when he was a youth and it has a curious story.

It was at Pentrich close by that a little band of poor stockingers and weavers turned rebels in the hard years after Waterloo, and their insurrection, which brought three of them to the scaffold and drove some of them into exile, caused much stir throughout the country. To stem the tide of irreligion and disaffection the vicar of Pentrich set about creating enthusiasm for a church at Ripley and raised a fund from which it was built in 1820, in the heart of the town.

From his home at Butterley Hall, Sir James Outram passed to a career in India which reads like that of a Crusader in a 19th century setting. While still a young man he became almost a legendary figure in the East. His first outstanding success was when, having subdued the lawless and savage Bhils, he won them to confidence and friendship, living unguarded among them, "sleeping under their swords", forming the pick of them into an efficient police force, and finally leaving them blessed with schools.

These men of the East like a man who can hunt with them, and this Outram could do; in ten years he killed 191 tigers (one after a sensational fight alone in a dark cave), 25 bears, and 15 leopards. The Afghan War called him away and he returned by perilous paths, disguised as an Afghan merchant, by a previously unknown route, bringing despatches to Sonmiani.

Although he found an unsympathetic influence in Lord Ellenborough, Outram was highly regarded by practically all other men on whom the safety of the Dependency hung. He was entrusted with romantic missions in which we see him navigating rivers thick with cataracts, crossing stony wastes on camels, carried through the mountains in a palanquin when a horse had shattered his leg, fighting in the hills, charging home in the plains, seizing sovereign banners, arresting refractory chiefs, here relieving an outpost, there redressing fiscal injustices, saving a rebel's life for the sake of his father who had been faithful, banishing sedition, righting wrongs, and everywhere winning the affection and confidence of native rulers and subjects alike.

"Gentlemen", said Napier at a public dinner given to Outram at Sakhar in 1842, "I give you the Bayard of India, without fear and without reproach! Major James Outram of the Bombay Army," and from that hour, by that name the world has since acclaimed him. He cared little for command, but much for right and justice. He pleaded the native cause when he thought he detected inequity in the treatment accorded them, but when he had to defend the Residency at Hyderabad against the Baluchis, so brilliant were his tactics that Napier promised a special despatch detailing what he regarded in Outram's policy as a model for all soldiers to imitate.

He refused to accept £3000 prize money awarded to him, and in operations of great moment to India he was ready to subordinate himself, as he did during the Mutiny, when he insisted on serving under Havelock so that that brave soldier should have the glory of relieving Lucknow. Outram joined Havelock's cavalry as a volunteer, and charged victoriously at their head with a cane in his hand for weapon. Lucknow having been relieved, he took command and withstood the second siege and, with a comparative handful of men, kept at bay 100,000 enemies from November 1857 until March of 1858.

He left India a baronet and bearer of many gifts. In Bombay, where he was well known, the natives said of him, "A fox is a fool and a lion a coward compared with James Outram." He died in 1863 in Paris, and his body was brought home to Westminster Abbey, where Napier's famous words are inscribed on his tomb.

Risley. Once on the busy Derby–Nottingham road, but now happily by-passed, it has fine trees and old buildings rich in memories of the Willoughbys who came here in the 14th century and are buried at Wilne two miles away.

The great house built on the site of their old home has disappeared, except for a gateway on a terrace and the long stone wall enclosing the grounds, brought from the ruins of Dale Abbey. The church, a rare example of an Elizabethan church, was built by Michael Willoughby in 1593 as a chapel for his house; the delightful schools and schoolhouses close by, founded by him and his family, were rebuilt in the early 18th century. The church has the Willoughby arms over the doorway, and they are carved on the fine alabaster font, which, like the chancel screen adorned with cherubim, is as old as the church. By the porch is part of an old canopied niche from Dale Abbey, turned upside down and used as a flower vase. A lane between the church and the schools runs to a pretty retreat where a footbridge crosses a stream near a group of old cottages.

Rowsley. It is on the doorstep of hill and valley, rock and moorland, delightful rivers and beautiful bridges, and fine old homes of England. Round about it rises Lees Moor, covered by lovely woods, the fine stretch of Beeley Moor, and Stanton Moor with its Nine Ladies stone circle. Down the valleys come the Derwent and the Wye to meet below the village, the Derwent fresh from the glory of Chatsworth, and the Wye having added to its crowded life of romance the joy of flowing by Haddon Hall and gathering the waters of two lovely streams, the Lathkill and the Bradford.

Rowsley Bridge has a charming view of the Derwent fringed by lovely trees. Twice has the bridge been widened since packhorse days, keeping five pointed arches on the side with the ancient masonry, and round arches on the new. The inn is a joy to see, a study of gables and mullioned windows, dating from 1652. Over the embattled porch is a fine stone peacock, the crest of the Manners of Haddon. Every Peak traveller knows the Peacock; Landseer and Longfellow have been here; but the road which climbs from it is often passed by. It leads to a little church which was built only in 1855, but has something worth finding both without and within.

A lychgate opens to a churchyard with a noble prospect and a magnificent elm whose mighty arms spread over a circle nearly 100 yards round. In the church is a fragment of a cross, said to be the head of a preaching cross set up before King Alfred's day. It is carved with braidwork and was rescued from the bed of the Wye.

The church is a pleasant place with arches and windows in the style of the Normans; its wide chancel arch has zigzag moulding and capitals with foliage. On a fine tomb in a chapel built for her coming lies a figure as in quiet sleep, a beautiful lady who would have been a duchess had she lived. She wears a simple gown and her hands are folded on her breast; at her side on the mattress is her baby. She was Catherine, wife of Lord John Manners who became seventh Duke of Rutland, but she died in 1859 when she was 23, too soon to share her lord's stately rank. In her memory the window in the chapel tells the story of St Catherine in four scenes.

A mile from Rowsley is Stanton Woodhouse, an Elizabethan house overlooking Darley Dale and set in a wealth of trees, among them ancient yew, chestnut, elm, and walnut. It was once the home of the Allens who had among their relatives a Lord Mayor of London and a great cardinal at Rome.

Sandiacre. Its fields have mostly given place to factories and houses. Yet a place of surprising contrasts it is, for to those who look for beauty the busy street soon leads to a winding lane climbing to where 1000 years ago the Saxons found a rocky outcrop on which to build their church. Some of their work remains in the church above the housetops, looking over the industrialised valley of the Erewash.

It is a beautiful church, full of years and interest. The simple 13th century tower has Norman work in its foundations, and a spire with two tiers of lights. Its 19th century porch has a restored Norman doorway in its keeping. The lofty nave has, unusually, a 15th century clerestory but no aisles, a 14th century window, a Norman window on each side (lengthened to give more light), and a little Saxon window with long-and-short work above a massive Norman chancel arch of great beauty. On each side of the arch are grotesques.

The fine arch opens into what is the glory of this place, a spacious 14th century chancel, lovely within and without, built by Bishop Roger de Norbury, prebendary of Sandiacre from 1342 to 1347. The windows are splendid with tracery; there is a charming priest's doorway, while rich buttresses carved with tracery and crowned with pinnacles, and a fine parapet with quatrefoils, enhance the beauty of the outer walls. Inside, the elaborate sedilia and the piscina under lofty canopies are richly pinnacled. From the 12th century comes a remarkable gravestone on the chancel floor, engraved with a cross and a curious animal on each side of it. It was found under the pulpit and may have marked the burial-place of the builder of the Norman church. The font is 600 years old.

Four stones remain of the Charltons, who have a long story from the time when one was M.P. in 1318. Sir Richard was slain on Bosworth Field; Sir Thomas was Speaker in 1453; Edward was a Commissioner in the Civil War. They were living at Sandiacre in the 16th century, and have lived hereabouts in our own century. A pathetic floorstone tells how John Manley died in 1658, and six of his brothers and sisters all died before they were 12. In the churchyard is a stone coffin 40 inches long.

Sawley. More than 1000 years have told their tale since a little band of monks came rowing down the Trent from Repton and brought their craft to rest by these green meadows. Something of the church they built is in the one between the road and the river, eloquent with the story of the years, yet with the strength that outlasts centuries and the charm of dignified simplicity. Here is work of the Norman builders, with traces of the 13th and much of the two next building centuries. Within these walls are memories of people who have passed this way; their figures are in stone and their portraits in enduring brass.

We come to it along an avenue of limes more than a century old, running through the rectory lawns like a lofty aisle not made with hands; 24 great trees make a church approach not surpassed in Derbyshire. And there in front is the fine 600-year-old north doorway with its massive old oak door, ribbed and studded. All this time the south door has kept its old bar-fastening; all this time the priest has been going through the chancel doorway, and the children of Sawley have been baptized at this primitive-looking font.

Who is not stirred with the thought of all this continuity of time and this enduring heritage of our countryside? Everywhere the outside walls are strong and clean, crowned with a sturdy 15th century tower and spire with four small windows. We come inside and find it bright and light with charming windows, most of them 600 years old, with a 15th century clerestory above the lofty 14th century nave arcades. The Normans built the plain round chancel arch; some of the masonry above it, and some in the north wall of the chancel, is said also to be theirs. Across the east end of the chancel is another wonder of our past, a stone screen 500 years old, seven feet from the east wall. Its oak door is panelled and studded and has a handle of fine iron work.

This mediaeval treasure house is rich indeed in craftsmanship, for it has a 15th century oak screen with an embattled cornice and some tracery under the chancel arch, old stalls in the choir, and some sturdy Elizabethan oak benches in the nave. It has a Carolean pulpit with a canopy, a 17th century altar table, an old oak chest, and remains of a 14th century oak screen now in the aisles. The roofs of the nave and the north aisle have much of their fine 15th century timbering, the nave roof with old bosses.

The church has a noble group of monuments. The 14th century stone figure of a priest has suffered much through lying outside for centuries. There are two other priests in the north aisle, one perhaps Ralph de Chaddesden who died while rebuilding the church in the 13th century, the other perhaps Hugh de Scoter, who carried on his work.

Five hundred years ago the Bothes or Booths settled at Sawley in a house of which some of the timbers are still in the cellars of Bothe Hall, near the church. A rich and famous family, they were great benefactors of this church, and gave England two archbishops, two bishops, and two archdeacons. The first of them was Roger, and his fine brass portrait showing him in armour with his head on a helmet and his feet on a boar is on an altar tomb under a canopy in the chancel. His wife is here, wearing a necklace with a cross, and in two groups are their 18 children. On another tomb are the brass portraits of Roger's son Robert, his wife, and a group of six girls; Robert a knight with a collar of suns and roses, and the wife in a widow's veil with her feet on a stag. In a handsome bay forming a recess in the chancel, built for his tomb, lies John Bothe, a treasurer of Lichfield cathedral, who was buried here in 1496. He wears the dress of a canon, and his head is on a cushion held by angels. A lady in flowing robes lies in brass on the floor of an aisle, with just the head of her husband left, showing his long hair; he was a merchant, dying in 1510.

In a small house (now demolished) near the church John Clifford was born. He was one of the most vital forces of modern Noncomformity, in the pulpit, on the platform, a man of charming character, who made himself what he was, the greatest Free Churchman of his day. He was born a poor boy at Sawley in 1836, and had the slenderest form of elementary education before he was working as a boy in a lace factory. From the first, however, his love of books and thirst for knowledge were insatiable. His personality not less than this anxiety for learning marked him in early youth as suited for the ministry, and his denomination, the Baptists, welcomed him into their Academy at Leicester and College at Nottingham. When he was only 22 he was invited to accept the pastorate at Praed Street, Paddington, where (and at the larger chapel built for him at Westbourne Park) he remained for 57 years.

John Clifford was particularly attracted to London because it gave him opportunities of study. In five years he took the degrees of B.A., B.Sc., M.A., and LL.B. at London University, and built up one of the biggest and most energetic Nonconformist churches in the country, whose devotion to him was unfailing. There was no denominational organisation that did not welcome him as its president. He believed in every man taking an active part in citizenship, and as he was a convinced Liberal in politics he was as well known on the platform as in the pulpit. Education on the broadest national lines, universal, free, and unsectarian, was his special subject. He held that the teaching of creeds was the duty of the sects and not of the nation, and that revenue contributed by everybody should not be used for them. Indeed he refused to pay for such purposes, and led a movement for passive resistance against such payments. The result was that, from time to time, some of his household goods were seized and sold. In this he was the embodiment of what was called the Nonconformist Conscience.

For what he believed was right he was a doughty fighter; but it would be a great mistake to regard him as a narrow-minded demagogue. His breadth of mind and gentleness of spirit was what most impressed those who knew him best. His charity was broad enough to allow every man to believe what he must, and to respect his honesty, but he declined to be made a participant in what he regarded as other men's errors.

A great worker all his life, he worked till the moment of his death, which came one day as he sat among his friends at Baptist House in Kingsway. His long brave life ended (at 80) as he would have wished it to end, on the platform where he had spent so much of it, fighting for every good cause and all downtrodden people.

Scarcliffe. It has the memory of a gracious lady for whom it rings its curfew every year for three weeks on each side of Christmas. It is said that the lady and her child were lost in the forest hereabouts, overcome with weariness and cold when the curfew bell of Scarcliffe led them safely home; and she left five acres of land to the church for the ringing of curfew for ever.

She was the Lady Constantia, probably one of the Frechevilles who held the manor in the 13th century; it was one of their ancestors who gave the church to the monks of Darley Abbey. The doorway through which the monks came is here to this day, with a tympanum over it carved with geometrical patterns of a design so varied that it seems as if the sculptor had been practising his art. Here also are four round arches and three pillars of varying shapes set up by the Normans; one of the three pillars is round, one octagonal, and one is four-clustered. The fine little priest's doorway is Norman too, buried in plaster until last century, and the tiny piscina in the corner of the chancel is the old one used by the monks. The roofs are partly old, and there is an enormous chest almost 10 feet long made out of four huge planks.

In this fine old church lie the mother and her child who were lost in the forest some 700 years ago. They lie in marble, the baby in the mother's arms, one of its hands up to her face. With her right arm the mother gathers up the graceful folds of the mantle she is wearing over her gown, which is fastened at the throat with a round brooch. Her hair is in plaited braids and on her head, which rests on a lion for a pillow, is a coronet telling of her high estate.

Scropton. It has a charming bit of road, shaded by trees, between two lychgates leading to the churchyard. The church was rebuilt in 1856 by Benjamin Ferrey, and all that remains of the older one are two memorials now under the tower which has an unusual pyramid roof. One is an alabaster stone with the engraved portrait of William Schower, a London merchant of Dick Whittington's day, his feet on a greyhound. On an altar tomb adorned with angels lie Nicholas Agard and his two wives, he in armour with a double chain round his neck, they with mantles tied with cords, little dogs touching the hems of their garments. They lived in early Tudor days at Foston, a mile or so away.

Very unusual are the altar and the reredos, with 12 paintings of the Disciples set in a framework of wood, all from Vienna. A window showing a kneeling figure on a ship at sea is a fitting memorial to one who was happiest when pacing the deck of his ship. He was Admiral Sir Arthur Cumming, who spent his last years at Foston and was buried in this church in 1893 after a life of much adventure. He distinguished himself at the storming of Sidon when he was 23, and he did something when he was 26 that was as wonderful as anything in romances of the sea. Cruising off South America, he fell in with a pirate ship with a cargo of slaves. He gave chase, shot the captain, leaped on board with seven other men and fought against 30. He drove the pirates below hatches, chained them all, and had complete control of the vessel until his own ship came up.

Shardlow. Road and river run through it side by side until the Trent swings under a modern bridge towards its meeting with the

Derwent near Wilne. This bridge replaces the fine Cavendish Bridge, built about 1760, which collapsed suddenly in 1947. Busy days began for Shardlow when this bridge (of which some stonework remains), was built, for it robbed the ancient Swarkestone Bridge of the stream of coaches and became itself part of the main highway from London to Carlisle.

It was busy with waterways, too, for downstream the Trent and Mersey Canal, constructed by James Brindley and opened in 1777, entered the river. In the late 18th and early 19th centuries, Shardlow was an important inland port. It still has old warehouses and a fine stone-fronted Hall of the 17th and 18th centuries, now a national agricultural advisory centre.

Shirland. The busy road to Chesterfield runs between its little green and the fine old church which has seen five centuries go by. It is adorned with battlements and pinnacles, eight of them crowning the fine tower. The porch, with a vaulted roof, has a niche over the door in which sits a modern St Leonard.

A recess in the chancel comes with its carved finials from the older church, where it sheltered the figure of a knight. The front stone of its alabaster tomb still remains, carved with 21 shields of the Greys, who held the lands in the time of King John. The vanished knight was perhaps Sir Henry Grey, who was summoned to Parliament about 1377.

An alabaster stone on the chancel wall has the headless figures of two men and two women wearing mantles and kneeling at desks; they are perhaps Reginald Grey with his wife and two children, and are over 600 years old. His father was kissed by Henry III for his willingness to travel with him to Holy Land in 1252, when very few men were prepared to go.

On the top of an alabaster tomb in an aisle are engraved the portraits of John Revell with his wife and eight children. He is in 16th century armour with his sword and a dog; his wife has a flowing gown with close-fitting sleeves and wide cuffs. The Revells of Ogston founded a chantry here in the 15th century. The church has a chained folio copy of Jewell's *Apology* (1609), an ancient Bible, and a pitch pipe used by the leader of the choir until about 1767.

198

Shirley. Two veterans have fallen on hard times in this village in so pretty a setting among the little hills. They are the old yew and the old cross in the churchyard, and both are past their glory, for, though the yew stands proudly high, with a trunk measuring about 17 feet round, its branches were sadly broken in a gale, and the cross has only a few feet of its shaft on its base and three steps.

The tower of the tiny church is of the 19th century, as is the north aisle and the arcade leading to it. The rest of the church is chiefly of the 14th century, with a font 500 years old. Its oldest possession is a stone in the outside east wall of the north aisle, once part of the tympanum of a Norman doorway, crudely carved with animals and foliage. On a floorstone near the altar rails is the worn alabaster portrait of a priest, Nicholas Bentley, who was vicar here till 1515. He would know the fine silver paten of Henry VII's day which is still in use.

Two 19th century memorials are of the Shirleys, an ancient family which took its name from the village 800 years ago, and were its lords until the 19th century. One of them, immortalised by Shakespeare as valiant Shirley, was killed in the Battle of Shrewsbury. A farmhouse near the church has part of their old homestead in a gable, some oak panelling, and the moat.

A brass cross is in memory of Canon Shirley of Christ Church, Oxford, where he was buried in 1873. A stone monument with three canopied niches is to Walter Augustus Shirley of 1847, a vicar here who became a bishop, greatly esteemed for his wide reading and scholarship, and much beloved for his kindly humour. Here his son Walter was born, one of Dr Arnold's most brilliant scholars at Rugby.

The charming Old Vicarage, to the north of the village, was the birthplace of John Cowper Powys and Theodore Francis Powys, two of a famous trio of literary brothers, the sons of the Reverend Charles F. Powys, who was vicar here in 1872–9.

Smalley. It has a fine view of the rolling Derbyshire hills and Stainsby House on the hillside, home of the Sitwells since 1785. But it has nothing more pleasing than its churchyard, a garden of flowers, with tree-lined walks, roses and rhododendrons, cypress and yew on every hand, the king of all being a magnificent old yew with stately trunk and spreading branches which lost two arms in a storm.

The church has seen much change in its life since it was built in 1793. At first just a nave and chancel, it had transepts added in 1844 but lost them less than 20 years after, when the aisles and a bigger chancel were built. The tower, like a pagoda, was built in 1912. The old turret it replaced had what was perhaps the only weather-cock in England which has been held as hostage at an inn. When the church was being built messengers were sent to bring the weathercock from Derby, but returned without it, having had so good a time at an inn there that the landlord kept it until they paid his bill. One relic of the older church is here still, a stone with an engraved cross perhaps 800 years old.

Smisby. Its small church, which looks over the housetops into Leicestershire, has monuments of the Kendalls who lived at the old Hall, now a farmhouse near the church.

One monument is an alabaster stone sculptured with the figure of a woman in a long mantle, her hands clasped on her breast. She was Joan Comyn, who died about 1350, heiress of the lord of the manor. Her face is much worn and one of her shields is gone, but she was for long the most important lady of Smisby, for it was through marrying her descendant that the Kendalls came to the hall. Here is William Kendall, his portrait engraved in stone when he died in 1500; he is worn away though his wife can still be seen. Here, too, is Henry Kendall, kneeling with his wife on a great monument against the chancel wall, their 16 children with them, two sons and one daughter in shrouds.

The low tower is of the 15th century, but the oldest work in the church is a 13th century lancet and a buttress. The nave arcade, the east window, and the font bowl are of the 14th century. Seven old tiebeams support the roof. The fine linenfold panelling in the chancel and the tower was once part of the glory of the castle of Ashby-de-la-Zouch.

The village still keeps its old lock-up, a tiny octagonal building with a studded door and a roof like a spire. In the fields to the south of the village, says tradition, was fought the famous tournament described by Sir Walter Scott in *Ivanhoe*, less than two miles from the castle round which some of the scenes in the story were laid.

Snelston. The River Dove divides it from Staffordshire, and this model village of brick cottages is sheltered by wooded hills and has delightful lanes. In one of them is a restored church, and though the great house has gone, the lodge survives and is a fine study of stone-roofed gables overhanging brick-and-timber walls.

The 19th century took the old church away, except for the low 15th century tower, with pinnacles, gargoyles, and heads on the dripstones of the windows, and the font, which is also mediaeval. The bright interior has fine woodwork, the chancel screen being extended to form a canopy over the pulpit. The carved and gilded reredos has figures in wood and alabaster, and the unusual War Memorial, of delicate Moorish carving, has arcades and lattice windows in red, blue, and gold.

Somersal Herbert. It nestles in a hollow of little hills at the end of winding lanes, with a small church by a charming old house, the half-timbered and many-gabled Hall of the Fitzherberts, who have lived in this place for 700 years. Much of the house is Elizabethan, and in the entrance hall are two oak tablets to John Fitzherbert and his wife which have been here since 1564, odd for being in two halves, one unreadable without the other.

The delightful churchyard of lawn and flowers is set among fine trees and orchards, where a rose-lined path leads to a cross with a tapering shaft. It stands on three steps and is perhaps of the 13th century, almost the oldest occupant of this tiny village.

The church with its sturdy exterior and low embattled tower, and its pleasing interior with black-and-white roof, has little left of the old work since the rebuilding in 1874. Its oldest possession is a Norman font, shaped like a tub and carved with 26 interlaced arches below a lattice border. In a chancel recess is the battered figure of a priest with a chalice, perhaps Robert By-the-Broke, who became rector here when Joan of Arc was fighting the English in Orleans.

South Normanton. Here (in a house now demolished) was born in 1726 Jedediah Strutt, who rose to wealth and fame by inventing the ribbed stocking frame, and who lies buried in the cemetery above the Derwent which turned his wheels at Belper.

A busy village has grown round a church begun in Norman days,

O

made new in the 14th century, and much refashioned in 1878. Of the 14th century there are left the north arcade of the nave, the font, and a piscina. One or two windows and the embattled tower with modern pinnacles are 15th century. The oldest relic is a Norman coffin-stone engraved with a cross, now in the floor of the porch; and the most beautiful relic is the 13th century carved arch of the doorway leading to the vestry. It was originally the priest's doorway, and was hidden until last century. There is a monument with weeping cherubim to Robert Revel, lord of the manor in Queen Anne's day, one of a family who lived at the old gabled Carnfield Hall, about a mile away.

South Wingfield. It takes to itself the church of the neighbouring hamlet of Oakerthorpe, lying on the old Roman road; but more important are the imposing ruins of Wingfield Manor, crowning a hill above the Amber, and among the finest remains in our land of a great house of the 15th century. It was built by one Cromwell and destroyed by another, and in the two centuries between them it had a remarkable history as a stately house, a prison, and a fortress.

Ralph, Lord Cromwell, began building the house after 1440, and it was still unfinished when he died in 1455. A man of great wealth, he was Lord Treasurer of England, Warden of Sherwood Forest and Constable of Nottingham Castle, and he built the castle and church at Tattershall in Lincolnshire where he is buried. The house was completed by the 2nd Earl of Shrewsbury, and became a favourite seat of the family. George Talbot, 6th earl and husband of Bess of Hardwick, had the custody of Mary, Queen of Scots, for nearly 16 years, and she was here in his care for a short time in 1569.

She was at Wingfield again in 1584 with 250 people as guards and retinue, and it was during this time that the plot was hatched which cost Anthony Babington his head and brought Mary to Fotheringhay. Young, handsome, and an ardent Roman Catholic, Babington had been a page to the queen in his boyhood, and had remained devoted to her cause. He lived only a few miles away at Dethick, and it is said that, in spite of the strong guard placed over the queen, he managed to visit her frequently disguised as a gipsy. News of the conspiracy leaked out through Walsingham's spies, and in 1586 Babington was executed in London.

The house was garrisoned for Parliament in the Civil War, and after falling for the king was taken by Sir John Gell and dismantled. After the Restoration, Immanuel Halton, an astronomer, settled here, turning the Banqueting Hall into a two-storeyed dwelling and allowing the rest to fall into decay. A century later his descendants used the ruins as a quarry for stone to build the house at the foot of the hill, as plain as the other was lovely. But in spite of the ravages of time and its use as a farmhouse, there is still enough dignity left in walls and gables, entrances and windows, to suggest Wingfield's ancient splendour, and what we see today is being preserved for all time.

The ruins spread over a space of a quarter of a mile round, 416 feet long and over 250 feet wide; the inner court devoted to state and dwelling apartments, the outer to accommodation for guards and retainers. The Banqueting Hall has still a projecting bay window of rare beauty, with exquisite tracery. The fine porch leading to the hall has a lovely archway and a small traceried window of most beautiful design; and there is a charming round window in a gable of the state apartments. Under the hall is a remarkable room with four entrances and a vaulted roof enriched with great bosses carved with tracery, resting on arches which spring from the walls and from pillars between two aisles.

In the range of buildings between the two courts is the great inner gateway with a turret on each side. The buildings east of the gateway have been modernised into a farmhouse, and at the other end stands the watch tower, 72 feet high, with steps leading to the summit. Often must the Queen of Scots have climbed these steps to reach her rooms, desolate now with only fragments of the walls which held her captive. Little is left of the outer court, but near the entrance gateway stands the grand old barn, 70 feet long and with massive timbers.

The church stands on its own, in pleasant meadows, with the Amber flowing by one side of the churchyard. Made new in Georgian days, it has still its 13th century nave arcades, and the 15th century tower with worn heraldry on the buttresses. From the 14th century comes the priest's doorway with its crude little figure. The bowl of the font is Norman, oldest possession of all. In the churchyard, below the east window, is a coffin stone with a battered 13th century knight in a tunic of mail, his hands folded on his breast. Long after his day the coaches came lumbering along the Roman road through Oakerthorpe, and there is still a platform at the 18th century Peacock Inn where 16 coaches changed horses every day.

Spondon. The pressure of the Artificial Silk Age has left it still a few quiet ways about its church, with 18th century brick houses, and still we may take a walk in the beautiful Locko Park with its stately Hall, partly of the 18th century, but greatly enlarged about 1850, its great lake and its charming waterfall sheltered by yews.

Here was born in 1830 Sir Drury Drury-Lowe, the famous soldier who served in the Crimea and the Mutiny and made a moonlight charge at Tel-el-Kebir. He received the surrender of Arabi Pasha, who gave up his sword to him. But nearly two centuries before him Henry Gilbert, builder of the chapel at Locko Hall, conferred a greater distinction on this place, for he brought home as his bride one of the three daughters of Sir John Barnard who had been brought up by his second wife Elizabeth, only child of Shakespeare's daughter Susanna. Elizabeth Gilbert died when only 35, and her stepmother was among the mourners when they laid her in Spondon church. Her monument, showing her with pretty ringlets, is on a wall of the north aisle, and it is thrilling to reflect as we look on it that once another pair of eyes were fixed on it, the eyes that fondly looked on Shakespeare himself—those of his own "dear sweet little Bess".

The church, with a spire as a landmark on the hilltop, was made new after a fire in 1340, except for part of the tower. Fine and lofty, with wide arches and great windows, it is a splendid example of a 14th century church, though with porches and aisle made new last century, and with three sedilia, a fine little piscina, and a stone lectern, of a kind seen only in Derbyshire, built into the chancel wall. In the churchyard is a noble elm and something centuries older, a massive fragment of a Saxon cross with knotwork carving.

Stanley. It has a great house, a glorious cedar, a cottage with a fine thatched roof, and a tiny church with a double bell-turret.

All that is left of the chapel that was here 800 years ago is a Norman priest's doorway now in the wall. A small lancet and some buttresses are from the 13th century building. The chancel was rebuilt about 1875, but its 14th century east window was in the old chapel. The font was made 600 years ago, and the pulpit 300. In the floor by the pulpit is a brass tablet to Sir John Bentley of Breadsall, who was buried here 20 years before the Civil War was to darken the countryside.

Stanton-by-Bridge. With a fine view from its windblown hilltop of the great Trent meadows, this tiny place is at the south end of the long, winding causeway which stretches over the low-lying land and links it up with Swarkestone.

Full of years is its little towerless church, for the "long-and-short" stones at the south-east angle are Saxon, and the plain round chancel arch, a tiny west window with a deep splay, and much masonry of the west wall are Norman work. Within the porch is a lofty Norman doorway with chevron moulding, the little cross over it being perhaps the consecration cross of the Norman church.

From the 14th century come a beautiful window and the priest's doorway in the chancel, the nave arcade, a piscina, and the font. There is a fine old oak chest, and in the west wall of the aisle are fragments of 12th century coffin-stones, one very rare with a little animal carved by the cross.

Under an arch in the aisle lies the stone figure of a priest who rebuilt the old church; he is perhaps Geoffrey or Thomas de Stanton, who followed each other here in the 14th century. On the wall of the chancel is a stone with the engraved portraits of William Sacheverell of 1558 and his wife; above it is another stone with their seven sons and seven daughters, a fine effect as of a bridge of kneeling children. Another alabaster stone against the chancel wall has the engraved figures of Katherine Francis and her husband Richard, in Tudor dress; six boys and seven girls are hidden.

Stanton-by-Dale. This charming village looks one way to the wide industrial Erewash Valley beyond the glowing fires of the great ironworks, and the other way across the Trent Valley towards Charnwood Forest. Its roads are up and down, with low stone walls crowned by hedges, and near the green where three ways meet is a village cross with a weatherworn shaft and a later head.

A row of almshouses over 250 years old, trim with lawn and flowerbeds, brings us to the church with flowers creeping up its walls, in a churchyard like a garden. Lighted by fine windows of deep splay, it has grown from a Norman church made new about 1300. There are fragments of Norman cross-stones built in the outside walls, and a tympanum of much interest over the south doorway. In the middle of it is a raised round boss believed to be a crude sundial, perhaps of Norman days, with lines cut out to mark the hours of 6, 9, noon, 3, and 6; round the boss has been cut at a later time a circle containing a cross outline in relief. The stone-roofed vaulted porch which shelters it is of the 14th century, and another old lancet is in the aisle. The nave arcade and the font are of about 1300, and the tower is of the 15th century.

We read here of Edward Holt who was 100 when he died in 1606, and among the Pilkingtons of the old manor house who are buried here is Matthew, the last of them, who died in 1765. He is remembered because he made an index of the Bible, a remarkable piece of work which appears to have passed into oblivion.

Stanton-in-Peak. Climbing the steep hillside to Stanton Moor, this model village of gabled stone houses has a wonderful view of the lovely valley where the waters of the Lathkill and Bradford dales run together to meet the Wye, fresh from its journey by Haddon Hall. Youlgreave's splendid tower and Bakewell's elegant spire are landmarks in the scene.

Its 17th century Old Hall is a farmhouse, with some remains of the ancient home of the Foljambes and the Plumptons. Stanton Hall, in a park with a herd of rare black fallow deer, was built in the 17th and 18th centuries by the Thornhills whose memorials are in the church they built in 1839.

Stanton Moor, a high plateau over a square mile in extent, is full of interest for its ancient remains of monoliths, burial mounds, and stone circles. Skeletons and calcined bones of the Bronze Age have been found in some of the mounds. Among the detached stones about the moor are the Andle Stone (a massive block 15 feet high), the tower-like Cork Stone, and the curiously shaped rock called the Cat Stone almost on the edge of the precipice overlooking Darley Dale. The small stone circle called the Nine Ladies, about 33 yards round, and with all but one stone upright, has its pointer (the King Stone) 100 feet away.

Not far from this circle is a square tower, a landmark from far around, with the inscription "Earl Grey 1832", a tribute to the man who carried the great Reform Bill through Parliament. Thankful the country should be for its share (through the National Trust) of this moor, for Stanton Moor Edge, a natural terrace 900 feet above sea-level, about a mile long and comprising 28 acres, is ours for all time; ours with all the glory of its magnificent views of encircling heather-clad moorlands, and of the winding Derwent valley from Chatsworth to Oaker Hill in Darley Dale.

Staveley. Famous for its coal and iron, and more recently for its chemical works, it has pleasant ways by the church, with the ancient cross restored in the churchyard, and the 17th century Hall close by. The Hall is now the rectory, much changed since the Freche-villes put their arms over the door and enriched its walls with splendid woodwork. They were here six centuries ago. Margaret founded the school at Netherthorpe in 1572, Peter built the little stone almshouses at Woodthorpe over 350 years ago. John lies in the great sarcophagus in their 17th century chapel in the church, the last of his line and its first and only peer. He garrisoned his house for the king and fought for it till the Parliamentarians took it. He filled a window in this chapel with glowing heraldry surrounded by cherubim and wreaths of flowers, the glass made by Henry Gyles of York in 1676. John's daughter, Christian, lies in the chapel, sculptured in white marble, a baby in her arms.

In the chancel is an earlier Peter Frecheville in brass, without his head, but still with sword and dagger, wearing armour adorned with his arms, and all his ancient dignities upon his tomb. He set it up here at the death of his wife in 1482, and when he died after 21 years more they put another brass on the chancel wall, where he kneels, facing his wife, with their eight boys and seven girls kneeling in fur-trimmed gowns. His oldest boy John died a few years after him, and he is buried between the chancel and the chapel.

The church, with something of nearly all our great building cen-turies, was made a large and stately place by 19th century restora-tion, which gave it a new porch, and a north aisle with an arcade dividing it from the nave. Its oldest possessions are fragments of engraved coffin stones. A long tapering stone with a cross and a sword, and a font with a man's head on it, bearded and crowned, are both of the 12th century.

The base of the tower with lancet windows and corner turret is of the 13th century, its 15th century upper storey was crowned with battlements and pinnacles 200 years later. The sides of the south doorway and their foliage capitals are also of the 13th century. From the 14th century come the south arcade, the two low arches and the pillar between the chancel and chapel, and the row of small clerestory windows above them, unusual in a chancel. A recess of this time, built into the new aisle, has crude little carvings on the pinnacle at each side, of a man with folded hands, one with a crown, and one in long gown. In the east window is an odd old man with his hurdy-gurdy, almost all that is left of a fine array of ancient glass. One of two roundels, he is a comical figure with his toes turned in as he turns the handle of his funny little organ.

The Rodes of Woodthorpe Hall were neighbours of the Freche-villes, and at the old Hall, of which fragments remain in the farm-house on the site, was born about 1530 Francis Rodes, a judge of Elizabeth's day; and there he died after beginning the building of the fine Barlborough Hall which became the home of his son, Sir John.

Steetley. Though scarcely a hamlet, it shelters one of Derby-shire's gems, hiding this with a veil of trees even from the narrow way that brings us to it. This Norman chapel of the mid 12th century is a temple of loveliness all alone except for a farm. It has only a nave and a chancel ending in an apse, 52 feet from east to west and less than 16 feet wide, but it is so rich in ancient beauty that it has been said to be "a gem of early architectural art, one of the most complete and beautiful specimens of Norman work on a small scale to be found in this country".

Not 100 years ago it was a roofless ruin, except for the roof of the apse, and cattle wandered in and out of the walls through doors made for them. In 1875, for the first time for 300 years, people met within the ruins to make plans for their restoration, and five years later it stood in its glory as we see it. The south doorway has been given two new pillars and mouldings. The old part of the arch has three orders of moulding, one plain on plain pillars, the second

ornamented with beak-heads and resting on pillars with deep-cut
nterlacing foliage, the third with chevrons, on pillars carved with
medallions.

In the interior, the glorious chancel arch has triple mouldings, the
first a scalloped border with a cone in every scallop, the second embattled, the third with chevrons. The capitals on which they rest
are quaintly carved; one with a double-bodied lion, another with
St George coming to the rescue of a prostrate figure under a winged
dragon whose long sweeping tail curls round the next capital and
branches into foliage.

The chancel arch is a fine frame for the charming apse, which
opens with an arch resting on capitals handsomely carved. The
four ribs of its vaulted roof are carved with beak-heads, with a holy
lamb in a medallion which they meet. The capitals of the pilasters
on which the ribs rest are elaborately carved with interesting designs, one showing the temptation of Adam and Eve with the serpent
curled round a tree loaded with fruit, and another with two doves.
It is lighted by three exquisite lancets filled with glass like patchwork in the colours of the rainbow. Below these windows on the
outside wall the apse is encircled by a beautiful string course carved
with foliage, and it has a cornice under the roof, continued round
the rest of the chapel, resting on brackets with grotesque heads and
other devices.

Stoney Middleton. It is a little singular and well named, for its
houses rise tier on tier on ledges of rock and under steep hanging
cliffs. But it has little crooked ways and sudden turns with unex-
pected bits of charm, one of them by the church in company with
gay gardens and a little brook on its way to the grounds of the old
Hall, the home of the Denmans.

Here lived Joseph Denman of Bakewell and his famous nephew
Thomas, one of the greatest reformers of the Victorian era. He was
an upright judge, a man of high moral character, and one of the
most persistent advocates of the abolition of slavery. His sons rose
to high positions, one an admiral, another a judge. The son Thomas
who succeeded him lived to be 89, and was long remembered in the
village for his queer hobby of keeping black pigs and taking them in
his carriage as presents to his friends.

An unusual building is the church, the nave and chancel being an octagon added to the low 15th century tower in 1759. There is a tribute to Urban Smith, for 53 years vicar last century, and when John Riddlesden retired after 47 years, he was only the second vicar in a century of continuous service. Near the church are the old stone buildings of the baths fitted up by Lord Denman on the site of what may have been a Roman bath, no longer used though the warm spring still flows.

At the doorstep of the village is Middleton Dale, to take us on to Tideswell, a gorge of wild scenery with great limestone quarries and stupendous rocks stretching in weird shapes along a mile of the road, with Lover's Leap and the mighty Castle Rock's projecting towers, a cave which kept for many years the secret of the murder of an old Scots pedlar, and the charming rocky glen which goes uphill to Eyam.

Stoney Middleton holds a Well-Dressing Festival (like that at Tissington), starting on the first Saturday in August.

Sudbury. It is in the rich meadows of the Dove, with old brick houses, an old inn, and a wayside green. Through it two busy highways join for a spell so that none shall miss its beauty, bringing us to the open lawns of the stately Hall, begun about 1613 by Mary Vernon, left unfinished at her death, and completed by George Vernon after 1670. A house of warm red walls, it is full of treasure within and beauty without; on one side it looks to fair parklands; on the other to gardens and lake, river valley, and Needwood Forest.

Since the 17th century it has been the home of the Vernons to whom the Montgomerys brought the lands in the time of Henry VIII. The Montgomerys held the manor soon after the Conquest, though they lived at Cubley a few miles away. In the church close by, set in a garden of wonderful yews, lie two of the Montgomery ladies of 700 years ago, carved in stone with wimples under their chins and hearts in their hands. They would come through the doorway which lets us in, for it is Norman and was incorporated in the church which was rebuilt about 1300, the time of the nave arcades, the chancel arch, and part of the tower, the upper stages of which are of the 15th century. Among the old carved stones built

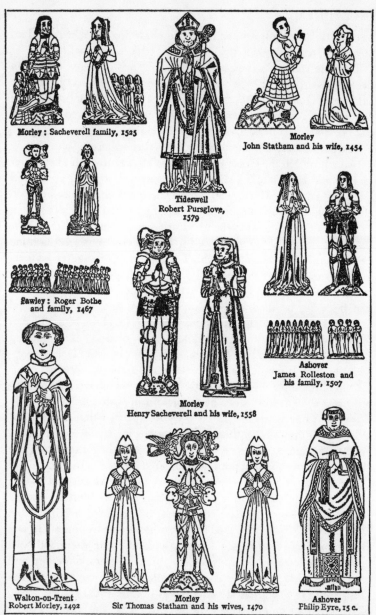

Morley: Sacheverell family, 1525

Tideswell
Robert Pursglove,
1579

Morley
John Statham and his wife, 1454

Sawley: Roger Bothe
and family, 1467

Morley
Henry Sacheverell and his wife, 1558

Ashover
James Rolleston and
his family, 1507

Walton-on-Trent
Robert Morley, 1492

Morley
Sir Thomas Statham and his wives, 1470

Ashover
Philip Eyre, 15 c.

DERBYSHIRE PEOPLE ENGRAVED ON BRASS

into the outside walls are the head of a charming floral cross and an angel with a shield which belonged to a 14th century roof.

The fine roofs of nave and chancel, one with winged angels on the stone corbels and one with fine bosses, are modern, as are the oak chancel screen, the sanctuary panelling, the stalls and the prayer desks. Among fragments of old woodwork fixed on to an oak chest are two from a 14th century chancel screen.

The church is rich in memorials of the Vernons, from John of 1600 to two who fell in the Great War, one the 8th baron. John lies under an heraldic arch, looking stately in his armour, wearing a ruff and a beard. His wife Mary, who lies on the tomb below, her head on an embroidered cushion, began the Hall and died in 1622.

There is a monument to the first Lord Vernon and his three wives, the third being the daughter of Sir Simon Harcourt who became Lord Chancellor. An epitaph to Lord Vernon's daughter Catherine, who died when she was 25, was written by the poet laureate William Whitehead. There are sculptured heads of the fourth lord and his wife; he died at Gibraltar in 1835, and they are buried under an old yew in the churchyard, a spot he chose himself. Another monument is to the fifth lord who died in 1866, having changed his surname to Warren. His son Augustus Henry is remembered by a window and the elaborate alabaster reredos.

One of the most illustrious of the Vernons who have known Sudbury was the 5th lord, born at Stapleford in Nottinghamshire. He was only a boy when he visited Italy for the first time, but he fell in love with the country the moment he saw it. He afterwards lived much in Florence, where he was a great student of Italian literature and history. As a young man he dedicated himself to the worship of Dante, and from that time until his death in 1866 he devoted a great part of his time and fortune to the making of a wonderful book.

With the help of his Italian friends, he prepared a remarkable work about Dante, published in three handsome volumes. It was an astonishing piece of scholarship, and has been described as a book which, for utility of purpose, comprehensiveness of design, and costly execution, has never been equalled in any country. It has illustrations by the greatest Italian artists of the 19th century, many of whom were employed for twenty years. It has Dante's great poem, *The Inferno*, together with a sort of encyclopedia of the poet's

Italy and a masterly account of his life. The third volume, with 112 engravings and a marvellous collection of facts about 14th century Italy, was not finished till after Vernon's death at Sudbury in 1866. In acknowledgment of his great tribute to their national poet, the Italians made him a member of one of their most distinguished orders of merit, but he was even then slowly dying in his lovely house here. Only a few copies of the book were issued and they are highly valuable today.

Sutton-on-the-Hill. The village is in a hollow but the church is on a hill, a fine landmark with a wide view of the countryside from Needwood Forest to the limestone uplands of the Peak. A lychgate and little avenue of fine yews brings us to the church made partly new, though a merry boy with his tongue out greets us, as we come inside, as he greeted people in the days of Agincourt and long before. He is of the 14th century, as old as the tower (whose spire was rebuilt in 1831), the priest's doorway and two windows in the chancel, and the nave arcade, which he adorns in company with a king and a bishop among other heads.

Fine corbel heads form the dripstones of the windows; the excellent 19th century reredos, desk, and pulpit were made from the alabaster of the old chancel floor. During the rebuilding, 13 silver coins of Henry III's day were found in the north aisle. On the sanctuary floor are alabaster stones to Sir Samuel Sleigh and his three wives: Judith of 1634, Margaret of 1647, and Elizabeth who died in 1738 aged 82, there being 104 years between the deaths of the first and last. The great marble monument in the chancel was erected in 1679 by Sir Samuel, the last of his line, to Judith. Unusual and very striking in its suggestion of death, it has a simple black coffin under an elaborate canopy with coloured arms. An inscription to Gervase Sleigh, Sir Samuel's brother, was added later to the monument. It is recorded in the registers that 200 years ago a man was paid five shillings a year for driving dogs out of this church with a whip, and for waking sleepers with a white wand.

The village, half a mile below the church, is a group of farms and houses with the Sutton Brook meandering through the fields. Here a charming bit of road sets off to Etwall, between stately trees and a fine house embattled like a castle.

Sutton Scarsdale. So secluded is it that we forget it lies so near the great industrial world, though a glimpse of the great house can now be obtained from the new M1 motorway. All about it are memories of lost splendour, for it looks out to the ruins of Bolsover Castle and to a gabled house which has taken the place of Oldcotes (one of the three great houses in Derbyshire built by Bess of Hardwick), while its own house is in pitiable ruins.

One of the grandest buildings in Derbyshire, Sutton Scarsdale Hall was built in 1724 by Francis Smith of Warwick in a classical style for an Earl of Scarsdale, on the site of the old home of his family, the Leakes, who came here in the 15th century. One of them was made earl for his services to Charles I. He fortified the old house and defended it against 500 men, and when he was eventually taken prisoner he was set free on giving his word to submit to Parliament at Derby. He broke his word, and the house was plundered and his estates seized. It is said that after the death of the king the earl went about in sackcloth, had a grave dug, and lay down in it every Friday. He was buried in the church in 1655.

Long before him there came here John Foljambe, a boy who died in 1499, and is here engraved on a floor stone, wearing armour with his head on a helmet. Here also is a bust of Samuel Pierrepont, in a long curled wig; he died in 1707, the last of a branch of the family which acquired the famous house of Oldcotes by marriage with Bess of Hardwick's daughter.

A few fragments of old glass are all that are left of that which a 15th century John Leake put in the church. The nave, the fine porch, and most of the chancel are of the 14th century; the tower is of the 15th century. An old bracket in the aisle is carved with a human face, and in a roof are bosses with the arms of the Leakes and the families they married with.

Swadlincote. It lies in the extreme south of Derbyshire, well south of the Trent, in that great wedge of the county which extends between Leicestershire and Staffordshire and has more the characteristics of those counties than of the rest of Derbyshire.

Though an urban district, Swadlincote is really made up of a group of industrial villages which includes Woodville, Newhall, and Church Gresley (which has a separate entry in this book). Its thriving industries, based on the coal and clay on which it stands, include large potteries (founded in 1795), as well as brickworks, and stoneware pipe manufactures.

Swarkestone. It has meadows in spring like the Field of the Cloth of Gold, and over them winds in and out, up and down, the famous Swarkestone Bridge. Five graceful arches, rebuilt in 1796, span the Trent; the rest runs as a raised causeway with low parapets full of nooks and curves, while arches here and there, ending in a fine group near Stanton-by-Bridge, accommodate the floods. The long causeway has 15 ancient arches, and some of the stones are believed to be from the 13th or 14th centuries.

We like to think of it as one of the favourite haunts of Derbyshire's great philosopher Herbert Spencer, who walked here one morning when the world was asleep and began fishing by moonlight. Here Sir John Gell routed the Royalists in 1643 when they were trying to hold this key to the north, and here the advance guard of the Young Pretender's disconsolate army turned back for their retreat in December, 1745.

Here is a fine farmhouse built in the 17th century from the ruins of the home of one of Queen Elizabeth's judges, Sir Richard Harpur; a barn, a gateway, and a stone building with a domed tower at each end are still left. The building, attributed to John Smithson, the architect of Bolsover Castle, was perhaps a banqueting hall or a summer house; it stands in a walled enclosure which may have been a playing-ground, and is sometimes called the Bowling Green.

It is the monuments of the Harpurs that are the pride of the little church, made new in 1876 except for its 15th century tower and the chapel with the Harpur tombs. Built into the east wall are fragments of the Norman chancel arch, and Swarkestone children are still baptized at the Norman font.

Sir Richard Harpur lies with his wife Jane, the last of the Finderns, on a fine alabaster tomb, he in his judge's gown with a cap, ruff, and collar, and three rings on his fingers. Charming is Jane, in a gown with many bows and a girdle from which hangs a pomander box, with a French cap and ruffs, a chain three times round her neck, and a posy of primroses in her bodice. At her feet kneel two children. On the brass inscription round the tomb are tiny figures of dogs, boars, stags, dragons, lions, an elephant, a fish, a mermaid looking at her reflection in a mirror, and a dog running off with a duck. Above the tomb hangs a helmet with the Harpur crest of a boar.

It is an engaging monument, and yet for richness of detail it is surpassed by the fine tomb of their eldest son, Sir John, who lies in armour with a fine head of hair and portrayed in detail true to life; there is even a wart on his cheek. His wife has a French cap on her hair, a ruff, and a long gown opened to show her embroidered petticoat. Their 12 children kneel at prayer on the front of the tomb, the sons in cloaks and kilts, the girls in tight bodices with wide sleeves, little caps, and ruffs.

Under a canopy in the chancel is a raised tomb with the engraved portraits of a 15th century knight and his lady; he is John Rolleston and is in armour. On the front of the tomb are two angels and two fine groups of seven sons and seven daughters. Their family were the great people here before the Finderns and the Harpurs.

Taddington. Charming is its approach from Ashford-in-the-Water, with changing scene of woodland glen and towering hill as the road winds with the Wye as far as Brushfield Hough and Fin Cop, the splendid guardians of the lovely Monsal Dale. From here the road climbs through Taddington Dale by dense plantation, and leaves with surprising suddenness the beauty of the valley for the bare uplands. Here the old grey village, one of the highest in England, over 1000 feet above sea-level, looks north across Millers Dale towards the heights of Kinder Scout. On Taddington Moor, higher up to the south, is the Five Wells chambered barrow of the New Stone Age, where many remains of skeletons have been found.

In the churchyard is a stone whose wonder is its age, the slender tapering shaft of a cross six feet high. Three of its four sides have chevrons and patterns like the designs on Celtic jewellery and pottery. Some say it was set up in the 7th century, either by Celtic missionaries from Lindisfarne or to mark the place where the first Bishop of the Mercians preached in the wilds of Derbyshire, but others think it may be Norman work.

The church, with its fine south doorway, is mainly of the 14th century, though the tower and spire are rebuilt from the old materials. Projecting from the north wall of the chancel is one of the stone reading desks peculiar to Derbyshire. The eight-sided font is of the 15th century, bowl and base tapering in unusual fashion towards the middle. On the west wall of the nave are remains of an old wall painting, but older still, perhaps the oldest thing in the church, is a floorstone with a Latin cross.

Set in a marble stone once part of a tomb are the brass portraits of Richard Blackwall and his wife, with groups of five daughters and six sons. Richard wears civilian dress of the early 16th century; his wife is in the dress of a widow. The Blackwalls held their lands at Blackwell, close by from the 12th century, but lost them through loyalty to Charles I. A floor-stone in the south aisle has the engraved portrait of a man thought to be Wendesley Blackwall.

Taxal. In its churchyard is a sundial on an old pedestal, and a magnificent yew 20 feet round. The small church was made new in 1825, but the tower is over 400 years old and has two merry stone men. In the nave is an inscription to Michael Heathcote, Gentleman of the Pantry and Yeoman of the Mouth to George II. The Royal Oak is an attractive 17th century inn with glorious views of the Goyt Valley, Eccles Pike in the east, and, away to the north, Cracken Edge, Chinley Churn, and the rugged heights of Kinder Scout.

Thorpe. It brings us to hidden glories at the foot of the hills all round, but it also has joys of its own. Its limestone houses and gardens are scattered at random on the hillside above the meeting of the rivers, the Manifold at the end of a romantic journey over and under ground, the Dove fresh from Derbyshire's most beautiful dale. The finest possession of the village is a little church which looks all tower and was built in the mid 12th century.

The sturdy tower is as the Normans left it (except for an altered doorway), with a plain round arch to the nave. Its battlemented parapet rests on a Norman corbel table with heads worn by eight centuries of weather. The bowl of the font is Norman, round and slightly tapering; it is said that it was used last century as a trough for cattle, and that bands of animals covering its surface crumbled out of doors.

The chancel arch is of the 13th century, but the chancel was made

P

new last century, when a window of 15th century masonry was set in its south wall. All that is left of the 17th century tomb of John Milward projects a foot from the chancel wall. In front are tiny figures of two daughters in gowns with embroidered bodices, and two sons in cloaks and wide-topped boots. Both the boys were soldiers, one a colonel for Charles I.

For 200 years and more the church has had two magnificent sycamores to keep it company in the churchyard; for all its long life it has looked out to the hills that call us to beauty beyond. Fine guardian heights are the great mass of Bunster rising 1000 feet, on the Staffordshire side of the river, and Thorpe Cloud like a cone on the Derbyshire side, holding in the stepping-stones between them the key to Dovedale which we come here to find. The road brings us to the dale from the Staffordshire side of the stream, where the Izaak Walton Hotel reminds us of one who loved these haunts.

Tibshelf. Its miners look up, on their way to the pit, to an embattled tower which has been standing here 500 years, its narrow archway reaching nearly to the roof of the nave.

The church itself, a spacious place with fine arcades, was rebuilt in 1888 by Bodley and Garner. The ornate marble font, its white bowl on coloured pillars, is of 1867. In a niche on the porch stands a weathered figure of John the Baptist, the patron saint.

Ticknall. With houses of warm-red brick or of red limestone from Breedon, it wanders pleasantly, a charming picture as we come to it from Stanton-by-Bridge or Melbourne. A stone bridge like a horseshoe crosses the road to the lovely park of Calke Abbey. Farther on is the village lock-up, with a pointed roof and a studded door, and by the church gate are the almshouses built in the 18th century, when the old cross was taken into the churchyard.

As if to lend the dignity of age to a church built only in 1842, two fragments of the previous church remain in the churchyard. They are a corner of the tower and the east end of the old north aisle, with a window of intersecting mullions, all standing since the 14th century, when the church was rebuilt. Of such great strength were its walls, especially in the tower, that they had to be blown up with gunpowder when the new church took its place.

The present church, an example of the Gothic Revival style, by

H. I. Stevens of Derby, has an embattled tower and lofty spire, fine windows filling the place with light, a hammerbeam roof, and lofty arcades. One window is in memory of a vicar whose 47 years here ended in 1885, and the sturdy oak seats are in memory of the vicar who followed him for half as long. Some of the old monuments have found shelter here. In a 14th century recess lies the stone figure of a civilian in a close-fitting hood, holding a heart in his hands and with his feet on a dog. He was perhaps William Frances, rebuilder of the old church 600 years ago. Against the north wall is a marble stone with the engraved portrait of John Frances in 14th century armour with a pointed helmet and a sword. Part of their old home is in the vicarage.

Tideswell. Between the limestone uplands and a chain of lovely dales is this small town, over 900 feet above sea-level, with many old houses and a great treasure house known as the Cathedral of the Peak. Like Tissington, it is one of about 15 Derbyshire places that hold a Well-Dressing Festival, in this case always in June.

A stately place without and within, built in the shape of a cross, the church has seen six centuries come and go, its builders disturbed by the Black Death. The handsome west tower was the last part to be built, rising 100 feet with a rather overpowering array of pinnacles like turrets with slender spires. It has a vaulted roof below the ringing chamber, and a lofty arch to the nave. The porch with a lovely modern door has an upper room panelled with 17th century pews, and on each side of the south doorway is a consecration cross.

The crowning glory of the interior, where lovely windows and the unusual 14th century clerestory shed light on the mellowed charm of lofty arcades, on monuments of brass and stone and on splendid woodwork old and new, is the glorious chancel, a gallery of light and beauty. It has handsome sedilia and a charming piscina, and a fine embattled stone reredos screen with two great canopied niches containing sculptured figures in lime-wood, added in 1950. The lower part of the oak chancel screen is almost as old as the church; the upper part was added in 1883.

One of the transepts has 10 stalls with misericords nearly 600 years old, originally the chancel stalls. Two tables have ancient tracery, some of it from Lichfield Cathedral. There is a fine old north door, and much mediaeval timber in the roofs. The splendid array of modern woodwork, much of it by a local craftsman, Advent Hunstone, is very effective. There are screens in both transepts and across the tower arch, and two oak porches. The choir stalls of 1880 have ends carved to suggest Confirmation, Ordination, Baptism, Prayer, and Praise. The beautiful chancel stalls have St Chad with a model of Lichfield Cathedral at his feet, John the Baptist, angels, a bishop, birds feeding their young, and a charming Annunciation. Two have misericords, one with a queen holding a heart in her hands, the other with a human between grotesques.

In the church lie the Foljambes, the great folk of Tideswell from soon after the Norman Conquest until the 15th century. Sir John, a 14th century benefactor, has his brass portrait on the chancel floor, showing him in chain armour; the brass is a copy of the old one, given by Cecil Foljambe last century. He also gave the glass of 1887 in the east window in memory of his ancestors buried here, and of his wife whose white figure we see at the top. In the floor of the south aisle are brass portraits of a 16th century ancestor of Bulwer Lytton, Sir Robert Lytton, and his wife, both in gowns trimmed with ermine. The Lyttons lived at Litton near by before they went to Knebworth.

In the chancel floor is a splendid brass portrait of Robert Pursglove, Tideswell's Vicar of Bray, who was born here, and was buried in the church in 1579. He wears the pre-Reformation robes of a bishop and has his pastoral staff; at the corners of the stone are symbols of the Evangelists, and there is a rhyming inscription. A brass plate tells of his life and how he founded Tideswell Grammar School, the old building still standing near the church, though a school no longer. In 1539 he received a pension for surrendering the Priory of Guisborough; he was a Protestant bishop under Edward VI and a strong Papist under Mary. In 1559 he lost all his appointments for refusing to take the oath of supremacy to Elizabeth, and lived his last 20 years at Tideswell, where his bequests still help the poor. The original brass plate was used for the tomb of a later vicar, and is now on the wall.

On the chancel wall is a brass in memory of Samuel Andrew, a much-loved vicar who ended the 19th century here and was buried near the church. We see his engraved portrait as he lies at rest after restoring the dignity of this church during his service here since 1864. The work was carried on by Canon Fletcher who followed him, and who gave the glass of the west window in 1907.

In the north transept are the oldest monuments in the church: two stone figures of women, one perhaps of the 13th century, the other of the 14th, both unknown. On a table tomb in the other transept lie the alabaster figures of a knight and his lady, much battered through being moved about, but with 14th century armour and dress of splendid workmanship. Though an inscription says they are the De Bowers, it is thought they may belong to the Foljambes or Lyttons. To the 15th century belongs the fine alabaster tomb in the middle of the chancel in memory of Sir Sampson Meverill, lord of the manor and Knight Constable of England, one of a family here for 400 years. His long story is told in a brass ribbon, of his birth, his christening, and marriage—how he was page to a lord and lady, served the Archbishop of Canterbury, and how he fought in 11 great battles against Joan of Arc. How he ended we all may see by peeping through the open tracery of the tomb, where he lies a corpse, carved in stone and in a winding sheet. On the top of the tomb are brass symbols of the Evangelists, heraldic shields, and the Trinity, God seated with a crucifix and a dove.

The 14th century font has come back to its own after some adventures, for it had been used for mixing paint and had been long in the churchyard. A small coffin-stone in the south transept is perhaps of the 12th century. Part of a stone altar with two consecration crosses, some tiles with heraldic devices and symbols, and a fine bell now pensioned on a transept floor, are all from mediaeval England. A 17th century sanctus bell hangs in a gabled turret, and on a transept gable is a 14th century crucifix. An old Dutch almsdish of brass shows the temptation of Adam and Eve.

Here in the churchyard are two graves of much interest to travellers. One is of Samuel Slack who died in 1822, once a chorister here and summoned to sing before the king. His great bass voice brought him celebrity but did not help him to lose his uncouth ways. The other is near the picturesque sundial on the ancient steps of the churchyard cross, and is of the carpenter-poet who was much loved hereabouts. Prosperity made him owner of the Cressbrook Mills at a time when the hard life of the pauper apprentices at Litton Mills brought many of them to untimely graves in this churchyard, and he was greatly beloved for his humanity.

He was William Newton, the Minstrel of the Peak. Born near Abney in 1750, he received his title from Anna Seward, the Lichfield poet, who herself was born at Eyam. Son of a carpenter, he had little education, but improved himself by reading the books he found at houses where he worked.

He was able to buy a few volumes, chiefly poetry, to read in the little home he set up with a village girl as his wife. He was a born poet of limited range, with a parson-poet, Peter Cunningham, as his patron, and Anna Seward as his ideal. To her he addressed flattering verses, and so began a correspondence and friendship ended only by her death.

Very little of his work survives, and that little we owe to the woman whose vanity was flattered by the tuneful praise of her rustic adorer. Eventually she was able to help him materially by assisting a fund which gave him the opportunity to acquire a minor partnership in a cotton-spinning firm. This became famous as the Cressbrook Mill, where, thanks to the poet, the horrible factory system, with apprentice children housed at the mill, was conducted on model lines, the children well fed and clothed, with proper rest and instruction, and with methods resembling those of a good modern boarding school as part of the day's work.

In course of time Newton, happy with his little workpeople and their elders, his own family at home, and the delights of excursions into verse, attained prosperity and some reputation as a poet. He died in 1830, a fortnight before his wife. One of his sons gave Tideswell a water supply at his own cost.

Tissington. If ever roads lead to sheer delight they are surely the roads to Tissington, where a splendid lime avenue, half a mile long, brings us to charming stone houses in gay gardens, gathered in haphazard array about a spacious road with wayside lawns, a fine old Hall of the early 17th century and a church as old again keeping them company.

All roads seem to lead to Tissington when Ascension Day dawns, bringing people from many miles away to see the celebration of a

custom as full of beauty as of years, a floral festival going back perhaps originally to pagan days. It is the great day of Tissington's
wells.

They have never failed in time of need. They are said to have
kept the village from the desolation of the Black Death when all
around were stricken, and again from a terrible drought in the 17th
century, giving abundantly to help the neighbouring countryside.
All this Tissington remembers; it is the first of the Derbyshire villages
to hold its Well-Dressing Festival, and here the custom is kept up
with all its ancient beauty.

The five wells are by the road which makes a circular tour of the
village; the Hands Well, taking its name from folk who once lived
near; the Hall Well under a stone canopy opposite the great house;
the Town Well; the pretty Yew Tree Well; and the Coffin Well
named from the shape of its trough, in a cottage garden. For
several days the folk who love their wells are gathering moss and
flowers and leaves in hedge and field and garden. The night before
the festival starts they spend in pressing them into beds of damp
clay, in designs worthy of a painter and his brush, in living pictures
of Bible scenes, the story of a parable, the picture of a church, often
with a text to speak its message in this charming fragrant way. On
the morning of Ascension Day, when the wells are literally flowering, a service is held in the church, followed by a visit to every well
in turn, a hymn or psalm being sung at each, a prayer offered, and
the water blessed by the vicar.

For more than 400 years the Fitzherberts, one of the oldest of
Derbyshire's families, have lived here. They built the charming
house which lends its beauty to the road and is full of treasures
within; its fine gates are said to be the work of the famous Derby
craftsman, Robert Bakewell.

In the church across the way are many of their memorials, one of
them an elaborate monument reaching nearly to the roof, and unhappily cutting off one side of the chancel arch which has been the
glory of the church for 800 years. The tomb itself is charming in
spite of its intrusiveness, divided into two compartments with kneeling figures of two generations of Fitzherberts, Sir Francis and his
wife and Sir John and his wife who followed them. The older figures
are in the Tudor fashion and convention; the younger are from

Stuart days, and delightful in their grace and freedom, John's wife being daintily dressed, with white sleeves that are very neat. There is an inscription to Alleyne Fitzherbert, Baron St Helens, the famous diplomat who spent his life making treaties.

Enlarged last century with a north aisle and arcade in the Norman style, the church is high above the road in company with majestic sycamores and fine old yews, and remains of the old churchyard cross. The sturdy tower is mainly Norman, but its buttresses are of the 13th century. The modern porch shelters a Norman doorway, over which is a tympanum with a quaint little figure on each side, its arms akimbo. Other Norman remains are the fine font, its round bowl with crude carvings of strange figures, among them a man, a wolf, a bird, and a bear.

A notable possession of the church is its great two-decker oak pulpit, with a canopy; and the oddest of its treasures is a clarionet used to lead the singing in olden days, now kept in the porch. On the chancel wall is one of the rare modern brasses, on which is a portrait of Wilhelmina Fitzherbert, of 1862, kneeling at a cross.

In Alleyne Fitzherbert, Thomas Gray's "Little Fitzherbert", who was born here in 1753, lived again the qualities of his father and mother, described in immortal language by Dr Johnson. Arriving at Cambridge University at 17, he charmed the solitary Gray into visiting him.

For a generation his wits were devoted to promoting the peace of Europe, beginning with his appointment, at 24, as British Minister at Brussels. At 30 he acted as peacemaker between France and Spain and the Netherlands, then going as ambassador to Russia, where he accompanied Catherine the Great on her tour of the Crimea, fortified by her gift of a fur pelisse, cap, and muff, for a great sledge journey, with huge bonfires burning along the route and horses waiting in relays.

He passed to Ireland as Chief Secretary and to The Hague as ambassador; effected a treaty as a substitute for war between England and Spain; and, while in St Petersburg again for the accession of the new Emperor, concluded a treaty with Russia, following this with equally happy results in Denmark and Sweden. Trusted by all parties, and a first favourite at Court, he retired on a pension to nurse his broken health and cultivate his friendships.

Trusley. The winding lanes bring us to a small place of unsuspected interest, a charming brick church little more than 250 years old; just a nave and a chancel and a bell-tower with a bell perhaps 500 years old, but with beautiful modern glass and fine old craftsmanship, and with something found in only a few other places.

The sanctuary is panelled in oak, the very fine three-decker pulpit towers with its canopy over the box-pews, and an oak eagle sits above the 18th century alabaster font. The four richly coloured windows are memorials to the Cokes and range in date from 1881 to 1951.

Among other memorials to the Coke family, who have known this village since the 15th century, is a stone to Sir Francis Coke of 1639. One of his brothers, Sir John, born here in 1563, was for many years Secretary of State to Charles I and his brother George became Bishop of Hereford. On an alabaster stone is the engraved portrait of Bridget Curzon, who died in the days of Charles I. Her sister was the wife of Sir Francis. The old home of the Cokes has gone, but the massive stone doorway of the church and the fine old lead water-pipes embossed with their arms and crest, are said to have come from it. Trusley's great house now is a fine brick gabled building not far from the church.

A pathetic relic is kept in a glass case in the vestry, one of the paper garlands of white flowers that were sometimes carried in the funeral procession of a betrothed maiden. It was the mark of a pure life cut off in youth, and it was usual for a handkerchief or a glove of the girl to be left with the garland, perhaps with her name and age. Such garlands can be seen at Ashford-in-the-Water and Matlock.

Turnditch. It lines a lovely hilly road, rich in wonderful views over the charming valley of the Ecclesbourne. The simple wayside church, with fine limes in the churchyard, and one bell in the turret, has little left that is old except some 13th century buttresses and a 15th century font. Some of the stones in the north wall are three feet long, unusual in so small a place. The west window is in memory of Francis Lambert Cursham, who was vicar here for 40 years and died in 1914.

Twyford. The Trent flows in calm reaches only a few yards from this tiny hamlet. The outside of the church, with a low tower and spire, and a nave rebuilt in brick and stone in the 18th century, is charming; even more charming is the interior, with a fine low Norman arch enriched with chevrons, framing the 14th century chancel, and a sharply pointed arch opening to the 13th century base of the tower, which has three lancet windows. The rest of the tower and spire are of the 14th century.

Here are buried some of the Harpurs, descendants of Sir Richard Harpur of Swarkestone, one of Elizabeth I's judges. George Harpur of 1672 and his wife have a monument with arms and crest. Some of the Bristowes lie in the church, but Simon Bristowe, who fought in the Civil War and lived almost to see his century out, dying in 1699, is buried in the churchyard.

Upper Booth. It is on a lane which leads to a pathway over Kinder Scout, a charming upland dell looking out to wild moorland heights which rise like waves of the sea, a Peakland hamlet in a haunt where the only sound is the music of mountain streams and the call of the moorland birds. Near a tiny one-arch bridge the wild Crowden Brook comes rushing to meet the little River Noe which descends from the lofty height of Kinder Low, both hastening to the fair Vale of Edale ahead.

Upper Langwith. Its little aisleless church has seen many changes since its birth over 800 years ago. The chancel lost a Norman arch last century but kept a 13th century lancet, and the 14th century east window is in the nave. The fine porch, with its stone roof and crocketed pinnacles, is 14th century, and so perhaps are the beams of the roof, with kingposts and struts carved with tracery. There is an old piscina and a medallion of old glass in a window.

Out in the sun and rain, under the east window, is an old coffin, and a coffin-stone with an engraved cross, a chalice, and an open book fading away. Until 1878 the stone was in a chancel recess, and may have marked the grave of the builder of the chancel 700 years ago.

Upper Padley. It is a charming spot where the Burbage Brook comes down a lovely dell with many cascades, hurrying from its moorland home to join the Derwent before it runs under Grindleford Bridge.

The little chapel has had its adventures, for it was long an old grey ruin used as a cowshed and a barn. Once it was part of one of the most important houses in the county, and through all its desecration it has kept a quaint piscina and four carved hammerbeams in an upper room which was the private chapel of the great Hall. Romance and tragedy these old stones have known. The romance brought the Eyres to Padley when Joan Padley married Robert Eyre, home from Agincourt, where he took prisoner a marshal of France; the portraits of Robert and Joan are in brass in Hathersage Church. The tragedy came to them through their faith, and it was because of it that Padley has become a place of pilgrimage.

The Eyres were staunch to the faith of their fathers, and so were the family of Sir Thomas Fitzherbert, who came to Padley when he married Anne Eyre. He was the eldest son of the famous judge, Sir Anthony Fitzherbert, and suffered terribly for his faith, dying in the Tower in 1591 after 20 years in prison. While Sir Thomas was in prison, two priests were found hiding in the chimney buttresses of his house. They were Nicholas Garlick and Robert Ludlam, and were imprisoned at Derby, where they came upon a third priest named Richard Sympson who had escaped death by recanting his faith. They persuaded him to be true, and the three were hanged in Derby in 1588. It is said that Sympson, who was first to approach the scaffold, seemed to lose courage, whereupon Nicholas Garlick went before him, kissed the ladder, and ascended it with ecstasy to encourage him. John Fitzherbert, who had been looking after his captive brother's estates, was condemned for harbouring the priests, and died in prison even as did Sir Thomas.

It is still a chapel in a farmyard, and in the east gable are the pigeon holes, now blocked. Simple within, it has a gallery at the east end with a flight of steps each side. The altar-stone, after lying in a cowshed for centuries, was set up again when the chapel was restored for Roman Catholic services in 1933. A window shows the arrest of the two priests at Padley Chapel on July 12, 1588, and scenes of their martyrdom on St Mary's Bridge in Derby.

On the north side of the chapel are the ruins of Padley Hall, shaded by three sycamores growing from the bank. Remains of walling show the outline of the rooms, and there are a few steps of a spiral stairway. The kitchen has a great open fireplace and hearthstones black with the smoke of centuries ago. On one side of it is the crude kitchen sink cut out of a solid block of stone, and on the other a tiny oven as it was when the bread was taken out of it long ago.

Walton-on-Trent. It seems that nothing could have disturbed the peace of the lovely Trent meadows since Edward II came riding hotly by, chasing the Earl of Lancaster and the rebellious barons. Church and rectory, flowered cottages and gardens, are all by the wayside, and looking over the river to Staffordshire is the 18th century Hall, built by one of the few men who grew rich out of the South Sea Bubble.

The church is among lovely trees, with a shapely yew near the chancel and a fine lychgate in memory of a 19th century rector who did much to restore the glory of his church. Its few remains of the one begun by the terrible Hugh Lupus, Earl of Chester, a friend of the Conqueror, are a doorway to the vestry, a little moulding on the outside wall near the porch and a fragment of a window over a pillar of the arcade. The pillars themselves, supporting pointed arches, date from the late 12th century.

The chancel takes up the story with four lancet windows, the sedilia, and the piscina, all of the 13th century. The chantry, charming with its windows, piscina, and three stone seats with clustered pillars, was built in the next century by Richard Waleys, who was rector for 59 years. He lies under a low arch in the wall, battered and headless but still in his robes, his stone figure having been cut when it was used under the floor as a resting-place for the joists.

The fine tower was built about 1400, and has a fine arch under which stands the old font. In the floor of the chancel is the excellent brass portrait of Robert Morley, a 15th century rector, in his robes, blessing the chalice and wafer. It is a rare brass, said to be one of only two known of a priest in this attitude. Over the priest's doorway is the bust of Thomas Bearcroft, a 17th century rector.

More modern days have given of their best in the woodwork here, in the screenwork of the chantry, the traceried chancel screen of 1896, with fan-vaulting supporting a gallery of 18 small figures in niches, in the stalls and reredos, the pulpit with carved panels, and the lectern with two doors opening to show three carved Bible scenes, an engaging piece of work. In glass of 1904 in the north aisle is a vivid gallery of illustrious familiar folk—Wilberforce the friend of slaves, the great talker Dr Johnson, Izaak Walton the fisherman, and Sir Thomas More who loved honour more than life.

West Hallam. It stands on a hilltop with little to suggest the great coalfield close by. A lovely avenue of limes bring us to the church set between the great house and the rectory. The rector's garden has a glorious lime tree, and looks out over the valley to a great windmill with its arms still working as they have done since the 18th century.

The massive tower was made new in the 15th century, and legend says that four stunted trees once grew at the top of it. Some of the stone inside the church is beautiful, its amber colour veined with purple tints. The north arcade is probably of the 13th century and the south a century younger, as are the chancel arch and the great font. Old glass in the chancel shows two small figures under canopies and tiny birds in quaint attitudes; and high up in a clerestory window is a figure of James the Less, holding a book and the club with which he was martyred. One window is in memory of John Scargill, who founded the village school.

On a stone on the chancel floor is engraved the portrait of Thomas Powtrell in armour of the 15th century. On a magnificent canopied tomb lie Walter Powtrell of 1598 and his wife Cassandra, both with ruffs; he wears richly decorated armour, and with her gown of many folds the lady wears a French cap with falling lappet, and round the tomb are seven children.

It was the Powtrells who rebuilt the tower. Their old home is gone, and the last of their men died in the year of London's Great Fire. Their home was a famous hiding-place for fugitive priests, and Father Campion is said to have often sheltered there. One priest taken at the house was condemned to death, but was banished after long imprisonment. Another sentenced for celebrating mass at West Hallam Hall died during his imprisonment.

Weston-on-Trent. It seems all twists and turns and little bridges, with cottages in gardens ablaze with colour, and the church in lovely isolation, looking down on meadows where the Trent flows under overhanging woods of the Leicestershire border.

Well worth finding are two gems of river scenery. A lane leads down to the bank of the Trent opposite King's Mill, at the foot of Donington Park, where the swiftly-flowing river plays hide and seek among the islands, making music as it falls over a great weir, and running today as it ran when the Civil War came and some of the soldiers were laid in Weston's churchyard. From the high banks not far from the church is a glorious view of valleys and hills, with Breedon church silhouetted against the sky.

The church is lovely without and within. The sturdy tower and slender spire are chiefly of the 14th century with younger battlements. Fine battlements adorn the continuous roof of nave and aisles, and the 17th century brick-and-timber porch shelters a doorway of about 1300. A fine effect is given to the nave by the exceptional height of the 14th century arcades, their pointed arches resting on tall graceful pillars which show up the warm tints of amber and purple in the stonework. The chancel is mainly of the 13th century, though the east lancets are new. Many of the windows, a charming feature of the church, are of the 14th century. The east window of the north aisle is especially fine, and the east window of the south aisle, unique in Derbyshire, has geometric tracery. There is a fine piscina in this aisle, and one in the chancel with the sedilia. There is a good Jacobean pulpit, a font of 1661, and a plain oak chest of 1662.

A delightful group of painted figures in the south aisle shows a rector's family of Shakespeare's day, Richard Sale and his wife Dorothy, their six girls and two boys, and two babies in bonnets tucked up in their cots. Proud and quaint they look, the father with his beard, the mother with almost a flush of life on her face, all but the infants in ruffs and kneeling at prayer.

Whaley Bridge. An old-established cotton-weaving town with clothing and engineering works, it has characteristic old grey houses and inns, and is beautifully situated at the entrance to the wooded upper valley of the Goyt, with its charming reservoirs. Standing guard around the town are the heights of Chinley Churn, Eccles Pike, and Black Hill, lofty outliers of the Peak District.

In the hillside to the east of the valley, below the sharp cone of Eccles Pike, is a strange depression known as the Roosdyche, about half a mile long. Thought by some to have been a Roman chariot way, it is perhaps a natural feature of the land, and if so, is a remarkable phenomenon.

The hilly twisting road to Buxton climbs above the Goyt reservoirs and passes near White Hall, a house among the trees, now used by the county council as a centre for open-country pursuits. Higher up is the broad moorland of Combs Moss, with its gritstone edges and its wide view extending from Axe Edge to Kinder Scout.

Whatstandwell. It has little but its place in the world, but that would be hard to beat. This tiny village lies in a land where nature is at her loveliest in vale and hill, where the earth is strewn with exquisite flowers that only wait for their season. It nestles in the valley of the Derwent, one of the loveliest valleys in England.

Whatstandwell lifts its eyes to the hills, the highest crowned with a War Memorial tower whose beacon shines over Nottinghamshire and Derbyshire. It looks up across the valley to Shining Cliff, a beautiful name for a glorious hill, whose woods are rosy in June with masses of rhododendrons. Its steep lanes climb to grey-stone cottages and farmhouses.

Florence Nightingale knew and loved the village, and it cherishes the memory of the goodwill message she sent to the school and the practical interest she took in the social activities of the community. Once it belonged to Darley Abbey, but since the monks lost their lands the road over the bridge has seen many changes, and the inn near at hand has seen varied fortune. A bustling place the inn and forge must have been when the Champion coach drew up at its doors before labouring up the steep hill, horses all a-lather. But the 19th century road along the valley has relieved the village of the heaviest modern traffic and left it a quiet backwater.

The cottages, built from the stone of its own quarries, merge quietly into the background of wood and cliff; and the gardens and hillsides are gay with flowers in summer. To know Whatstandwell properly you must love it the whole year round, but no season will fail you: the loveliness of the English countryside is always here.

Wheston. In this small village on the limestone uplands, where the old Hall has long been a farmhouse, is one of the most interesting mediaeval survivals in the Peak, a wayside cross which marked the road to the Forest some 600 years ago. It stands in a walled-round group of trees, its tapering shaft on a great stone and a flight of three steps; its head showing the Crucifixion on one side and the Madonna and Child on the other.

At the Tideswell end of the village is the stone of another wayside cross, known in the neighbourhood as the Wishing Well.

Whittington. It has an exciting story, and a surprising little gallery of famous people. The story is of a band of men who planned to overthrow a king and change a dynasty. It was in 1688, when Protestant England was incensed with the policy of James II and his attempt to change their faith, that William Cavendish, fourth Earl of Devonshire, the Earl of Danby and a few honest friends met on Whittington Moor to arrange to bring William of Orange to the throne. They were driven by a storm, it is said, to find shelter at the village inn, then a busy calling place for packhorse and travellers on the old road from Chesterfield to Sheffield.

A new Whittington has grown up since then, as a suburb of Chesterfield, but the inn still stands in the quiet haunts of the old village. Restored and altered, and the Plotting Parlour gone, it is now a little stone house with a thatched roof, and has a tablet on the wall telling the story of how it came to be called Revolution House.

The gallery of famous people is in the church which was rebuilt in 1896, on the site of the older one where Dr Pegge, the famous antiquary, was buried in 1796, after preaching here for 45 years. It is at a quiet end of the village in a churchyard clothed with trees, and the portrait gallery is in the windows. Here are the great Earl of Shaftesbury, the great Liberal leader Mr Gladstone, heroic Hugh Latimer, and Thomas Cranmer, and Bishop Ridding of Southwell, John Milton, and John Wesley. The east window, a War Memorial, has figures of St Margaret and the Black Prince, with King Alfred and St George.

Whitwell. Its great possession, adding to the glory of its view of Sherwood Forest and its own wood of over 400 acres, is a proud church high above the busy village. It is a fine monument to the builders of eight centuries ago, and to the local quarries from which they took their stone; and is much as the Normans left it, except for the transepts which gave it the shape of a cross in the 14th century, the chancel then rebuilt, and the aisle windows added in the 15th century.

It is an impressive sight, with its round arches and round pillars. The Normans built the tower, except for the 15th century belfry, and set in the little window above the west doorway with chevron moulding round the arch; they set up the great chancel arch and the nave arcades, made the massive bowl of the font, put in the west window of the south aisle, and carved the corbel table of quaint heads along the side walls of the nave; and they did what Norman builders rarely did in building the clerestory windows.

From the 14th century come the fine windows of the chancel, the beautiful sedilia with lofty canopies and pinnacles, two piscinae, and three old brackets on which are set modern figures of St Lawrence with a gridiron, the Madonna, and Paulinus. A 14th century recess in a transept is adorned with tracery under a hood with a woman's head in square headdress and a man's head with a beard and curls. Here and in the chancel are fragments of old glass.

On a pretentious alabaster monument lies Sir Roger Manners, son of Dorothy Vernon of Haddon Hall; he lived at the gabled manor house near the church. Better than his monument is the simple memorial in brass with a little heraldry and a quaint inscription to Tobie Waterhouse who died a few years after Shakespeare, aged four years, but even then "full of grace and truth".

Willington. Now dominated by a huge power-station, it looks from the banks of the Trent across the meadows to Repton's slender spire, and we remember that in Repton church porch is kept the old toll board of Willington's five-arch bridge, one of the last main road bridges in the country to be freed from tolls. The church, with a tower of 1824, when much other alteration was done, has three 13th century lancets in the chancel and a Norman doorway with a crudely carved tympanum.

Wilne. A quiet lane brings us to this hamlet in the meadows, near where a toll-bridge crosses the Derwent and the river says goodbye to its last mill-wheel. Farther downsteam it joins the Trent, the most important of all that river's tributaries. It has come from the barren peaty moors through a run of sustained beauty such as no other English river has, for most of its 60 miles are attractive to

Q

various tastes in scenery. It is surprising to find a church in so remote a spot, but winter floods have driven the folk to higher ground at Draycott.

Yet more surprising is to find in this small church so great a treasure, one of the oldest fonts in the land, fashioned from a solid stone by a Saxon craftsman. Said to be part of a round column or the shaft of a cross, and hollowed out to make a font in early days, its beauty was unimpaired until fire swept through the church in 1917. It has been restored, and a great part of its old surface, carved with interlaced knotwork and other intricate designs, can still be seen.

The old church was made new in the 14th century, but the lower stage of the sturdy tower is of the 13th century; its upper part is a century younger, with battlements later still. The fine stone-roofed porch is of the 15th century. Bright with deep-splayed windows of the three mediaeval centuries, the church has its old piscina and two brackets close by, and an Elizabethan chest six feet long, elaborately carved. A great treasure is a silver chalice older than the Armada. When the church was restored after the fire, the pillars and arches of the arcade were rebuilt, and the nave re-roofed in oak. Plain oak screens took the place of the simple 15th century chancel screen and of an elaborate Jacobean screen which opened to the Willoughby chapel.

For centuries the church was the burial place of the Willoughbys of Risley. An alabaster floorstone in the chancel has the engraved figures of Hugh Willoughby of 1491 and his wife; on a wall are tiny brass portraits of Hugh of 1514, his wife and their five children. Old glazed tiles are in the floor of the Willoughby chapel which was built in 1622, and the brilliant glass of its windows, brought from abroad and restored after the Civil War, shows the Nativity, the Crucifixion, and the Ascension. Here, on a tomb with a canopy like a triumphal arch, lies Sir John Willoughby of 1605 in armour, with his wife in a gown with finely pleated bodice, their four children kneeling on the front of the tomb. It was their son Henry who erected this monument, and to his daughter Ann is a monument with two weeping children.

Wingerworth. Into its wide view come the crooked spire of Chesterfield and Bolsover Castle on its high ridge.

In a churchyard with fine yews and the base of an old cross, stands the embattled church, whose old glory is in what is left of early Norman days. A Norman doorway is sheltered by a 19th century porch, the Norman arcade of three arches is on massive round pillars, the archway into the chancel, under nine feet high and seven feet wide, is one of the smallest the Normans left in the county, and theirs also is the great font bowl, which was found on a farm. Rare paintings of the late 12th century were uncovered on the chancel arch in 1959. The fine tower, with two gargoyles on every side below the parapet, is of about 1500; two of the gargoyles are an ape and a muzzled bear.

A remarkable relic, unique in Derbyshire, is the timber structure on which the rood was raised about 1500. It projects two feet from the wall above the chancel arch and is 15 feet long. The upper edge is embattled, while the front is panelled and adorned with leaves. The rood stairway to the platform is still here. In the chancel lies the stone figure of a priest with a narrow fringe of hair round his head and a chalice below his folded hands; he is of about 1200, and is perhaps the priest who was here when the chancel was first built. In a north aisle window are fragments of old glass patterned with crowns and diamonds. A fine new nave, to the designs of Bernard Widdows, was added in 1964 on the north side of the old nave, and is filled with glowing modern glass.

Winster. It hides itself from the world among lovely hills, finding a wealth of interest all around in rocks and dales, and lovely views at the end of delightful walks to the limestone uplands and to the moors with ancient graves.

Old houses of the 17th and 18th centuries tell of its prosperity in lead-mining days, and though its market is no more, the picturesque old market-house still has its stone walls nearly 300 years old, though the round arches are filled in. Close by is the old Hall, with pilasters and a balustraded parapet, its stone brought by packhorse from Darley Dale 300 years ago. It was for a time the home of Llewellyn Jewitt, the 19th century antiquary to whom Derbyshire owes much and who is buried in Winster churchyard.

A skilled engraver, Jewitt illustrated a famous book on architecture, but he is best remembered for his scholarly book on ceramic art and his *History of Derbyshire*, a great work he did not live to finish. He was an expert in many subjects, founding and editing an antiquarian magazine, and writing handbooks on coins and tokens, burial mounds, historic buildings, and the stories and ballads of the county he served so well. He was a practical man, too, helping in the scheme to bring pure water to Winster.

The church was made new last century except for its 18th century tower. An arcade of pointed arches on very slender clustered pillars divides the nave, so that the chancel has two arches between it and the nave. Nothing is left of the Norman chapel, unless it is the fine font with cable moulding round the top, vigorously carved with quaint and varied figures. It has two children with an open book, a lily in a pot, the Madonna and Child, and a figure in a font which is said to represent the dedication of the church to John the Baptist.

Wirksworth. As we come to it over the hill from Whatstandwell, this old-fashioned stone-built market-town is a delightful picture. It stands at the head of the green Ecclesbourne Valley, surrounded by hills, some richly wooded, some riddled with old lead workings and scarred with huge quarries echoing with the thunder of falling stone. Its lead mines were worked by the Romans and the Saxons, and it was long the centre of the lead-mining district known as the King's Field, in which any man might search for lead, subject to the quaint laws and customs which governed the mining. At the time of Domesday Book, Wirksworth was prosperous both with the mining and smelting of lead, the ore being smelted in the tops of the hills around. The name of these hilltop hearths still survives in Bolehill a mile away, where Olive Schreiner lived for a time while writing her *Story of an African Farm*. It is said that the lead coffin sent to Croyland in 714 for the body of St Guthlac was from the Wirksworth mines.

In the 19th century Moot Hall, with the miner's arms (his scales, pick, and trough) carved on the front, is kept the massive brass dish once used as the standard measure for lead ore. Said to be the only old one left in the country, it has an inscription telling us that it was made in the time of Henry VIII. The Great Barmote Court, established for the settling of mining disputes, is still held here twice a year, in April and October. In a lead mine a mile away, known as the Dream Cave, was found the almost perfect skeleton of a rhino-ceros.

Wirksworth still keeps up at Whitsuntide the old custom of Well Dressing, as at Tissington, though there are no longer any wells and the water is all piped into the town. In the marketplace is an old inn with an 18th century front and a fine Elizabethan chimneypiece carved with fleur-de-lys, unicorns, and Tudor rose. Close by are the almshouses and the grammar school, both looking on to the ancient church, where the man who founded them in the 16th century is buried.

A treasure-house indeed is Wirksworth church of 1000 years, for it has a marvellous Saxon relic which would be considered a treasure even in the British Museum. Set in a north wall, it is a sculptured coffin-stone, slightly coped and measuring five feet long and about three wide. It was found near the altar, upside down over a vault in which lay a perfect skeleton. It has about 40 figures, all part of scenes in the Life of Christ, carved above and below a ridge along the middle of the stone. Along the top we see Christ washing the feet of the disciples; next comes a sturdy cross with a lamb in the middle, figures thought to be Peter and John above the arms, and below the arms two extraordinary birds. Then is what appears to be a quaint entombment scene, with Joseph of Arimathea and a companion carrying Christ on a bier, under which lies a figure perhaps sym-bolising Victory over Death; while above the bier are six head-like birds in a nest, representing the guard placed over the body. Three standing figures, one with a palm branch, complete the top row. The lower half has one of the most captivating Saxon processions. It begins with a representation of the Nativity; in the middle is an enchanting sculpture of angels with stately wings bearing Our Lord, who holds a cross, to Heaven; and this impressive piece of pageantry ends with a row of figures returning to Jerusalem after the Ascension.

An expert has said of this stone that it differs from all other work of early Christian times, and has the distinction of Roman work with traces of Byzantine influence, and that perhaps some craftsman from a Roman town in Britain, or some sculptor who had seen the mar-vellous work of the Romans on similar stones, here tried to introduce the spirit of something he had seen. It is older than Alfred, coming from the beginning of the 8th century or even earlier.

The interesting church, built in the shape of a cross, has a 13th and 14th century central tower supporting a modern spirelet. The charm of the interior is in the arches on clustered pillars; they are everywhere, for the nave, the chancel, and the transepts all have aisles. The nave arcades are of the 14th century, and eight fine lancets are a century older.

As if all this richness were not enough, the walls inside have been made captivating with many carved stones of Norman days: fragments of moulding, heads of shafts, quaint faces and figures peep out unexpectedly here and there. Among a medley in one transept is a pair of legs without a man, in the other is a tiny impish figure above a head with a bearded face. Another stone has on it a crowned king and a lady almost covered by a heart; she has one hand raised and a book in the other, and they look like a king and his queen of hearts. A fragment in the north aisle seems to show the Temptation of Eve, with a serpent coiling round a tree with an apple in its mouth, and Adam and Eve on each side rather worse for wear. Another stone has the quaint figure of a miner with his pick and bucket. A large coffin-stone in the wall of a transept was engraved, perhaps by a Norman craftsman, with a fine cross, a sword, and a horn.

The church has a large font with a bowl 700 years old, and another font dated 1662. A reredos in a chancel aisle is a mass of carving, coloured and gilded, by the peasants of Oberammergau.

There is a fine group of 16th century monuments. Set in the wall of a chancel aisle are brass portraits from two different monuments of the Blackwalls. There are 29 portraits in all, with 18 tiny figures of children above Thomas Blackwall and his wife, and seven children with another Blackwall and his wife below, the groups of children having found the wrong parents when being moved. An alabaster tomb has the engraved portraits of Ralph Gell and his two wives, and figures of their children round the tomb. Ralph, who was one of the Gells of Hopton and died in 1564, is bareheaded and has a long gown, and his wives have round caps and dresses tied with bows. Ralph's son Anthony is a fine figure as he lies on a handsome tomb, with moustache and beard, and a long gown with ruffs at his neck and wrists. He died in 1583 after founding the almshouses and grammar school. There is an inscription to Sir John

238

Gell, the Parliamentarian general and a monument to Sir Philip, the last baronet, who died in 1719. Anthony Lowe of Alderwasley lies on a fine Renaissance tomb in his armour and helmet, a skull under his feet; he was servant to four monarchs and died in 1555.

Many come to Wirksworth, not for the glory of the church or the beauty of the monuments, but for an unmarked grave in the church-yard where there is still the massive shaft of the old cross ten feet high. In this grave lies Elizabeth Evans, George Eliot's aunt. Wirksworth claims that the town was the Snowfield of *Adam Bede* and that Elizabeth Evans was Dinah Morris, Seth Bede's bride.

Those who love this great story will find much interest here, for there is still standing the Methodist chapel where Elizabeth Evans would preach sometimes. In it is this inscription:

To the memory of Elizabeth Evans, known to the world as Dinah Bede, who during many years proclaimed alike in the open air, the sanctuary, and from house to house, the love of Christ; also of Samuel Evans her husband, a faithful local preacher.

The cottage where they lived for several years still stands a mile south of Wirksworth on the Derby road, opposite the Tape Mills where Samuel was manager.

Sir John Gell, who was born at Hopton in 1593, married at 16, left Oxford without a degree, and from an early age took a prominent part in county affairs. As Sheriff he had to collect Ship Money from Sir John Stanhope of Elvaston, who refused payment and died defying authority, whereupon Gell, now a widower, married the victim's widow.

The pictures of Gell and his conduct during the Civil War are drawn by Royalist pencils, and represent him as a man without ardent convictions leading men whose delight was plunder; but both sides plundered, and the fact stands out that Gell was a military commander of skill and courage, who successfully led his forces to the overthrow of every fortified place he attacked, kept his own county loyal to Parliament, and helped to preserve Nottingham and Leicester as Commonwealth strongholds.

After the Royalist rout at Naseby he was accused of neglecting to destroy the fugitives, but nothing came of the charge. Five years later, however, he was held guilty of plotting against the State, and committed to the Tower of London, with forfeiture of his estate. He was released after two years, and was given a full pardon.

Wormhill. It lies in an upland hollow, sheltered from the coldest winds by a line of limestone hills. At one end of the village is a lovely grove of trees, and at the other a gabled stone Hall, an Elizabethan house restored by the Bagshawes who have known this village for centuries. A well is dressed in the village (as at Tissington) on the Saturday before the Summer Bank Holiday.

The prettiest corner is by the church, where the churchyard and vicarage grounds make a charming garden of lawn and evergreens. Its oldest stones are in the tower, which has looked down on the churchyard for 700 years, except that it has changed its gabled cap for a copy of the steep-pitched cap of the famous Saxon tower at Sompting in Sussex. In the tower hangs one of the smallest peal of bells that rings out anywhere in our countryside. There are six of them, and they were made as models at the famous Loughborough foundry. The churchyard has the foundations and a little of the shaft of the old cross, and an extraordinary tomb with five huge layers of stone like a pyramid.

In the interior is the little oak sanctuary with panelled walls, an altar table carved with wheat and vines, and a reredos with a scene of the Last Supper. In keeping with this fine work are the pulpit, litany desk, and choir-stalls. The Ascension in the east window and some of this woodwork is in memory of the Bagshawes, and it was here that William Bagshawe, the Apostle of the Peak, preached his first sermon. Of his family no doubt, was that Nicholas Bagshawe of whom we read in the registers here that in 1674 he was clerk and schoolmaster "for want of a better".

By the wayside is a drinking fountain in memory of a man born about a mile away to the north, another poor son of Derbyshire, who could hardly read or write yet became the greatest canal engineer of his time. He was James Brindley, born in 1716 in a cottage at Tunstead, where is still an ash known as Brindley's tree. It began to grow through the floor of the cottage where he was born, and grew until the cottage was sacrificed because of it. Tunstead has but a farm or two, yet is rich in the memory of this famous man of whom Carlyle said:

"The English are a dumb people. They can do great acts but not describe them. Whatsoever of strength the man had in him will be written in the work he does. The rugged Brindley has little to say for himself. He has chained seas together. His ships do visibly float over valleys, and invisibly through the hearts of mountains; the Mersey and the Thames, the Humber and the Severn, have shaken hands."

Down a precipitous path lovely with trees and flowers is the beautiful gorge of Chee Dale, where the River Wye is at its loveliest in a wild romantic setting, making a horseshoe curve between the mighty Chee Tor and the crescent rocks of the other side before reaching the more open Millers Dale. And in Great Rocks Dale, a mile to the west of Tunstead, is the largest limestone quarry in Europe, with the main Derby–Manchester railway almost running through it.

Yeaveley. This quiet village, set in rich pastoral country, is thought to have been the birthplace of Henry Yevele, the great architect of the naves of Westminster Abbey and Canterbury Cathedral, who died in 1400. The little brick church, built in 1840, has an east window filled with War Memorial glass, but its oldest possession is a mediaeval font of unusual shape set on a modern base.

A mile away to the west, in a delightful green hollow reached by a field path, are the scanty ruins of a chapel of the crusading knights of the time of Richard I, a fragment of wall with two graceful lancets, a curious font with a tapering bowl, and a coffin-stone on the grass carved with a cross and a sword. In company with the ruins is another relic of the past, the fine red-brick house called Stydd Hall. With embattled stone parapet and embattled stone windows, it comes in part from Tudor England, but is now a farmhouse.

Youlgreave. It lies between the enchanting valleys of the Lathkill and Bradford Rivers, whose waters meet at winsome little Alport a mile away. It looks out to the ancient stone circles of Stanton Moor and Harthill Moor, while only three miles away is Arbor Low, the most important stone circle in the county.

Long before we reach the village we see the splendid 15th century tower of one of the most delightful of all the Peakland churches, lovely in its structure and rich in the treasures it shelters. Of its

Norman days there still remain the fine south arcade of three bays with round arches, sturdy pillars, and capitals, and the pillars and capitals of the north arcade supporting the graceful arches of the 14th century.

The chancel was rebuilt 500 years ago, keeping its 14th century arch. The east window has been filled with lovely glass by Burne-Jones and William Morris, in radiant colouring of orange and yellow, silver and gold; it shows Christ blessing the world, with figures of the four Evangelists. The fine oak roofs are of the 15th century. The north aisle has the remains of an ancient piscina and one in the south aisle has its drain carved into a face.

The tower is one of the chief joys of the church, and one of the finest in the county. Square and massive, with stepped buttresses rising to the embattled summit, it has eight crocketed pinnacles, eight belfry windows, a window over the fine west doorway, and a charming little stair turret with battlements of its own.

The splendid font is very unusual and has a round bowl resting on a central column and four small shafts. From the side of the bowl projects a tiny bowl seeming to be held by the mouth of a strange animal carved upside down on the font itself. Its purpose is not certain, but it was probably a stoup for consecrated oil. Coming from the late 12th century, it belonged originally to Elton church, and was thrown into the churchyard there last century. It was taken into the vicarage garden at Youlgreave, and later brought into the church, the squire of Elton having a reproduction of it made for his village when it pleaded in vain for its return.

In the north wall of the nave is a stone 17 inches long with the figure of a draped woman, her hair parted in the middle, and holding a staff. It is not known what the stone represents, but it is probably much older than the 15th century wall in which it is set.

In the middle of the chancel is one of the loveliest things in the church, an exquisite alabaster tomb only three and a half feet long. Its sides and ends are adorned with angels holding painted shields, and on it lies a knight in plate armour. Round his neck is a collar of suns and roses (the emblems of the Yorkists); his feet are on a lion and his head is on a helmet with a cock's head, the crest of the great Derbyshire family of Cokayne. He is Thomas Cokayne, who lived at Harthill Hall close by and died in 1488. The oldest monument is a cross-legged knight in the chancel, wearing a quilted coat of over 700 years ago; he has a sword and holds a heart in his hands. He is perhaps Sir John Rossington, who married with the Cokaynes and the Gilberts.

The Gilberts were at Youlgreave for 10 generations, and the north aisle has a remarkable monument with 21 little figures sculptured in alabaster, showing Robert Gilbert (who died in 1492) with seven sons, his wife with ten daughters, and the Madonna with the Christ Child among them all. Near the monument is the small brass portrait of Fridswide Gilbert in a long-sleeved gown with the skirt open to show the patterned petticoat. She was a descendant of Robert and died in Shakespeare's day. Another monument in the north aisle shows Roger Rowe of Alport and his wife kneeling at a desk, he bareheaded and in armour, she with a curious tall hat, and below them tiny figures of six boys and two girls, all wearing Tudor ruffs. Roger died in 1613.

It is pleasant to find the modern woodwork well worthy of its place in this light and spacious church; the pulpit is finely carved, a fine tower screen has panels of linenfold, and the benches have linenfold ends. A War Memorial window has a medley of stained-glass fragments which were once in Ypres Cathedral and other Belgian churches destroyed in the Great War.

Youlgreave keeps the steps and massive base-stone of its old cross, and its registers and parish books are the most complete and interesting local records in Derbyshire. The village (like Tissington) maintains the old custom of Well Dressing, and five wells are decorated in a festival which takes place every year in June.

APPENDIX

Places of interest open to the public

(* Indicates National Trust Property)
(† Indicates Department of the Environment Property)

Bakewell: Chatsworth, open all day April–Oct., Weds., Thurs., Fris. and Bank Hols.; weekends 2–5.30.

Haddon Hall: open daily April to September (except Suns. and Mons.), also Easter, Spring and Late Summer Hol. Suns. and Mons. (Suns. 2–6).

Old House and Museum: Easter Sat. to Sept. 30 daily 2.30–5.

Barlborough: Barlborough Hall, open Aug. 5–26, Weds. and Sats. afternoons only.

Bolsover: †Bolsover Castle, open all the year daily.

Castleton: †Peveril Castle, open all the year daily.

Chesterfield: *Hardwick Hall, open April–Oct. Weds., Thurs., Sats., Suns. and Bank Hol. Mons. 2–6; May, June and July Weds. and Thurs. from 12.

Derby: Kedleston Hall, Easter Sun. and Mon., then Suns. from April 30 to Sept. 24 and Bank Hol. Mons. 2–6.

Duffield: *Duffield Castle foundations, open all the year daily.

Foremark: Foremark Hall, open June 12–July 1, daily 2.30–4.30.

Matlock: *Winster Market House, Easter Sat. to end Sept., Weds., Sats., Suns. and Bank Hol. Mons. 2–6.

Melbourne: Melbourne Hall, open Easter and Spring Bank Hol. weekends; Suns. and Weds. only May–June; open daily (except Mons. and Fris.) July–Sept.

Middleton: †Arbor Low stone circle and Gib Hill tumulus, open all the year daily.

Sudbury: *Sudbury Hall, open April–Oct. Weds., Thurs., Fris., weekends and Bank Hol. Mons. 2–6.

DERBYSHIRE TOWNS AND VILLAGES

In this key to our map of Derbyshire (which appears at the front of this volume) are all the towns and villages, etc., treated in this book.

Abney	D4	Chapel-en-le-Frith	B3	Glossop	B2
Alderwasley	E7	Chatsworth	E5	Great Hucklow	D4
Alfreton	F6	Chellaston	F10	Great Longstone	D5
Alkmonton	D9	Chelmorton	C5	Grindleford	D4
Allestree	F8	Chesterfield	F5		
Alport	D5	Church Broughton	D9	Haddon Hall	D5
Alsop-en-le-Dale	C7	Church Gresley	E11	Hardwick Hall	G6
Alvaston	F9	Clay Cross	F6	Hartington	C6
Ambergate	F7	Clowne	G4	Hartshorne	E11
Ashbourne	D8	Codnor	G7	Hassop	D4
Ashford	D5	Cressbrook	C4	Hathersage	D3
Ashover	F6	Creswell	H4	Hatton	D10
Aston-on-Trent	G10	Crich	F7	Hayfield	B3
Ault Hucknall	G5	Cromford	E6	Hazelwood	E8
		Cubley	C9	Heanor	G8
Bakewell	D5	Curbar	D4	Heath	G5
Ballidon	D7			Higham	F6
Bamford	D3	Dalbury	E9	Hilton	D10
Barlborough	G4	Dale Abbey	G9	Hognaston	D7
Barlow	F4	Darley Abbey	F9	Holbrook	F8
Barrow-on-Trent	F10	Darley Dale	E6	Holloway	E6
Barton Blount	D9	Denby	F8	Holmesfield	E4
Baslow	D4	Derby	F9	Hope	C3
Beeley	E5	Dethick	E6	Hopton	E7
Beighton	G3	Dove Holes	B4	Horsley	F8
Belper	F7	Doveridge	C9	Hulland	D8
Birchover	D6	Dronfield	F4		
Blackwell	G6	Duffield	F8	Idridgehay	E7
Bolsover	G5			Ilkeston	G8
Bonsall	E6	Earl Sterndale	B5	Ingleby	F10
Boulton	F9	Eckington	G4		
Boyleston	D9	Edale	C3	Kedleston	E8
Brackenfield	F6	Edensor	D5	Killamarsh	G3
Bradbourne	D7	Edlaston	D8	King's Newton	F10
Bradley	D8	Egginton	E10	King Sterndale	B5
Bradwell	C3	Elmton	H4	Kirk Hallam	G8
Brailsford	D8	Elton	D6	Kirk Ireton	E7
Brassington	D7	Elvaston	F9	Kirk Langley	E9
Breadsall	F8	Etwall	E9	Kniveton	D7
Breaston	G9	Eyam	D4		
Bretby	E10			Ladybower Reservoir	
Buxton	B4	Fairfield	B4		D3
		Fenny Bentley	D7	Little Eaton	F8
Caldwell	E11	Findern	E10	Little Longstone	D5
Calke	F11	Foremark	E10	Littleover	E9
Carsington	D7	Foston	D9	Litton	C4
Castleton	C3	Froggatt	D4	Long Eaton	G9
Chaddesden	F9				

245